The Pattern Companion:

Beading

The Pattern Companion:

Beading

Edited by Cassia B. Farkas

With material by
Ann Benson, Gay Bowles,
Valerie Campbell-Harding, Jane Davis,
Elizabeth Gourley, Ellen Talbot,
and Carol Wilcox Wells

Sterling Publishing Co., Inc.
New York

Library of Congress Cataloging-in-Publication Data Available

2 4 6 8 10 9 7 5 3 1

Material in this collection was adapted from:
Beaded Cross-Stitch Treasures, by Gay Bowles © 1999, by Chapelle Ltd.
Beaded Tassels, Braids & Fringes, by Valerie Campbell-Harding © 1999 by Valerie Campbell-Harding
Art of Seed Beading, by Elizabeth Gourley, Jane Davis & Ellen Talbott © 1999 by Elizabeth Gourley, Jane Davis & Ellen Talbott
Beading for the first time®, by Ann Benson © 2001 by Ann Benson
The Art & Elegance of Beadweaving, by Carol Wilcox Wells © 2002 by Carol Wilcox Wells

Detailed rights information on page 192.

Edited by Cassia B. Farkas
Book design by Alan Barnett
Cover design by Alan Carr

Published by Sterling Publishing Co., Inc.
387 Park Avenue South, New York, NY 10016
© 2004, Sterling Publishing Co., Inc.
Distributed in Canada by Sterling Publishing
c/o Canadian Manda Group, 165 Dufferin Street
Toronto, Ontario, Canada M6K 3H6
Distributed in Great Britain and Europe by Chris Lloyd at Orca Book
Services, Stanley House, Fleets Lane, Poole BH15 3AJ, England
Distributed in Australia by Capricorn Link (Australia) Pty. Ltd.
P.O. Box 704, Windsor, NSW 2756, Australia

Manufactured in China

Sterling ISBN 1-4027-1271-5

Contents

Introduction

No doubt about it, beading is an addictive craft. There is something appealing about stringing little bits of shining color together into an elegant glass fabric or a small treasure of detail and design; into elegant jewelry or eye-catching accessories with dangling fringes that catch the light on their iridescent surfaces. The history of the use of beads as decorative accents can be dated back to the earliest human cultures from pieces that have been found by archaeologists. It spans thousands of years and not only connects every continent, but every civilization of the world.

This book is packed with patterns for many different techniques. It is for those who love working with those sparkling beads, and for eclectics with an urge to try it all. It is a great resource if you've already caught the beading bug; you will find the wide variety of patterns provided may show you new tricks or variations you haven't tried, and they will definitely spark your imagination, inspiring you to create your own designs. But if you are new to the craft, there are basics enough here to use it as a "how to."

Variations abound—they can be learned in the basics; they're offered up in the project instructions—and if an idea comes to you, don't let it pass because there's no precedent. Try it! Try another way of doing a stitch; try using different colors or beads.

Directly following is a review of all the techniques needed for the projects included in the book. Variations specific to a project will be included in its instructions, but many tips and tricks of technique in this section will equip you to make variations of your own. After the techniques you will find information on supplies and on how to plan and calculate the number of beads needed for a project of your own.

Techniques

NETTING

Netting is a quick way to cover a surface with beads. Made up of interconnected loops of beads, netting allows both speed in the making and more variety in the surface texture than many other stitches. The loops can be made using accent beads or combining different sizes of beads to create new effects. The finished fabric can be open and lacy, or close and dense. The size and spacing of the loop repeat determines the density of the finished fabric. Although netting can be made in any color combination, it is most easily accomplished when the bead that links the loops together is a different color from the other beads in the fabric.

The following are instructions for a review of circular netting. The white beads are used here to illustrate the links between the loops.

Round 1: String three green beads and one white bead. Repeat nine times. Tie the tail end and working end of the thread into a circle with a square knot.

Round 2: String two green beads, one white bead, two green beads, and PNT the next white bead on the first round. Repeat all the way around.

Round 3: PNT the first three beads in Round 2. The needle will be coming out of a white bead. Repeat Round 2.

Continue repeating Round 3 for as long as you wish the tube to be. To increase the diameter of the tube, string three or more green beads instead of two in each side of each loop. To decrease, string fewer green beads on each side of each loop. This allows the netting to hug the surface of a container or flatten out into a circle.

Flat netting is the same principle as circular netting, except the rows are completed back and forth. More beads need to be strung at the beginning of each row to account for the edge of the net, and you must pass through some beads at the end of the rows to get the needle in the proper position for the following row.

Thread can make a difference in netting. Netting made flat tends to stay bunched up vertically unless you use thread almost the width of the bead hole rather than thin nylon beading thread. Silk, linen, or fine cotton cord are good choices.

Netting in size 11/0 seed beads

Netting in Delica beads

CHEVRON CHAIN

Chevron chain is woven similarly to, and can have the open look of, netting, or be tightly woven with beads right next to each other. The stitch can be increased in width and depth; flat chains are the normal use of chevron chain but it can be worked dimensionally, with a tight tension, forming really strong structures. Other techniques can be worked directly off the chevron chain, expanding the possibilities even more.

Note: The illustrations show two colors of beads. If this stitch is new to you, follow the color placement in each drawing. If you're practiced or feeling adventuresome, use colors of your choice in any bead position.

To make a sample, pick up one bead, and slide it to within 6 inches of the tail, then loop back through it; string on nine more beads, following the color pattern in figure 1. Now PNUT bead 1, forming a triangle. (See Figure 2.)

Pick up six more beads, and PNDT bead 8, then pick up six beads again and PNUT bead 14. Continue this sequence for the desired length. (See Figure 3.)

JOINING THE CHEVRON CHAIN

Before joining the ends of a chevron chain make sure that there are an equal number of sets on each side of the chain. A set is a group of beads that makes up the outside edge of an individual triangle within the chevron chain. (See Figure 4.)

To join the two ends together pick up three of the six beads of a stitch (A, B, C), PNUT bead 4, and pick up two more beads (D, E); finish the stitch. Now pick up beads F, G, and H and PNDT beads 1, 10, 9, and 8. (See Figure 4.)

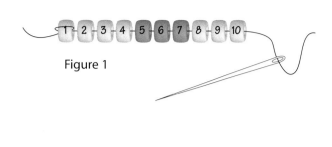

Figure 1

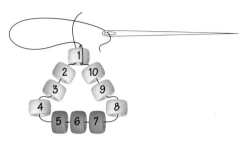

Figure 2

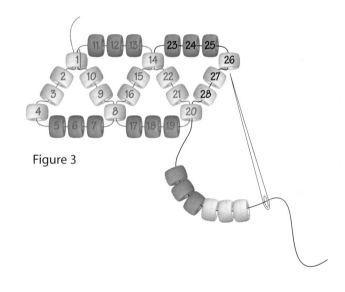

Figure 3

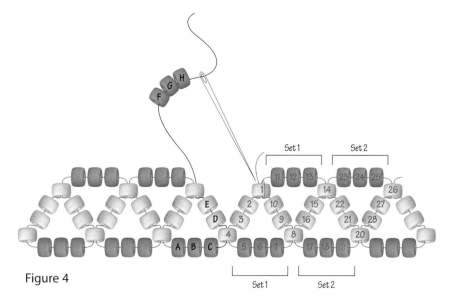

Figure 4

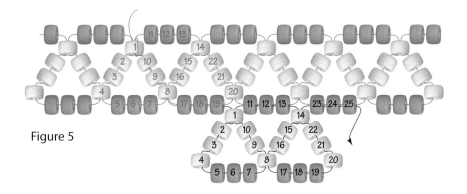

Figure 5

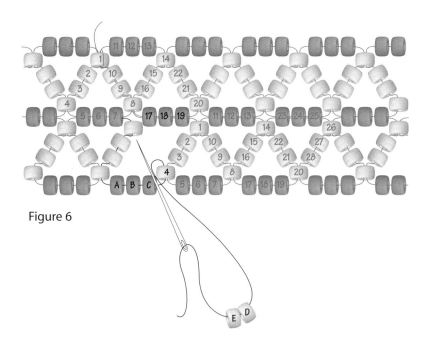

Figure 6

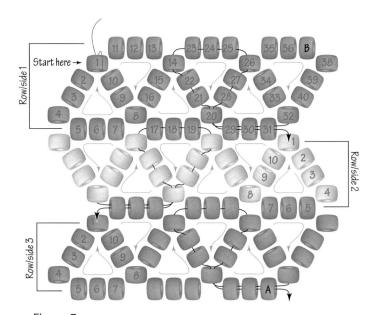

Figure 7

ADDING ROWS TO JOINED CHAIN

Add width to any chevron chain by adding another row to the existing chain. The needle must exit a set of edge beads (17, 18, and 19 in figure 4). Make a beginning triangle of chevron chain, then join it to the next set of edge beads in the original chain.

To begin the next row, pick up ten beads and PNUT bead 1. Now PNT beads 11, 12, and 13; consider these beads as the first three beads of the next stitch. Pick up the remaining three beads (14, 15, and 16), then PNDT bead 8. With the next stitch pick up six beads, and PNUT bead 14. Every other stitch will use beads from the previous row. (See Figure 5.)

To close the second row of chevron chain, pick up beads A, B, and C, and PNUT bead 4. Pick up beads D and E, and PNUT the bead at the top of the triangle. Weave through beads 17, 18, and 19 to finish the stitch. (See Figure 6.)

TURNING AND ADDING ROWS TO UNJOINED CHEVRON CHAIN

Add another row of chevron chain by turning and stitching back the other way. (See Figure 7.) For the sample, stitch three sets of chevron chain; the needle exits bead 32 when this is completed. To make the turn, weave through beads to reposition the needle so that it exits from a set of beads on the outer edge. The diagram shows the thread path. To start the next row, string on ten beads, PNBT bead 1 and beads 31, 30, and 29, and continue stitching across the row. When you reach the end you will need to weave through beads to make the turn as you did before; follow the thread path shown in the diagram. Stitch row 3, then position the needle as if you were going to stitch another row.

DIMENSIONAL CHEVRON CHAIN

Using chevron chain in a dimensional manner produces a structure that's strong yet open, one you can add to with more chevron chain or with other stitches. Make it open-ended, as in this sample, or with the ends joined to form a circle. You will need to keep a very tight tension.

MAKING A FOUR-SIDED TUBE

After completing figure 7, fold the sample so that rows 1 and 3 are perpendicular to row 2. With the needle coming out of bead A in row 3, string on four beads and PNT bead B in row 1, heading left. (See Figure 8.) Pick up three beads, and PNDT bead 1. Now PNBT bead A and its two neighbors, pick up beads 8, 9, and 10, and weave up through bead 5. Continue across the row in this manner, closing the tube.

ADDING ROWS

When adding another row of dimensional chevron chain, you'll stitch three sides. The fourth side is part of the previous chain.

Continuing to work from the completed sample tube, make the turn and have the needle exit the bead marked with a black dot, heading to the left. (See Figure 9.) Weave three sets of chevron chain to make row 5. Turn and add row 6. Make the turn and pick up four beads; the needle should be exiting bead C. Fold the work so that row 6 is over and parallel to row/side 4. PNT bead D and its two neighbors. Stitch the second tube closed in this way, weaving from the edge beads of rows 3 and 6. (Refer to Figure 8.)

MAKING A THREE-SIDED TUBE

Make two attached rows of chevron chain. Following figure 10, make the turn and pick up four beads, then pass the needle into

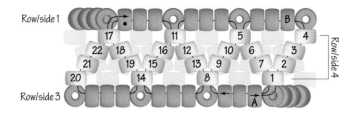

Figure 8

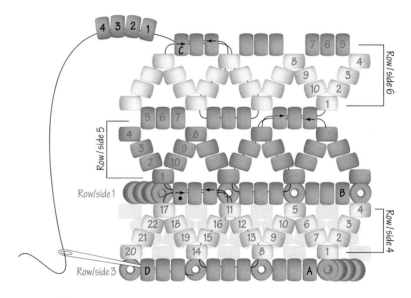

Figure 9

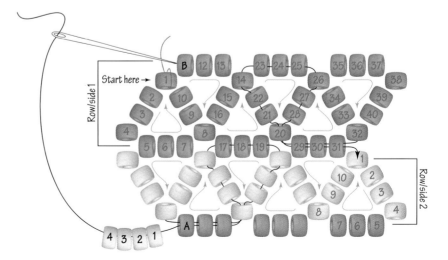

Figure 10

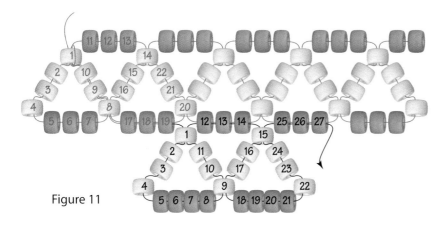

Figure 11

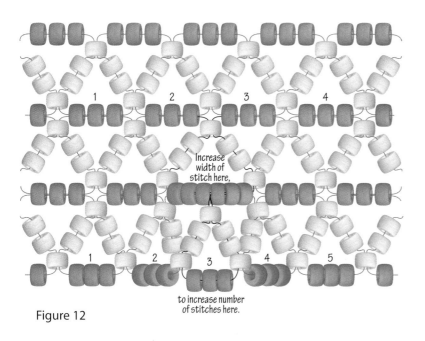

Increase width of stitch here,

to increase number of stitches here.

Figure 12

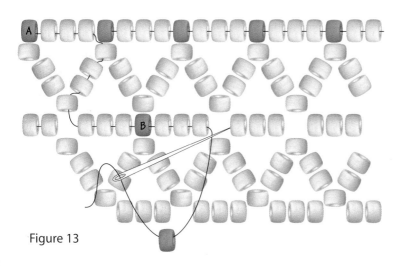

Figure 13

bead B and close the chain, working from side to side. The process is the same as for closing the four-sided tube. You can add more three-sided tubes to form a structure that looks like rows of pyramids on one side and is flat on the other.

INCREASING THE WIDTH OF A STITCH

Each stitch may be increased by adding more beads to the outside edges. (See Figure 11.) You can also increase the stitch at random. If the ends are joined, increasing causes the work to flare out towards you. If they're not joined, the increased edges will be curved.

INCREASING THE NUMBER OF STITCHES

Planning is important when increasing the number of stitches per row. First the width of a stitch must be doubled on one row, then that stitch is split and a new stitch is added between that group of beads when doing the next row. (See Figure 12.)

ADDING BEADS TO THE SURFACE

You may add beads to the surface of the chevron chain to fill in the gaps between edge bead sets. Adding these beads helps to tighten and strength the weave, and it also provides the beginning step to adding peyote stitch to a piece.

A row of dark surface beads has been added to the top row of chevron chain. (See Figure 13.) Bead A is the last bead to be added to that row. Follow the thread path shown to add surface beads to the next row (bead B is the first surface bead added to the second row). Continue in this manner as desired for your design.

PEYOTE STITCH

Peyote stitch, also called gourd or twill stitch, is simple and versatile, but with many possible variations, idiosyncrasies, and nuances.

The basic stitch begins by stringing a length of beads that will become the first two rows of the project. Begin the third row—which organizes the first three rows when complete—string one bead, PNBT the third bead from the needle towards the tail end of the thread, pull tight. (See Photo 1.) This lines two beads up vertically on top of each other at the end of the row with the next bead halfway between.

Next, string one bead, skip one bead, PNT the next bead, pull tight. (See Photo 2.) This creates a pattern of two beads vertically on top of each other and one bead stepped between.

Continue each new row by positioning the thread so that it is coming out of one of the upper beads; string one bead; skip the bead that is stepped down half a space, PNT the next bead that is stepped up half a space. (See Photo 3.) Pull the thread tight to fit the bead in place. (See Photo 4.) Each row is made up of every other bead on a horizontal line.

TIPS ABOUT PEYOTE STITCH

1. Counting rows: Begin at one corner of the piece or graph and count diagonally, or in a zigzag fashion vertically, so that you count every row.
2. The odd-count turnaround: When beginning with an uneven number of beads in a flat project, you will always have to PNT several beads at the end of a row on one side to get the thread in the proper position to add the next bead on the new row.
3. The shifty first bead: When adding the last bead in a round of circular peyote, you PNT the first bead in that round to prepare for the next round, moving the first bead in each round over by one bead (a diagonal line on the graph indicates the first bead in each round). However, some people stitch with the developing piece below; others with the developing piece above; some right-handed; others left-handed. Depending on which direction you stitch, the diagonal line for the first stitch in each round may be reversed.

Peyote stitch with
size 11/0 seed beads

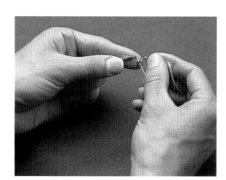

Photo 1

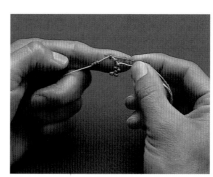

Photo 2

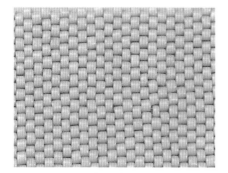

Peyote stitch with Delica beads

Photo 3

Photo 4

SQUARED NEEDLE-WEAVING

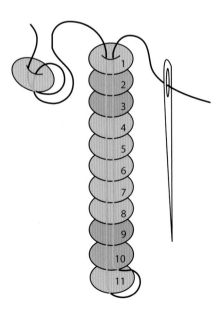

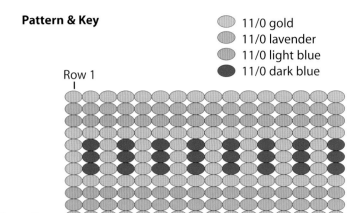

Pattern & Key

⬤ 11/0 gold
⬤ 11/0 lavender
⬤ 11/0 light blue
⬤ 11/0 dark blue

Row 1

Figure 2

This technique shares something with the principle of crochet. After the first row is worked, subsequent rows are looped onto it. It is worked from a gridded pattern and the results resemble loomed bead-weaving.

Thread a needle with a length of thread. To keep design pattern beads from slipping off the thread, create a "stopper bead." Slip one bead on your needle and let it slide down thread to 3 inches from the end of the thread. Loop thread and PNBT the bead and pull taut. (See Figure 1.) Secure stopper bead to a surface with a bit of tape to stabilize the thread.

Note: The stopper bead will be removed after the first few rows.

String beads for Row 1 from top to bottom, following your pattern grid. (See Figure 2.) Skip the last bead and insert needle back through all beads. The needle should emerge from the top bead of Row 1.

String beads for Row 2, from top to bottom. Insert the needle into the loop exposed at bottom of Row 1. Pull thread gently until entire second row is taut, but not tight, and beads rest against first row without puckering.

Note: The work in needle-weaving always proceeds in the direction of the beadworker's dominant hand.

Insert needle into last bead of Row 2, and bring thread out until it is taut, but not tight. Loop thread around Row 1 so it is nestled between beads 11 and 10 of Row 1. (See Figure 3.) Insert needle into beads 10 and 9 of Row 2, bringing needle out between beads 9 and 8 on Row 2. Again, thread should be taut, but not tight.

Loop thread around Row 1 so it is nestled between beads 9 and 8 of Row 1. Insert needle into next three beads on Row 2—beads 8, 7, and 6—bringing needle out between beads 6 and 5 on Row 2. Tighten thread again.

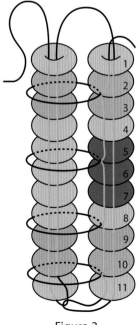

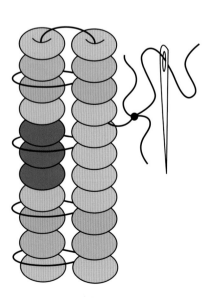

Figure 1

Figure 3

Figure 4

Loop it around Row 1 so it is nestled between beads 6 and 5 of Row 1. Insert needle into next three beads on Row 2—beads 5, 4, and 3—and repeat looping and inserting process until thread emerges from bead 1 of Row 2.

Repeat Steps 4–7 for all subsequent rows until band is long enough to wrap snugly around candleholder. Note: The weaving gets easier to handle as the design grows.

When you are down to about 3 inches of thread on the needle, it is time to add new thread. Remove needle from thread and cut a new length. Thread needle.

Note: About 30 inches of thread is a good length; longer thread tends to tangle, and a shorter thread necessitates frequent re-threadings.

Tie a square knot (page 29) so that the knot lands 1 inch from where the old thread emerges from beadwork. (See Figure 4.) Place a tiny dot of glue on the knot and wipe off any excess. The glue need not be dry before proceeding.

Continue beading as if one continuous thread were being used. Allow thread ends to protrude from work until new thread is well established within the weave. Pull gently on thread ends and clip them close so they disappear into the woven design. *Note: It might be necessary to use a smaller needle until the area of the knot has been passed.*

When you have completed the design, bury excess thread in weave and trim any excess threads. If what you are making calls for the piece to be joined, line up beads of last row next to beads of Row 1 and loop the two end rows together as shown in Figure 3.

TUBULAR RIGHT-ANGLE WEAVE

Right-angle weave is a stitch made up of units with four sides. The thread passes through the beads at right angles, never straight, and because of this the stitch flows in a clockwise, then a counterclockwise motion. The directional arrows in the illustrations show this movement.

String four beads onto the thread and tie them into a circle with a square knot. (See Figure 1.) Beads 2 and 4 become the top beads and beads 1 and 3 become the side beads. This is one unit of four.

Pass the needle up bead 1, and pick up three beads (5, 6, and 7), then pass the needle up through bead 1; note the clockwise motion. (See Figure 2.) This is a unit of four; three beads added to one from the previous unit. To do the next stitch to the right, first pass the thread through beads 5 and 6.

Pick up three beads (8, 9, and 10), and pass the needle down, counterclockwise, through bead 6. (See Figure 3.) Weave through beads 8 and 9 to get ready for the next stitch. Stitch unit 4 in a clockwise motion.

To join the two ends together, you'll add top beads but not side ones. The side beads will come from the end of the row and from the beginning of the row. (See Figure 4.) With the thread coming from bead 12, pick up bead 14, pass the needle into side-bead 3, pick up bead 15, and pass into side-bead 12. To set up for the next row, weave through beads 14, 3, and 15.

Three beads are always added when beginning a new row. String on beads 16, 17, and 18. (See Figure 5.) Stitch in a clockwise motion back through bead 15. At this point you could weave up through bead 16 and stitch to the left, or weave through beads 16, 17, and 18 and stitch to the right. All upcoming stitches in this row will use two beads from previous stitches and add two more.

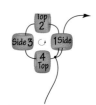

Figure 1

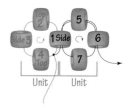

Figure 2

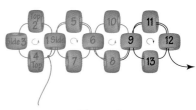

Figure 3

For the counterclockwise stitch, pass the needle through the top bead of the next unit (bead 2), pick up two beads for the side and top, and pass back through side bead 18. Weave over to the next side bead (19).

The clockwise stitch will be coming out of a side bead. Pick up two beads for the top and side, and pass through top bead 5. (See Figure 6.) Weave around to the side bead of that unit to begin the next stitch.

To join the two ends of row 2 only the top bead will be added, because the other three beads are already there. (See Figure 7.) Pick up bead 25, and weave through beads 16, 11, and 23 to complete the row. Go back through bead 25 to set up for the next row.

KEY THINGS TO REMEMBER

1. A new row begins with three beads and ends with one.
2. There are always four sides to a unit.
3. Stitches are always at right angles—never straight.
4. With counterclockwise stitches, if you are exiting a side bead from the bottom, pass through the previous row's top bead, then add a side and a top.
5. With clockwise stitches, if you are exiting a side bead from the top, add a top and a side, then pass through the top bead of the previous row.

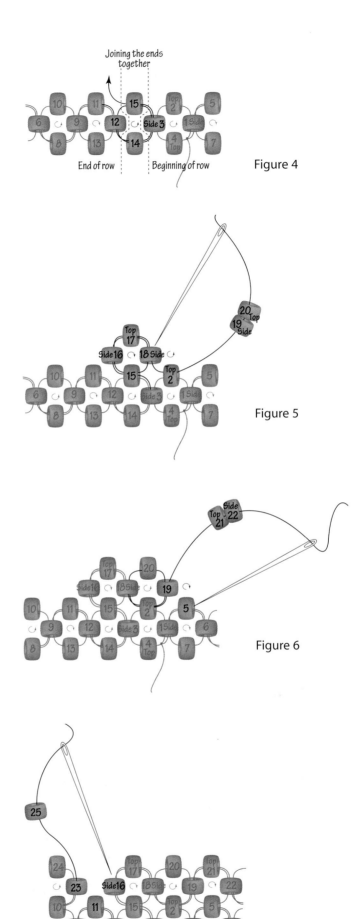

Figure 4

Figure 5

Figure 6

Figure 7

LADDER STITCH

Ladder stitch with bugle beads

The ladder stitch is used to make a base for the brick stitch (see next stitch). Bugle beads are usually used for this stitch, but you can also use seed beads. You will need two beading needles for this stitch.

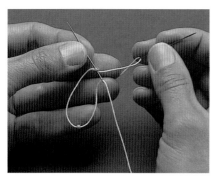

Photo 5

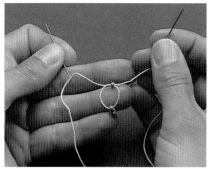

Photo 6

First, thread each end of a length of thread with a beading needle. Then string one bead and position it in the middle of the thread. Pick up another bead and PNT one end of the bead. PNT the opposite end of the bead with the other needle. (See Photo 5.) Pull thread tight until the second bead is positioned in the middle next to the first bead. (See Photo 6.) Continue in this manner until you reach the desired length. To form the ladder of beads into a circular shape, pass each needle through opposite ends of the first bead in the ladder. Pull tight.

BRICK STITCH

Brick stitch with size 11/0 seed beads

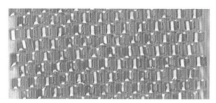

Brick stitch with Delica beads

A project done in the brick stitch looks similar to a brick wall—hence, its name. The beads lie in a vertical position, and the stitch is usually worked in the round. To work the brick stitch, you must first have a ladder-stitch base (see previous stitch).

Pick up two beads with your needle, then stick the needle under a loop of thread that is connecting the first pair of beads on the ladder stitch base. (See Photo 7.) PNBT the second strung bead and pull tight. (See Photos 8 and 9.) ★String one bead. PNT loop of thread that is connecting the next pair of

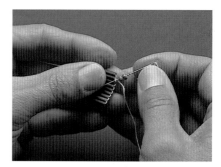

Photo 7

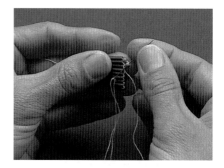

Photo 8

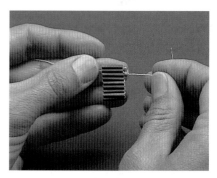

Photo 9

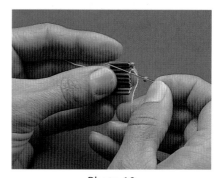

Photo 10

beads. (See Photo 10.) PNBT the bead and pull tight.★ (See Photos 11 and 12.) Repeat between asterisks until the end of the round. To finish a row when working in the round, PNDT the first bead in the row and back up through the second bead.

Photo 11

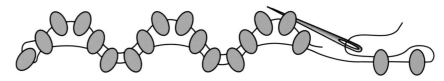

Figure 1

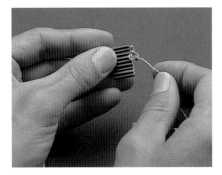

Photo 12

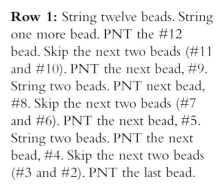

Figure 2

HERRINGBONE STITCH

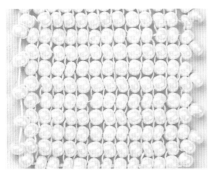

Herringbone stitch with size 10/0 seed beads

Herringbone stitch with Delica beads

This stitch originated in Africa and is also called Ndebele. It gives the finished project a beautiful woven or knitted look. After mastering the first few rows, it is an easy stitch to do. You must have at least four beads per row, or a number divisible by four, because the herringbone stitch is done in groups of two with single beads on each end. Always keep the thread tension tight, except in Row 1, where you can adjust the stitches evenly.

Row 1: String twelve beads. String one more bead. PNT the #12 bead. Skip the next two beads (#11 and #10). PNT the next bead, #9. String two beads. PNT next bead, #8. Skip the next two beads (#7 and #6). PNT the next bead, #5. String two beads. PNT the next bead, #4. Skip the next two beads (#3 and #2). PNT the last bead.

Row 2: String two beads. PNBT the first bead strung. (See Photo 13.) Skip next bead. (See Figure 1.) String two beads. PNT next bead.

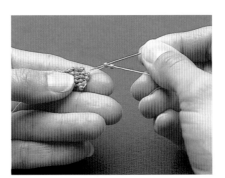

Photo 13

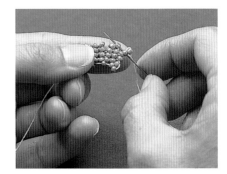

Photo 14

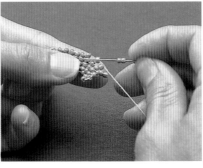

Photo 15

Photo 16

★Skip one bead. PNT next bead. (See Figure 2.) String two beads. PNT next bead.★ Repeat between asterisks until end of row. Every other two-bead set will be hanging down. Since these were the two beads skipped in the first row, they must be pushed up above the thread so that they are ready for the needle to pass through them. This only happens on Row 2.

Row 3: String two beads. PNBT first bead strung. ★PNT the first bead of the next two-bead set. (See Photo 14.) String two beads, PNT the last bead of the two-bead set. (See Photo 15.)★ Repeat between asterisks until end of row.

Row 4: Same as Row 3.

As you will notice, the beads of each row are not in a straight line. Each group of two makes an inverted U-shape. When pulling your stitches tight, especially with matte Japanese tubular beads, make sure one bead is on one side of the "U" and one is on the other. (See Photo 16.)

Ending Row: There are two different ending rows used in the projects in this book. One makes the edge even. The other makes the edge look the same as the beginning edge—singular beads topping each group of two beads.

Even Edge: String one bead. PNT next two beads of two-bead set. ★String one bead. PNT next two beads of two-bead set.★ Repeat between asterisks until end of row. To make both ends look the same, turn piece over and do the same thing to the beginning edge.

Singular Bead Topping: String two beads. PNT first bead of previous row. String one bead. ★PNT next two beads. String one bead.★ Repeat between asterisks until end of row.

SQUARE STITCH

Beads worked in the square stitch have a very similar appearance to loomed work. It is sometimes called the false loom weave stitch.

To do the square stitch, start by stringing the desired amount of beads on your thread. Do not make a knot at the end of your thread, because the tension of the thread may need to be adjusted. If the tension of the thread is too tight, your work might curl. For the second row, string two beads, then PNBT second-to-last bead on the first row in the opposite direction. (See Photo 17.) Then PNBT the second bead on Row 2. (See Photo 18.)

String a bead and PNT third bead from the last on the first row in the opposite direction. (See Photo 19.) Then PNBT third bead on second row in the same direction as the row. (See Photo 20.) Continue in this manner, adding on one bead at a time until end of row. At the beginning of each row, add on two beads at a time.

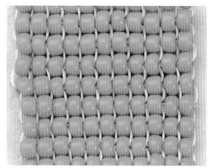

Square stitch with size 11° seed beads

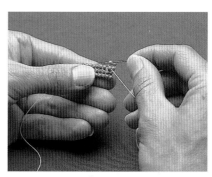

Square stitch with Delica beads

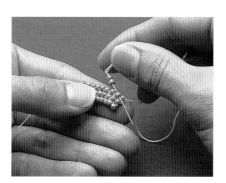

Photo 17

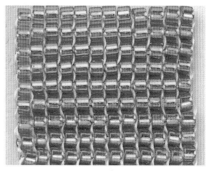

Photo 18

Photo 19

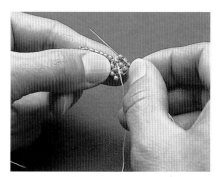

Photo 20

LOOM BEAD WEAVING

Loom bead weaving requires two sets of threads; warp threads and weft threads. The warp threads run vertically and are set up on the loom; the weft thread runs horizontally back and forth and carries the beads.

Note: Seed beads can vary dramatically. For loom work, choose beads of a uniform size and shape. If the beads are irregular your work will have a very uneven appearance.

WARPING THE LOOM

You will need one more warp thread than the number of beads in the width of your design. For example, if you have five beads across in your design, you will need six warp threads.

To calculate the length of the warp threads, figure the desired finished length of the project, add 12 inches for finishing the work and another 12 inches for tying to the loom. If you wish to make fringe, add the length of the fringe for both ends, then double it.

If you are doing a project that is longer than the loom and your loom has rollers, calculate how long to make your warp threads and how many you will need. Then cut the desired length and number of warp threads and tie one end of the group of warp threads to one or more tack heads on the roller at the top of the loom. Loosen the roller and wind up the warp threads while holding the other end of the warp threads in one hand and keeping the threads taut. Continue winding until there is just enough thread left to tie the warp threads to the tack heads on the bottom of the loom. Before tying the warp threads to the bottom of the loom, line up the threads in the spring

Loom bead weaving
with size 11/0 seed beads

coils at both the top and bottom of the loom. Tie the warp ends to the tack heads on the bottom roller.

Leave enough space on the warp threads at the beginning to use later for fringe and/or finishing your project. You may need to wind your warp thread from top to bottom until you reach the desired measurement. To do this, loosen both top and bottom rollers and wind both at the same time while keeping the warp threads taut, but not too tight. Tighten the wing nuts. Remember that you will be weaving from the bottom of the loom to the top. Start weaving about 1 or 2 inches from the bottom coils.

When your project is smaller than your loom and you don't need lots of thread for fringe, you can warp your loom by making a loop knot at the end of the thread on the spool. Hook this loop over a nail or tack head at the top end of the loom. Calculate how wide your project will be and where to start the warp threads so that the work will be centered on the loom. Then line up the warp thread through the top spring coil and bring it down to the corresponding coil at the bottom spring. Wrap the thread around the nail or tack head at the bottom of the loom and take the thread up through the coil right next to the one you just used, bringing it up to the top of the loom and placing the thread into the corresponding coil. Next, loop it around the nail head again. Continue back and forth in this manner, keeping an even ten-

Loom bead weaving
with Delica beads

sion on the threads until you have the proper amount of warp threads on the loom. Then tie off the thread end to a nail head with your favorite knot. Cut the thread from the spool.

WEAVING

When you start weaving, remember to leave enough space at the beginning of the warp threads for finishing and tying off your work. Cut the desired length of weft thread (about 2 yards) and pass through beeswax. Thread the needle and tie the end of the weft thread to the left outside warp thread with an overhand knot, leaving about a 6-inch tail. (See Figure 1.)

Note: If you are left-handed, you will tie the end of the weft thread to the right outside warp thread and reverse all following instructions.

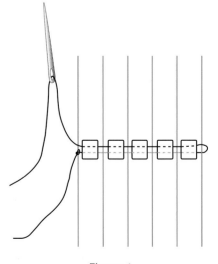

Figure 1

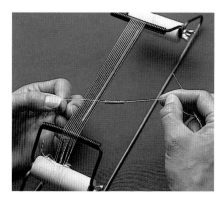

Photo 21

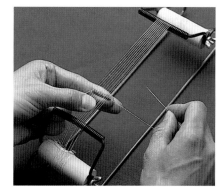

Photo 22

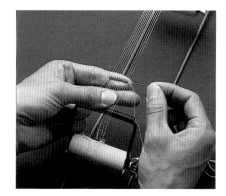

Photo 23

Reading the pattern chart from left to right and from bottom to top, string desired number and color of beads according to the design chart. (See photo 21.)

Take the beads for the first row on the weft thread and place them under the warp threads. Push the beads up with your left index finger so there is a warp thread on both sides of each bead. (See Photo 22.) The first row or two can be tricky, but after that, the warp threads will hold the beads in place while you pass your needle through the beads. Then, PNBT the beads, going from right to left. Make sure the holes of the beads are pushed up above warp threads so the needle goes back through beads above the warp threads. (See Photo 23.) If your needle goes under the warp threads, the beads will not be secured. If your needle goes through the warp threads, you won't be able to adjust the bead row up or down, which you may need to do.

Continue in this manner, following the design chart. When you have about 5 inches of weft thread left on your needle at the end of a row, it is time to get new thread. Take the needle off the thread and leave the tail of thread hanging for now. You will weave it in later. Thread the needle with new thread and PNT the last three or more rows of beads, making sure to end at the 5-inch tail. This will secure the

new thread. Continue beading with the new thread. After you have made three or more new rows, thread the 5-inch tail and PNT the three or more new rows. Cut off excess thread. Weave in the beginning tail the same way.

FINISHING

There are several different ways to finish, depending on your project.

Back of the work will not show/no fringe: Use your weft thread without any beads on it to weave several rows at the ending edge of the work and at the beginning edge. This will create a thread cloth that you will fold down to the back of the work and glue or sew in place. (See Figure 2.) After making the thread cloth at the end of the project, go back to the beginning of the work and add a

new weft thread. Weave several rows without beads to create a thread cloth at the beginning of work. Remove the work from the loom and tie pairs of warp threads together using a surgeon's knot. (See page 30.) Continue until all warp threads have been tied. Trim threads and fold to the back of the work and glue or sew in place.

Front and back will show/no fringe: Do not make thread cloth ends. Remove finished work from the loom and weave each warp tail back into the body of the work by threading it into a needle and PNBT several rows of beads. Do not pack beads too full of threads as the beads can break from the pressure. If beads get packed too full, weave any remaining warp thread ends back along the warp threads in the beaded fabric. (See Figure 3.)

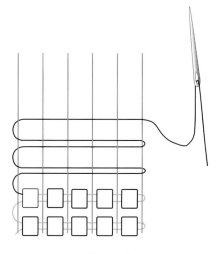

Figure 4

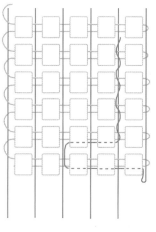

Figure 3

Piece will have fringe: Remove work from the loom and use the warp thread ends to create the fringe. Thread a warp thread with a needle and string the desired amount of beads on it. Skipping the last bead, PNBT the rest of the beads to the edge of the work. (See Figure 4.) Make a double half-hitch knot near the edge of work. (See page 29.) Weave the excess thread back into the body of the work by wrapping it around the warp threads and going through the beads. (See Figure 5.) Be creative! There will be lots of warp ends to weave in and not much space to do it. It can be discouraging, but don't give up. It will be over before you know it!

DECREASING IN LOOM WORK

To decrease in loom work at the beginning of a row, go to the end of the row preceding the row that you wish to decrease and take the needle back through the number of beads to be decreased. Make sure to pass the weft thread under the outermost warp thread before going back through beads. Bring the weft thread to the back of the work and start the next row as you normally would. (See Figure 6.) To decrease at the end of a row, add desired amount of beads and, ignoring excess warp thread, take needle to back of work and continue as you normally would. (See Figure 7.)

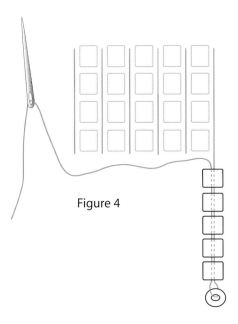

Figure 4

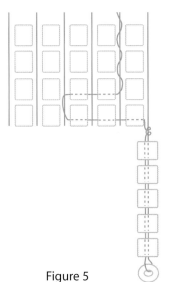

Figure 5

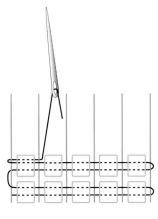

Figure 6

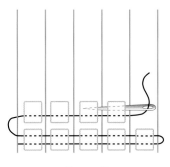

Figure 7

PRE-STRUNG BEAD TECHNIQUES

The following three techniques assume a certain skill level in the crafts of knitting and crochet. If you do not yet possess these skills, it is suggested that you find a manual, a teacher, or a friend who will demonstrate them for you. You will want to gain some mastery of them before attempting projects that rely on these techniques.

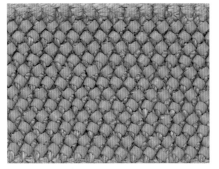

Bead knitting with
size 11/0 seed beads

Bead knitting with Delica beads

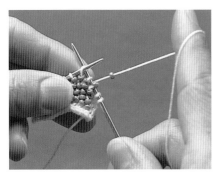

Photo 24

Photo 25

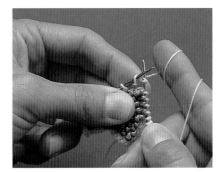

Photo 26

BEAD KNITTING

There are several types of knitting with beads pre-strung onto thread. The projects in this book use bead knitting in plaited stockinette stitch, where each bead is pushed into the stitch as the stitch is made. There are no beads on the wrong side of the fabric, and the beads on the right side of the fabric sit close together to cover the whole surface. In plaited stockinette stitch, the beads slant to the left on the right side of the knit row and slant to the right on the right side of the purl row. This way, they fit together neatly in a zigzag pattern, and the fabric doesn't bias.

In bead knitting, the tension needs to be tight in order to lock the beads in the stitches on the right side of the fabric. It helps to wrap the thread around a finger several times with about five or ten beads between the knitting and your hand. This way, you can slide a bead into place for the next stitch without having to let go of the right needle.

To make a sample of bead knitting, string about sixty-four size 8/0 seed beads onto size 5 perle cotton. Use a Big Eye needle to string the beads, or thread a size 10 beading needle with nylon or strong quilting thread, and tie it in a square

knot around the perle cotton. Cast on twenty stitches to size 0 knitting needles.

Row 1: Knit one row without beads. You make a plaited knit stitch by inserting the knitting needle in the back of the stitch and wrapping the thread around the right needle clockwise before completing the stitch.

Row 2: Purl the next row without beads. You make a standard purl stitch by inserting the needle into the front of the stitch and wrapping the thread around the right needle counterclockwise.

Row 3: Knit two stitches in plaited knit stitch (as explained in Row 1), then insert the needle into the back of the next stitch and slide one bead about ½ inch away from the knitting. (See Photo 24.) Wrap the thread with the bead clockwise around the right needle and slide the bead down to the junction between the two needles. (See Photo 25.) At this point, pull the left needle towards you and the right needle away from you to create a space between the stitch in progress. Now push the bead through the opening where the right needle will go to make the knit stitch (blue bead in photo for clarity). (See Photo 26.) Pull the needle through and complete the

Photo 27

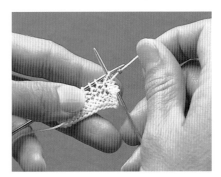

Photo 28

stitch. (See Photo 27.) Repeat the plaited bead knit stitch fifteen more times, then make two plaited knit stitches without beads.

Row 4: Purl the first two stitches (as explained in Row 2), then insert the needle into the front of the next stitch, and slide one bead about ½ inch away from the knitting. (See Photo 28.) Wrap the thread with the bead counterclockwise around the right needle and slide the bead down to the junction between the two needles. (See Photo 29.) This time, pull the right needle towards you and the left needle away from you to create a space in the stitch. Push the bead through the opening where the right needle will go to complete the purl stitch. Now push the right needle through and finish the stitch. (See Photo 30.) Repeat the bead purl stitch fifteen more times, then purl the last two stitches without beads.

Photo 29

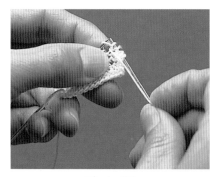

Photo 30

Repeat rows 3 and 4 until you are comfortable with bead knitting. More beads can be added by cutting the perle cotton about 2 feet (or more) away from the knitting and stringing the beads onto that end.

To bead knit using smaller beads and needles, the only variation is to slide the bead about ¼ to ⅜ inch away from the knitting before wrapping the thread around the needle to make the stitch.

CROCHET

The flat crochet method used in this book allows the beads to come out on the same side of the piece for each row.

Bead crochet with Delica beads

Bead crochet with
size 8/0 seed beads

Before you begin to crochet, string the beads to be used for the project onto the thread in the desired pattern. After the beads have been strung on, start crocheting with a simple chain stitch row of cotton thread; as many stitches as desired.

Row 1: SC without beads.

Row 2: Start SC by sticking hook under top of stitch from previous row (two strands). Grab thread and pull through. (See Photo 31.) You now have two loops on the hook. Slide a bead down and push the bead with your fingers through the

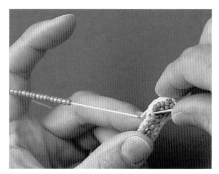

Photo 31

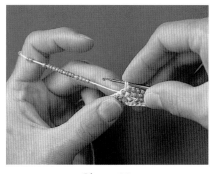

Photo 32

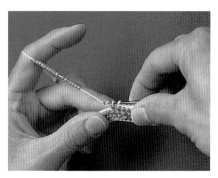

Photo 33

hole (in the top of the stitch from the previous row) where you just brought your hook through. (See Photo 32.) Then finish stitch by grabbing thread and pulling it through both loops on the hook. (See Photo 33.) Repeat this stitch until the end of the row. The beads will be on the front of the piece.

Row 3: This row is easier than Row 2. The beads will appear on the back of the piece, which is really the front of the piece. Stick the hook under the top of the stitch from the previous row (two strands). Slide a bead down until it hits the piece. Grab the thread with the hook, making sure that the bead is caught between the hook and the piece. (See Photo 34.) Pull the thread through. (See Photo 35.) Now there are two loops on the hook, and the bead is attached behind the stitch. Finish the stitch by grabbing the thread and pulling it through both loops. (See Photo 36.) Repeat this stitch until the end of the row.

Repeat Rows 2 and 3 until desired length.

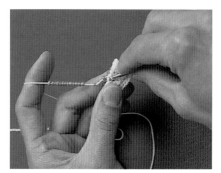

Photo 34

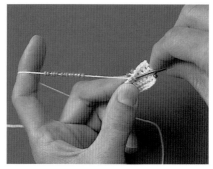

Photo 35

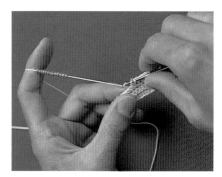

Photo 36

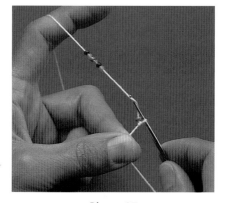

Photo 37

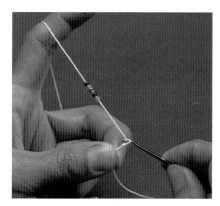

Photo 38

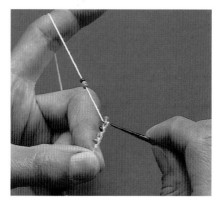

Photo 39

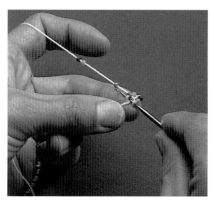

Photo 40

TUBULAR BEADED CROCHET

Tubular beaded crochet is one of the simplest techniques to master for anyone who likes to crochet. The tube is made of slip stitches that spiral up, forming a cord, while the beads are simply held at the base of the thread before each loop is pulled through to complete the slip stitch. By varying the types and sizes of beads, or the thread thickness, you can create many different effects. The thicker the thread used in relation to the bead size, the more space will show up between the beads.

Tubular crochet with Delica beads

Tubular crochet
with size 11/0 seed beads

To make a practice sample of this technique, string four colors of size 8 beads on size 5 perle cotton in the sequence of one bead in color 1, one bead in color 2, one bead in color 3, and one bead in color 4. Repeat this same sequence about ten to twenty times. Make a slip knot. Then, using a size 7 crochet hook, make four bead chains by sliding a bead into each chain stitch as it is made. (See Photos 37–39.)

Begin the spiral by making a beaded slip stitch into the first beaded chain stitch you made. To do this, put the crochet hook through the beaded loop of the first chain stitch, keeping the bead to the right of the hook. (See Photo 40.) Slide a new bead down the thread so it is behind, and to the right of, the bead on the loop. The new bead will be the same color as the bead on the loop the crochet hook is through.

Wrap the thread over the crochet hook and pull it through both loops. (See Photo 41 and Figure 1.) The new bead will be locked in the stitch to the right of the bead below. Continue in this manner by making a beaded slip stitch in every stitch. Every stitch you put the hook through will have the same color bead as the stitch you are making. The bead colors will spiral around the cord.

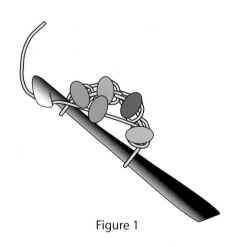

Photo 41

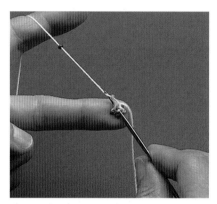

Figure 1

EMBELLISHMENT TECHNIQUES

BACKSTITCH

The backstitch is an excellent way to embellish fabric with beads. It is an embroidery stitch that attaches lines of beads to fabric, felt, or leather.

Backstitch

Knot a length of beading thread and PNUT back of fabric. ★String one to three beads. The straighter the line, the more beads you use. PNDT fabric, then PNUT fabric at a point in between the last two beads strung. (See Photo 42.) PNBT the last bead strung. (See Photo 43.) Pull tight. (See Photo 44.)★ Repeat between asterisks on entire area to be covered with beads.

COUCHING

Couching is a type of appliqué where beads are strung on one needle and sewn to a surface with another.

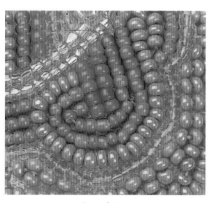

Couching

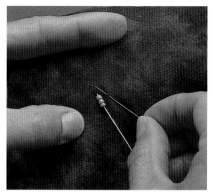

Photo 42

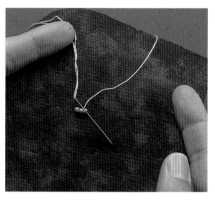

Photo 43

Photo 44

Thread two needles and make a knot at the end of each thread. Push one needle up through the fabric and string on a length of beads. Push up the other needle from the bottom to the top of the fabric and tack down the thread of the bead strand. (See Photo 45.) Push the working needle back down through the fabric on the other side of the bead strand thread. (See Photo 46.) Bring the working needle back up through the fabric between the two beads where you want to tack down the next bead strand thread. (See Photo 47.)

Photo 45

Photo 46

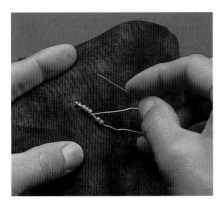
Photo 47

NEEDLEPOINT

To needlepoint with beads is very simple. Pick a needlepoint canvas size that will go with your bead size.

You can needlepoint with virtually any type of thread: beading thread, cotton crochet thread, embroidery floss, or whatever suits your project and beads.

Work one horizontal row at a time for uniform appearance—from the right in short backstitches or from the left in long backstitches. PNUT from back of canvas (See both points A in Figure 2.) Slip one bead on needle and PNDT to back of canvas (B). Bring needle from back of canvas (C). Secure thread by holding it against back of canvas and stitching over it as you attach the first few beads. Continue in this manner to the end of the horizontal row. Start the next row and return in the opposite direction using appropriate stitch. Repeat, using different color beads according to your graph or design chart. Mark off each row on the graph after completion, as it will help you to keep track of your place.

If the canvas doesn't fit the beads, or the beads look crowded, adjust by skipping a hole or two every stitch. When finished with one color (if you are matching the color of thread to the color of bead), or if you run out of thread, PNBT a few same-colored stitches on the underside of the canvas.

Note: Experienced needlepointers will notice that the thread is running in a different direction. In order to make the bead slant to the right, the thread must slant to the left. Additionally, the fine needle required to get through the beads will feel very tiny to someone accustomed to the firm bulk of a tapestry needle.

Short Backstitch
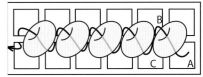

Long Backstitch
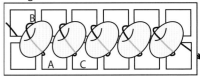
Figure 2

Bead needlepoint with Delica beads

Bead needlepoint with size 11/0 seed beads

CROSS-STITCH

Counted cross-stitch is worked on even-weave fabrics manufactured specifically for counted-thread embroidery. They are woven with the same number of vertical as horizontal threads per inch, so that each stitch will be the same size. The count of threads per inch in even-weave fabrics determines the size of a finished design.

To determine the size of the finished design, divide the stitch count by the number of threads per inch of fabric. When design is stitched over two threads, divide stitch count by half the threads per inch. For example, if a design with a stitch count of 120 in width and 250 in height was stitched on a 28 count linen over two threads (making it 14 count), the finished size would be 8⅝ x 17⅞ inches.

120 ÷ 14 = 8⅝ (width)

250 ÷ 14 = 17⅞ (height)

Finished size = 8⅝ x 17⅞ inches

Cut fabric at least 3 inches larger on all sides than the finished design size to ensure enough space for desired assembly. To prevent fraying, whip-stitch or machine-zigzag along the raw edges or apply liquid fray preventive.

Fold the fabric in half horizontally, then vertically. Place a pin in the intersection to mark the center. Locate the center of the design on the graph. To help in centering the larger designs, small arrows mark left- and right-side center and top and bottom center. Begin stitching all designs at the center point of the graph and fabric.

Insert needle up from the underside of the fabric at starting point. Hold 1 inch of thread behind the fabric and stitch over it, securing with the first few stitches. To finish thread, run under four or more stitches on the back of the design. Avoid knotting floss, unless working on clothing.

EMBROIDERY STITCHES TO KNOW

BACKSTITCH (BS)

1. Insert needle up between woven threads at 1.
2. Go down at 2, crossing two threads to the right.
3. Come up at 3. Go down at 4, crossing two threads to the right.
4. Repeat to fill design area.

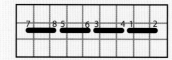

BEAD LOOPS

1. At each marked symbol on the graph, pick up the amount of beads indicated.
2. Insert the needle up between woven threads and through the first bead, go down in the same hole to form a loop. Adjust each loop before going on to the next one.

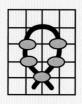

CROSS-STITCH (XS)

Worked one at a time in a row.
1. Insert needle up between woven threads at 1.
2. Go down at 2, forming a diagonal stitch.
3. Come up at 3 and down at 4, etc.
4. To complete the top stitches creating an "x", come up at A, go down at B. Come up at C, go down at D, etc. All top stitches should lie in the same direction.

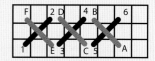

FRENCH KNOT (FK)

1. Insert needle up between woven threads at 1.
2. Loosely wrap floss once around needle.
3. Go down at 2, crossing one thread next to 1. Pull floss tight as needle is pushed down through fabric.
4. Carry floss across back of work between knots.

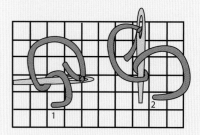

Another method of securing floss is the waste knot. Knot floss and insert needle down from the top side of the fabric about 1 inch from design area. Work several stitches over the thread to secure. Trim knot later.

To carry floss, run floss under the previously worked stitches on the back. Do not carry thread across any fabric that is not or will not be stitched. Loose threads, especially dark ones, can show through the fabric.

HERRINGBONE STITCH (HB)

Worked with two strands in diagonal and horizontal stitches.
1. Insert needle up between woven threads at 1.
2. Go down at 2. Traveling horizontally across the back, come up at 3, go down at 4, making an "X".
3. Come up at 5, go down at 6. Come up at 7, go down at 8, etc.
4. Repeat to fill design area.

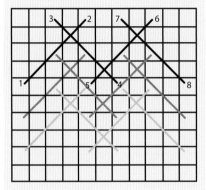

SATIN STITCH (SS)

Worked with two strands.
1. Insert needle up between woven threads at 1.
2. Go down at 2, forming a straight stitch.
3. Come up at 3, go down at 4, forming another smooth straight stitch that is slightly longer than the first.
4. Repeat to fill design area.

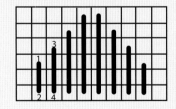

MISCELLANEOUS TECHNIQUES

KNOTS

Knowing different knots when doing beadwork can really come in handy. Each one handles a specific job and is easily tied.

Clove-hitch or Double Half-hitch knot: Bring the working thread under and over the stationary thread, then under and over the stationary thread again, and through the loop formed by the working thread. (See Figure 1.) Pull tight.

Figure 1

Overhand knot: Take the left end of the thread, pass it over and then under the right end. (See Figure 2.) Pull tight.

Figure 2

Slip Knot: To start any crochet project you must use a slip knot. Hold the tail thread in your left hand, leaving about 6 inches (15.2 cm) hanging free. Make a loop with the working thread that lays over the tail thread. Now use the hook to reach through the loop, and pull up the working thread. (See Figure 3.) Tighten the knot and you're ready to work.

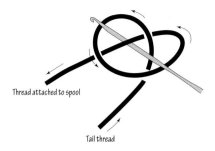

Thread attached to spool

Tail thread

Figure 3

Square Knot: The square knot is one of the easiest knots to tie, because it's simply two overhand knots. Be careful when doing the second half of the knot, or it can go wrong and turn into a granny knot, which will not lie flat and is not secure.

With thread A in the right hand and thread B in the left, lay A over and then under B. (See Figure 4.) Thread A is now on the left and thread B on the right. Lay thread A over and under thread B, and pull to tighten. An easy-to-remember rule is: "right over left, under and tie; left over right, under and tie." This creates one loop that goes over both threads on one side and another loop that goes under both threads on the other side.

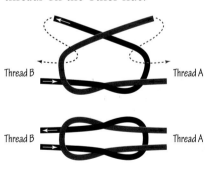

Thread B   Thread A

Thread B   Thread A

Figure 4

Surgeon's knot: Take the left end of the thread and pass it over, under, over, and under the right end. Next, take the right end, and pass it over, under, over, and under the left end. (See Figure 5.) Pull tight. This knotting can be used to secure the ends of loomed bead-weaving.

Figure 5

Weaver's Knot: Joins a new thread to an old thread, making a continuous strand throughout the project; this knot is handy if working with tight tension, when ending or adding a thread by weaving back into the work isn't practicable. Try to position the knot as close to the work as possible, reducing the number of times it must pass through a bead that is already full of thread.

Place the tail end of the new thread under the tail end of the old thread. (See Figure 6a.) Using the long portion of the new thread, wrap it around and behind the short end of the new thread, forming a loop around the old thread. (See Figure 6b.) Place the new thread over the old one. Pass the old thread end over the new and down into the loop. (See Figure 6c.)

Close the loop by pulling on the new thread end, then pull the two old threads away from the two new threads. If the knot has been tied correctly it won't slip. Don't cut the ends; let them be woven in as you stitch. Later, if any ends are sticking out, clip them very close to the work.

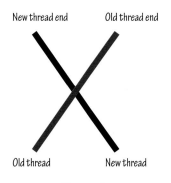

New thread end   Old thread end

Old thread   New thread

Figure 6a

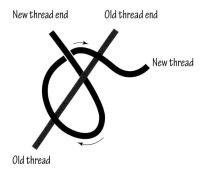

New thread end   Old thread end

New thread

Old thread

Figure 6b

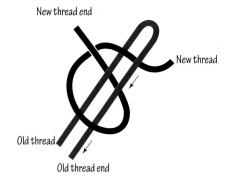

New thread end

New thread

Old thread

Old thread end

Figure 6c

BLOCKING

After you knit, crochet, or needle-point a piece, it is sometimes necessary to block it in order to set (and sometimes adjust) the stitches, to ensure that the piece is square and the edges lie flat. This often improves the look of a finished item by eliminating any unevenness. An easy way to do this is in your home oven. Turn the oven on to 200° F. Wet the needlework in cool water until the thread is soaked throughout. Blot out the excess water with a dish towel and then place the needlework right-side up on a clean cookie sheet. Adjust the rows of stitches, beads, and selvedge edges so that they are flat and line up vertically and horizontally. Place in the oven and turn the oven off. Leave project in the oven for several hours, or overnight, until the piece is dry.

For beaded cross-stitch or beaded embroidery on linen or other washable cloth, it is often desirable to gently wash the piece after completion, as the floss and fabric can become dingy from the concentrated hand-work. Soak the fabric in cold water with a mild soap for five to ten minutes. Rinse well and roll in a towel to remove excess water. Do not wring. Place the piece face down on a dry towel and iron on a warm setting until the fabric is dry.

BEADS

How many beads will you need for a project? This becomes a math problem, so here's a little bit of information to help you figure out how many beads to buy. Most bead sellers sell their beads by the gram, so knowing how many beads are in a gram is important. It's also good to know how many beads of a certain size will fit in an inch (or centimeter), and in a square inch (or square centimeter), so that you can do the math.

There are no standard packages for beads. Each company that sells beads to an individual consumer has its own put-up size. The following may help you determine the number of packages to purchase, but bear in mind that all beads don't weigh the same; a metallic 11/0 seed bead will weigh more than a transparent 11/0 seed bead. Each manufacturer's 11/0 seed beads are of a different size, so this is approximate. All of the beads weighed in this list were from one manufacturer, and they were all opaque black.

BEADS PER GRAM

type of bead	per gram
15/0 seed beads	290
Cylinder seed beads	190
11/0 seed beads	110
8/0 seed beads	38
6/0 seed beads	15

BEADS STRUNG PER LINEAR MEASUREMENT

type of bead	per inch	per cm
15/0 seed beads	24	9
Cylinder seed beads	20	7
11/0 seed beads	18	7
8/0 seed beads	13	5
6/0 seed beads	10	4

BEADS PER SQUARE AREA

type of bead	per sq. inch	per sq. cm
15/0 seed beads	330	54
Cylinder seed beads	285	42
11/0 seed beads	216	35
8/0 seed beads	108	20
6/0 seed beads	70	12

EXAMPLE

To make an amulet purse that's 2 inches (5 cm) wide and 2½ inches (6.4 cm) deep, first find out how many square inches (or square centimeters) there are in the piece, and don't forget that there's a front and a back.

2 x 2½ = 5 square inches
(5 x 6.4 cm = 32.5 cm²)
for one side

5 x 2 = 10 square inches
(12.7 x 5 cm = 63.5 cm²)
for both sides

Look at the list for beads per square area measured, decide which type of bead you'll be using (cylinder beads for our example), and multiply the number of square inches (or square centimeters) by the number of beads in the square area:

10 inches squared x 285
(63.5 cm squared x 285) =
2850 beads.

Now see how many beads per gram there are for the beads you're using, and divide that into the total number of beads: 2850 ÷ 190 = 15 grams of cylinder beads that will be needed to stitch the body of the purse.

TRAYS AND CANISTERS

Trays are essential for spreading out your beads while you work so that you can easily pick them up with your needle and inspect them to determine the bad ones from the good. Plastic divided plates, pie tins, plastic or ceramic watercolor palettes and mixing trays, or any type of shallow container is good. Plain white or a light color is best so that you can see the beads easier, but if you're working with light-colored beads, a darker color tray will work best.

Some can be stored in the original tube or small ziplock bag that they come in. Other beads, which come in hanks or little plastic bags that have to be cut open, will need a storage container. You can buy empty tubes or small ziplock bags, or you can use little jars or plastic bottles such as empty 35mm film canisters. Fairly transparent ones are the best to use because you can see what's inside.

NEEDLES

Beading needles are thin and straight with very small eyes. This can make threading the needle a bit of a challenge. A helpful hint is to cut your thread at an angle before you try to thread the needle.

The needles are sized according to their length and thickness. There are short needles (1¼ inches long), long needles (2 inches long), and loom needles (3 inches long). Most beading needles come in sizes #10, #11, #12, #13, #15, and #16. Size #10 needles are the thickest and size #16 are the thinnest. The numbers approximately correspond to bead sizes. Size #10's are usually good for size 9–10 beads, size #12's are good for beads 11 and 12, and size #15's are good for 14, 15, and smaller beads. Since beading needles can break and bend easily, it is a good idea to have a ready supply.

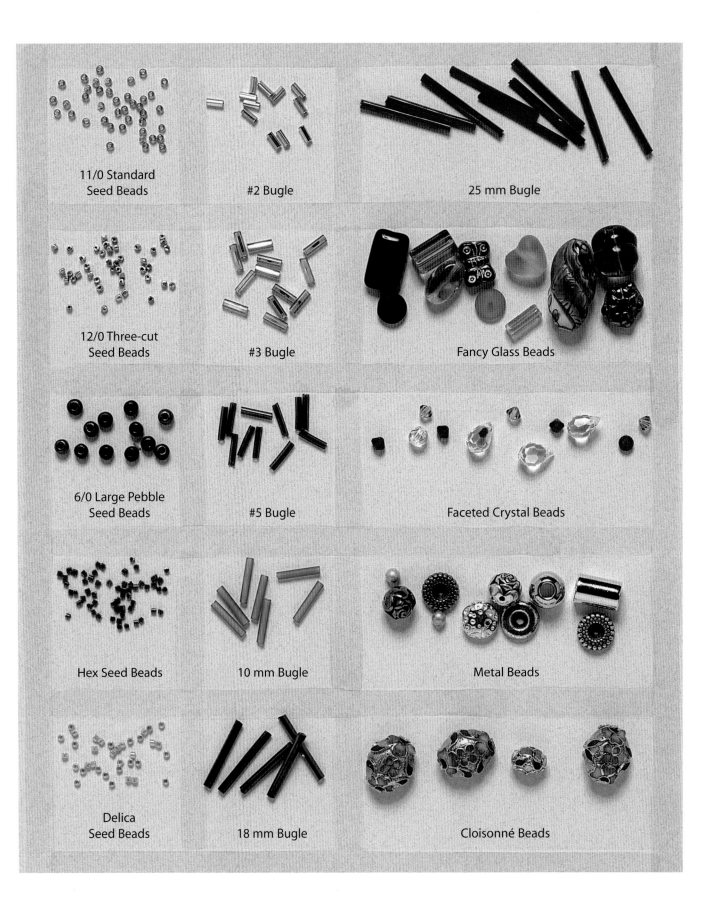

11/0 Standard
Seed Beads

#2 Bugle

25 mm Bugle

12/0 Three-cut
Seed Beads

#3 Bugle

Fancy Glass Beads

6/0 Large Pebble
Seed Beads

#5 Bugle

Faceted Crystal Beads

Hex Seed Beads

10 mm Bugle

Metal Beads

Delica
Seed Beads

18 mm Bugle

Cloisonné Beads

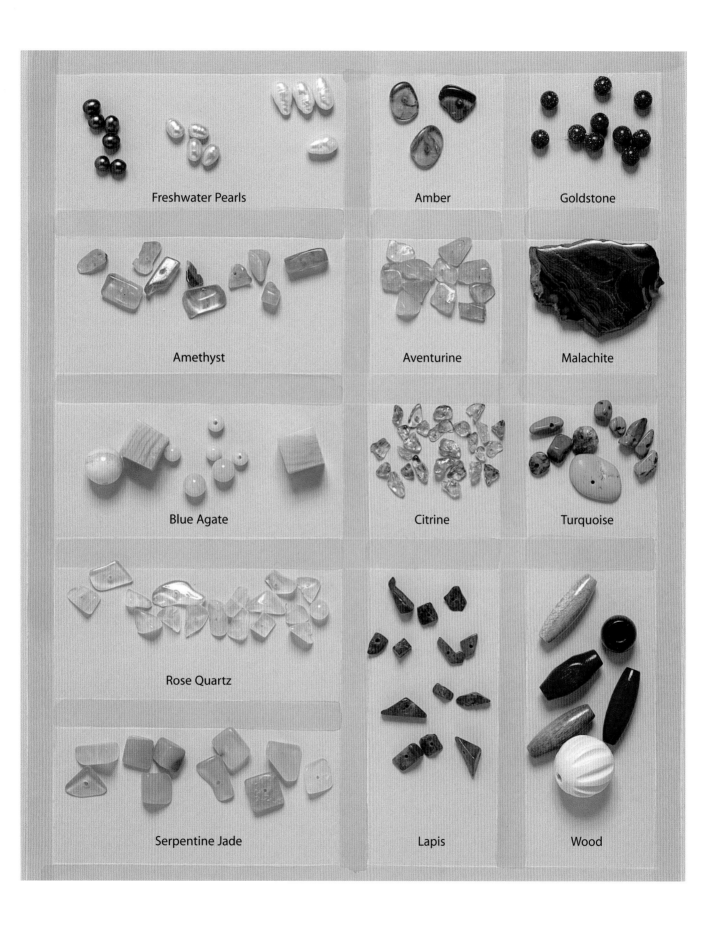

Freshwater Pearls

Amber

Goldstone

Amethyst

Aventurine

Malachite

Blue Agate

Citrine

Turquoise

Rose Quartz

Serpentine Jade

Lapis

Wood

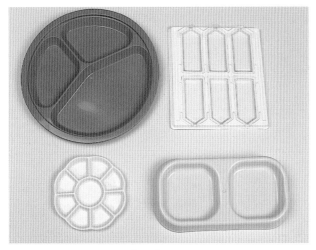
Bead trays

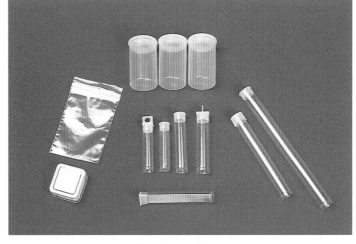
Bead containers

Use twisted wire and Big Eye needles for stringing beads on the thick thread used for knitting and crocheting beads. Twisted wire needles have large, collapsible eyes and come in sizes #6 ultra thin, #10 medium, and #12 heavy. They are made of a thin wire twisted together. They do not have a sharp point; therefore, they are not good for embroidery or leatherwork. Big Eye needles are easy to thread because the eye runs down the entire length of the needle except for the points at either end.

NEEDLES FOR CROSS-STITCH

Blunt needles should slip easily through the fabric holes without piercing fabric threads. For fabric with 11 or fewer threads per inch, use a tapestry needle #24; for 14 threads per inch, use a tapestry needle #24, #26, or #28; for 18 or more threads per inch, use a tapestry needle #26 or #28. Avoid "parking" the needle in the design area of the fabric when not working. It may leave rust or a permanent impression on the fabric.

CROCHET HOOKS

The small, steel crochet hooks needed for crocheting with beads are sizes US 7–13, but not all steel hooks are created equal. The size might read US 9/1.15-mm on a hook from one manufacturer, but another brand might read US 9/1.40-mm because in the US all metric-sized hooks that fall within a certain range of diameters are stamped with a single US hook number.

Everyone crochets with a different tension. If you have a pattern to follow, a gauge will be given. In such a case, the hook size will be determined by your tension. It is best to experiment with the thread of your choice and different-sized hooks until you get the look and gauge you desire.

KNITTING NEEDLES

To do the knitting projects in this book, you will also need knitting needles. The knitting needles used for beadwork are very thin, double-pointed needles. They come in sizes 00–000000, with 00 being the thicker needles and 000000 being the thinnest.

THREAD

Nylon, kevlar, linen, silk, and cotton are some of the fibers used to make beading thread. Nymo is nylon thread that ranges in size (thinnest to thickest) from 000, 00, 0, A, B, C, D, E, F, FF to FFF. Size of the thread to use will depend on the size of bead you are using. Nymo thread comes in different colors and is good for loom weaving, off-loom weaving, and embroidery.

Silk thread comes in several different colors and gauges (thin, medium, and thick sizes). It is good thread for stringing necklaces, knotting, knitting, and crochet.

Kevlar thread is thin and very strong. It is available in a size similar to size 0 Nymo thread. It is

available only in black or beige, but it is good to use when strength is essential.

French linen thread is 100% linen. It comes in two sizes: #60 fine (good for use with beads 13/0, 14/0, 16/0, and 18/0) and #100 medium (good for use with beads 8/0, 10/0, 11/0 and 12/0).

Perle cotton thread is used for knitting and crocheting with beads. It is 100% cotton and available in sizes #50–#3; the smaller the number, the thicker the size. Most bead knitting uses size #8.

BEESWAX

Beeswax strengthens and protects your thread and helps keep it from tangling. Before threading beads, just run your thread through the beeswax, then pull the thread through your fingers to remove excess wax. Also available is thread conditioner called Thread Heaven.

FINDINGS

Findings are metal components used for jewelry. They can be purchased at a bead or craft shop, from mail order catalogs, or craft websites, and they come in a variety of metals.

Keep an assortment of findings on hand made from sterling silver, gold-filled, and some karat golds, for that special piece.

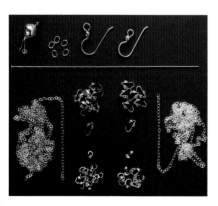

SCISSORS AND TWEEZERS

A small pair of very sharp scissors is essential. Don't cut paper with them, save them for thread only to make clean, close cuts; you want to see beads, not thread ends.

Small tweezers are handy to help you untangle knots, pick up individual beads, and grab a dropped stitch.

LARGER TOOLS

A good set of jeweler's pliers is needed if you're going to make anything that involves metal findings. (Remember when buying that you get what you pay for.)

Chain nose pliers: Available as straight or bent nose, they are rounded on the outside with a flat smooth surface on the inside; used to open and close jump rings, pull the needle through a tight spot, squeeze chain links to a smaller size, break beads, and attach findings.

Round nose pliers: The tips are shaped like small cones, and are used to form a loop on the end of a wire.

Flat nose pliers: (optional) These have a rectangular jaw with square edges. If you want to bend a wire at a right angle, these pliers do it.

Flush cutters: Useful for cutting wire; a file may be needed to smooth the rough ends.

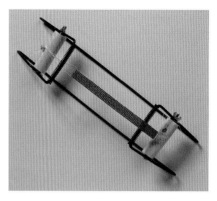

Loom with warp and weft threads

BEAD LOOMS

There are several different bead looms on the market. Most bought looms are designed for narrow, long projects, such as belts and headbands. If you are going to make a wider project, you will probably have to make your own loom. There are several different types of looms that you can make. You can even use a plain wooden picture frame as the base of the loom. Remove the glass, nail springs across opposite ends, then hammer in three nails to the sides of the top and bottom of the frame, leaving about ½ inch of the nails sticking out.

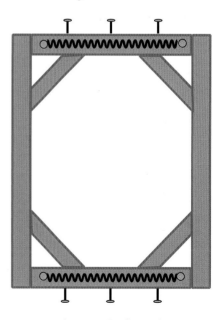

Simple-to-make frame loom

SECTION I

Netting

Netted Christmas Ornament

MATERIALS

Delica Japanese tublar beads:
- 4 grams silver-lined red, #602
- 5 grams silver-lined emerald, #605
- 1 gram silver-lined gold, #42
- 2 grams silver-lined violet, #610

1¾ inch x 2½ inch glass ball or 2¼ inch round glass ball
6 red center-drilled glass disks
12 ½ inch bugle beads
6 bugle beads ⅜-inch long by ⅛-inch thick
18 round red glass beads, 3mm
Beading thread, size B
Beading needle, size 12
Scissors

The samples shown were beaded on hand-blown, egg-shaped ornaments approximately 1¾ inches x 2¼ inches. Instructions follow for the ornament on the right. To use a 2¼-inch round glass ball, use size 11/0 seed beads instead of the Delicas, and follow the basic instructions after making the adjustments listed at the end of the project.

For the first six rounds, work the netting in a flat circle on a table. On Round 7, place your beading on the glass ball. On Rounds 7, 9 13, and 16 (decrease rounds), adjust the netting by pulling it tightly down so that it clings to the ball and the beads in the decrease round do not have gaps of thread.

Round 1: String twelve repeats of three violet beads and one gold bead. Tie the tail end and working thread into a square knot to form a circle, leaving a 6" tail to knot and weave into the netting.

Round 2: Position the circle so that the thread is coming out the right side of a gold bead. String three violet, one gold, three violet. PNT the next gold bead on Round 1. Repeat all around the circle. PNT the first three violet beads and the first gold bead in the round.

Rounds 3–4: Following the design chart, complete Rounds 3 and 4 in the same manner as Round 2, using three red, one gold, and three red for Round 3, and four green, one gold, and four green for Round 4.

Round 5: Complete Round 5 the same as the previous rounds, using five green, one gold, and five green beads around. However, at the end of the round, instead of passing through the first five green and one gold bead to prepare for the next round, only PNT the first green bead strung at the beginning of the round. Now you are ready for Round 6.

Round 6: String seven green, one gold, seven green beads, and PNT one green, one gold, and one green bead. Repeat around. At the end of the round, PNT the first seven beads in the round and one gold bead.

Rounds 7–15: Following the design chart, complete these rounds the same as Round 2 using the appropriate number and color of beads.

Round 16: String one red, one gold, one red, and PNT the next green bead. Repeat around, then string through the whole round again. Tighten this round by pulling the netting down snugly around the ball. PNT one red and one gold bead.

Bottom Fringe Round: String three red, one bugle, one 3mm round, one violet Delica. Skip the violet Delica and PNBT the 3mm round and bugle bead. String three red Delicas and PNT the next gold bead on Round 16. Repeat around.

Middle Fringe: Begin a new thread or PNBT the beads up to Round 5. PNT the beads on a section of Round 5 so that the needle is coming out the left side of a gold bead as shown on the middle fringe round of the design chart. String fourteen red Delicas, one disk, three red Delicas. PNT the fourth Delica on the other side of the disk. String ten red Delicas. Skip the second hanging gold bead on Round 5 and PNT the third hanging gold bead on Round 5. Repeat five times. PNT the beads on Round 5 so that the thread is coming out the next hanging gold bead. String twelve red Delicas, one ⅛-inch-thick bugle bead, three red Delicas, one 3mm round, three red Delicas. PNBT the bugle bead. String twelve red Delicas. Pass the needle under the strand of beads with the disk and through the gold bead. Repeat around. PNUT the beads to Round 1.

Top Picot Edge: Position the thread so that it is coming out of the middle violet bead in one of the Round 1 sections. String two red, one gold, one violet, and PNBT the gold. String two red and PNT the next middle violet bead on Round 1. Repeat this sequence around the top of the ornament, alternating a green bead and a violet bead for the tip of the picot. Tie off and weave in thread.

Adjustment for a 2¼-inch Round Glass Ball:

Rounds 7–9 have five beads, one bead, and five beads in each repeat.

The next four rounds have four beads, one bead, and four beads in each repeat.

The next round has three beads, one bead, and three beads in each repeat.

The next two rounds have two beads, one bead, and two beads in each repeat.

The last round, bottom and middle fringe, and top picot edge are the same as in the listed instructions.

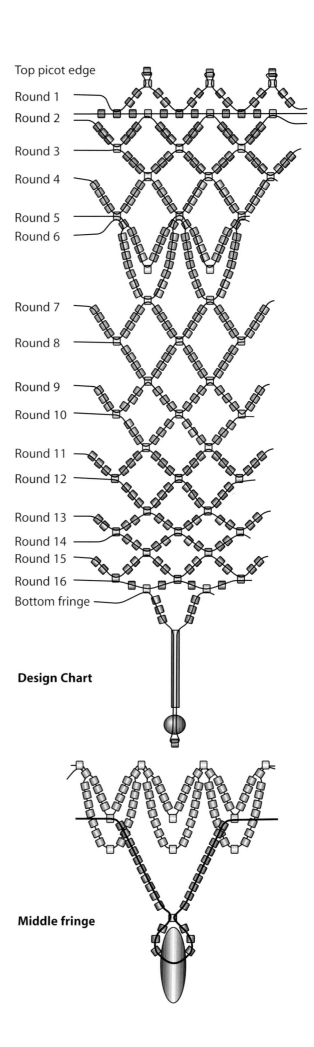

Top picot edge
Round 1
Round 2
Round 3
Round 4
Round 5
Round 6
Round 7
Round 8
Round 9
Round 10
Round 11
Round 12
Round 13
Round 14
Round 15
Round 16
Bottom fringe

Design Chart

Middle fringe

Variations of Chevron Chain

Variation 1. This chain is compact, with only one outside edge bead.

Pick up six beads in the color order shown in Figure 1, looping back through the first bead before adding the others. Pass back up through bead 1, and pick up one light and two dark beads. Weave down through bead 5. (See Figure 2.) Continue in this manner for the length of the piece.

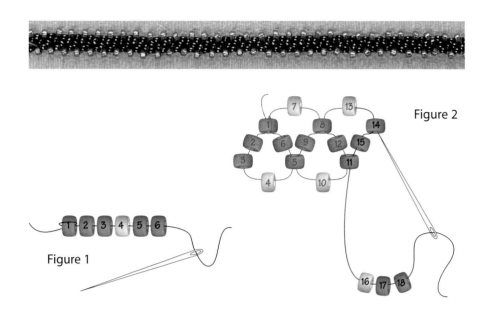

Figure 2

Figure 1

Variation 2. This narrow version is so tight that you can't see the telltale V of the chevron. Here, two beads are stitched through in every interior position, and the outside edge bead stays at one.

Pick up seven beads in the color order shown in Figure 3, looping back through the first bead before adding the others. Pass the needle back up through beads 2 and 1, and pick up two dark and one light bead. Now pass the needle back down through beads 7 and 6. Continue adding three beads, passing through two for each subsequent stitch. (See Figure 4.)

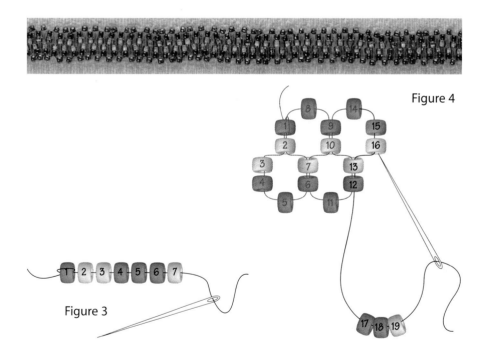

Figure 4

Figure 3

Variation 3. Here, the length of each leg of the V has been extended, and there are two outside edge beads, giving the chain an open and wider format.

Pick up nine beads in the color order shown in Figure 5, looping back through the first bead before adding the others. Pass the needle back up through bead 1 and pick up two light and three dark beads. Now pass the needle down through bead 7. (See Figure 6.) Continue in this manner until the desired length is reached.

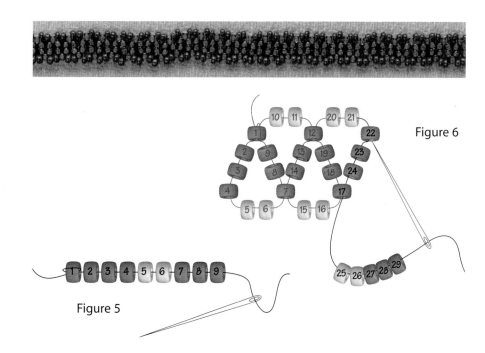

Figure 6

Figure 5

Variation 4. This very symmetrical variation is the one that I used in the basic instructions and the one that I seem to use the most when making dimensional chevron chain vessels. The outside edge beads have increased to three, pushing the V open.

Pick up ten beads in the color order shown in Figure 7, looping back through the first bead before adding the others.

Weave back up through bead 1 and pick up three dark and three light beads. Now pass the needle down through bead 8. Continue in this manner until the desired length is reached. (See Figure 8.)

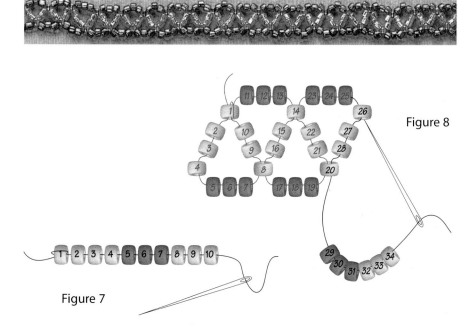

Figure 8

Figure 7

Variation 5. In this version, the chain widens and the shape of the V changes somewhat because two beads are used to join each stitch instead of one.

Pick up thirteen beads in the color order shown in Figure 9, looping back through the first bead before adding the others. Pass the needle back up through beads 2 and 1, and pick up three dark and four light beads. Now pass the needle down through beads 11 and 10. Continue in this manner, referring to Figure 10, until the desired length is reached.

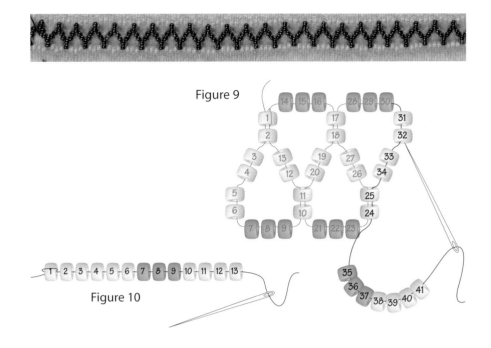

Figure 9

Figure 10

Variation 6. This chain is similar to Variation 1, but with a count of three edge beads and a different color placement, which gives it a braided look.

Pick up eight beads in the color order shown in Figure 11, looping back through the first bead before adding the others. Pass the needle back up through bead 1, and pick up five dark beads. Now pass the needle down through bead 7. Pick up four light beads and one dark bead, and pass up through bead 12. Pick up five light beads and pass down through bead 17. Pick up four dark and one light bead, and pass through bead 22. (See Figure 12). Repeat the pattern from bead 9.

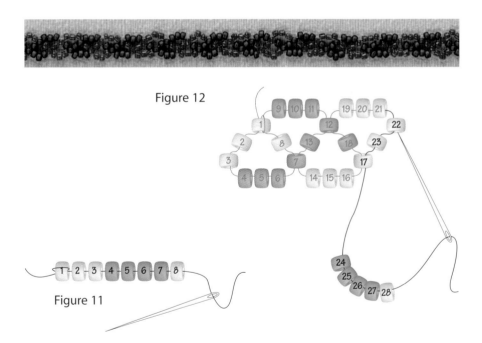

Figure 12

Figure 11

Variation 7. This variation changes the color of its center bead for a different look.

Pick up eleven beads in the color order shown in Figure 13, looping back through the first bead before adding the others. Pass the needle back up through beads 2 and 1. Pick up three dark beads, two light, and one dark. Now pass the needle down through beads 10 and 9. Repeat the pattern for the desired length, referring to Figure 14 as you work.

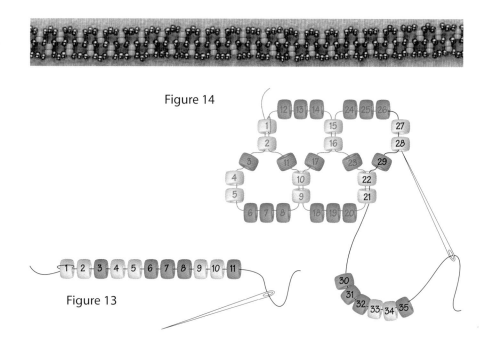

Figure 14

Figure 13

Variation 8. Instead of having a row of beads on the outside edges, tiny fringes were formed at the turns for a very different look.

Pick up nine beads in the color order shown in Figure 15, looping back through the first bead before adding the others.

Pass the needle back up through bead 1. Pick up two light beads and one dark bead, pass back through the second light bead, and pick up two light beads and one dark bead. Now pass the needle down through bead 8. Repeat the pattern, referring to Figure 16 as you work.

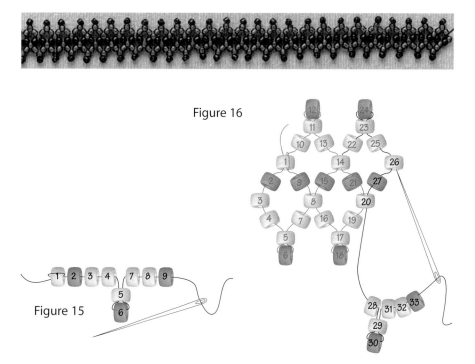

Figure 16

Figure 15

Variation 9. It seems that the variations are endless. This one has the tiny fringes on one side only, using an 8/0 bead at the drop point. The count has increased in the interior section, and the needle passes through two beads on the up stitch and one bead on the down stitch.

Pick up fourteen beads in the color order shown in Figure 17, looping back through the first bead before adding the others. Pass the needle back up through beads 2 and 1. Pick up seven dark beads, and pass down through bead 12. Pick up two dark beads, one 8/0 bead, and one dark bead, then pass back through the 8/0 bead, and pick up five dark beads. Now pass the needle up through beads 19 and 18. Repeat the pattern, referring to Figure 18 as you work.

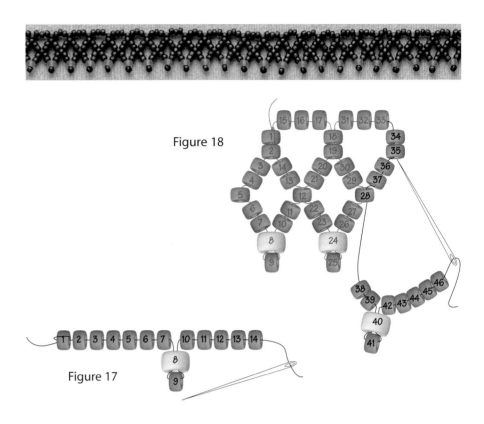

Figure 18

Figure 17

Ribbon Choker

FINISHED SIZE
13½ inches (34.3 cm)

WHAT YOU'LL NEED
11/0 cylinder seed beads:
    15 grams transparent light gray iris
4 mm Czech fire-polished trimbeads:
    83 dark ruby iris
Light gray beading thread, size D
Beading needle, size 12
Satin or velvet ribbon

INSTRUCTIONS
Row 1. Using the cylinder seed beads, stitch a chevron chain 83 sets long; follow Figure 1 for bead placement. The size of the chevron chain is the same for the first three rows.

Row 2. Turn (see Figure 7 on page 10 in the basic instructions for chevron chain), then stitch back across the length of the initial chain.

Row 3. Turn again, and stitch the third row. The thread path is shown in Figure 2 in black.

Row 4. The size of the chevron and the addition of a trim bead make row 4 a little different. After you make the weaving turn, string on five cylinder seed beads, one trim bead, and four more cylinder seed beads. Pass back up through the first cylinder bead, and continue across the row with this bead count. (See Figure 2.) When you're finished, weave and knot the thread back into the main body of the work.

ADDING THE CLASP LOOPS
If the thread is long enough, weave up to bead 1 of row 3, and string on 15 cylinder seed beads. Attach this loop of beads to bead 1 of row 1. Reinforce the loop by passing back through all of the loop beads and each of the #1 beads several times. Weave and knot the thread into the main body of the work. Repeat the process of adding a loop to the other side of the choker. To wear the choker, pass the ribbon through one loop, position the choker on your neck, and thread the other loop with the ribbon; tie the ribbons into a bow.

Figure 1

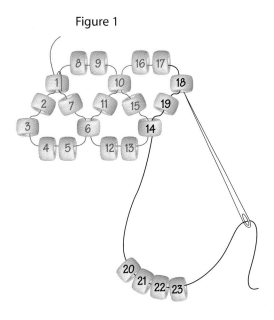

Figure 2

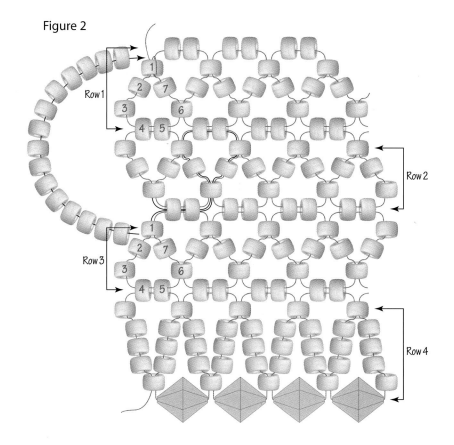

Row 1

Row 2

Row 3

Row 4

Pagoda Basket

FINISHED SIZE

3¾ inches (9.5 cm) tall x 2¼ inches (5.7 cm) diameter

WHAT YOU'LL NEED

11/0 seed beads:
  70 grams opaque light orange
  14 grams opaque orange
  14 grams lined blue/magenta
Rose tan beading thread, size F
Beading needles
Sizes 12 and 13
Sharps, size 12

Begin this basket at the top and work your way down. Its design is a series of dimensional triangular chevron chain tubes spaced apart with flat chevron chain. Each piece is worked directly from the previous section. A tight tension is very important! Close the bottom of the basket with peyote stitch. Use a weaver's knot (see page 30) to add thread, making sure that the knot lies inside interior beads only, as the edge beads are used for attaching upcoming rows.

THE BODY OF THE BASKET

1. Thread the needle with a long piece of thread, and stitch a one-color version of variation 3, using the light orange beads. (See Figure 1.) Do 29 sets of the chain, and join the two ends with the 30th set. (See Figure 2.) Weave to the top edge to begin the second row. Tie off the tail thread, remembering to unloop the first bead.

2. Stitch the second row in two colors; use orange beads for the interior and three magenta ones per set for the edge. Begin the second row with a 10-bead triangle, and stitch all the way around the first row, attaching the second row to it. (See Figure 3.)

3. Weave through beads until the needle exits bead 7, heading right. (See Figure 3.) Now close the dimensional three-sided chain, using all magenta beads. String on 4 beads, and pass the needle into beads A and B, folding rows 1 and 2 so that row 3 fits snugly between the other two. Pick up three beads, and weave back through beads 1, C, D, and E. Continue picking up beads and weaving between the two rows to form the third row. When you've finished, weave to the top edge.

4. Add beads along the top edge to fill in the gaps between sets. (See Figure 4, page 49.) Do this only along the top edge of the basket; adding these beads will help open the top of the basket. Weave through the beads in row 1 to the bottom edge, exiting a set of edge beads. Stitch row 4, using light orange beads and chevron chain variation 3. Attach it to the bottom edge of row 1.

5. Repeat these four rows five times, but end with rows 1–3 only. You'll have a total of seven triangular tubes and six plain chevron chain sections.

THE BOTTOM OF THE BASKET

6. Use peyote stitch to make the bottom of the basket. The bottom of the basket needs to be flat. To get that, you may have to

put in a row then take it out, because there are just too many beads. If this is necessary, restitch the row, decreasing its size by either reducing the stitch width or dropping a stitch altogether. Trial and error works well here.

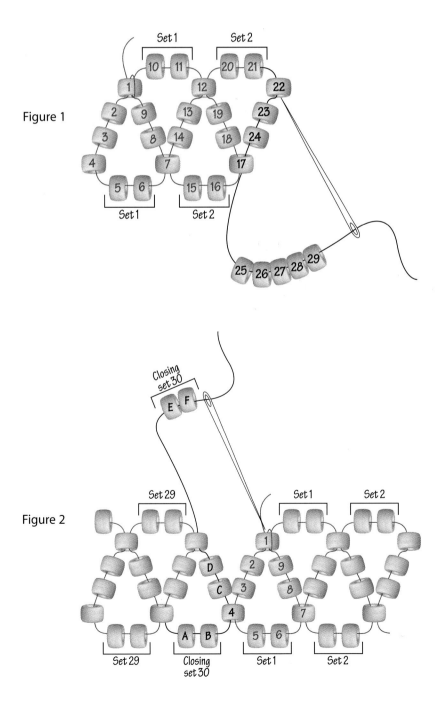

Figure 1

Figure 2

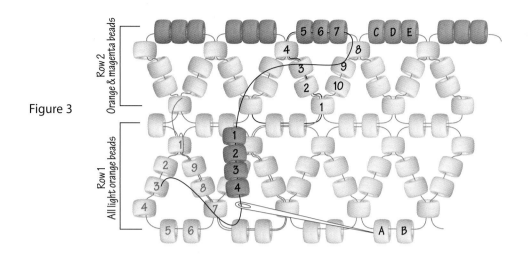

Figure 3

Row 2
Orange & magenta beads

Row 1
All light orange beads

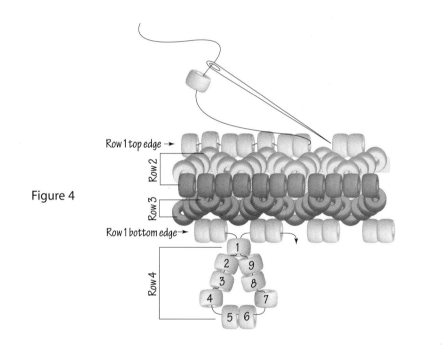

Figure 4

Row 1 top edge →

Row 2

Row 3

Row 1 bottom edge →

Row 4

Rainbow Collar

FINISHED SIZE

12 inches (30.5 cm) diameter

WHAT YOU'LL NEED

There are approximately 20 different colors and seven different types of beads used in this broad collar; the majority are size 12/0 and 11/0 seed beads, plus 3- and 4-mm Czech fire-polished beads and small bugle beads. The palette in the chevron chain sections uses colors from the rainbow, with the black and white rondels creating contrast in color and visual texture. You can use beads that you happen to have on hand, and adjust the fit as necessary.

Beading thread, size B
Beading needle, size 13
3 small decorative buttons
Macrame board
Straight pins

This collar is made up of four rows of chevron chain and two rows of needle-woven small rondels. Each strip is connected by interweaving the bottom-end beads of one strip with the top-end beads of the second, adding beads as necessary to create a smooth curved line. Pinning and shaping your work to the macrame board is essential. Use large-hole beads at the beginnings and ends of the strips, as you'll be passing through them many times, and don't cut the end threads—they'll be needed later.

THE BODY OF THE NECKLACE

Row 1: Chevron Chain. Enlarge the template (opposite) to the final size indicated on the drawing, and attach it to the macrame board. You can use a plastic lid in the center as a guide. Stitch the first strip of chevron chain to fit the circumference of the inner circle minus 2 inches; see Figure 1 for the style and basic colors, and also look closely at the photograph. Using straight pins, attach the chevron chain to the macrame board to fit the curve of the inner circle. Adjust the length for a better fit to your neck, if necessary.

Working from the middle, add beads between the end beads of the chevron chain to form a solid curved line that lies flat. (See Figure 2.) It will take some patience to get the right number of beads between each section.

Row 2: Rondels. Make a total of 37 black and white rondels: 19 with white centers and black points, and 18 with black centers and white points (your total number may vary, according to the length of row 1). Don't trim the thread ends away just yet, as they'll be used for linking one rondel to another to form a chain.

To make a rondel, string 12 beads, then pass the needle through all of the beads again, forming a circle.

Weave through beads 1 and 2, pick up three beads, and pass through bead 4; pick up three beads, and pass through bead 6. Continue picking up three beads and passing through one bead all the way around the circle, forming six points. (See Figure 3, page 52.) To make the center bead of each point stand out, weave through these beads again, bypassing each center bead. As an example, pass the needle through beads 13, 15, and 4, bypassing bead 14, and pull the thread tightly to pop bead 14 out. (See Figure 4 on page 52 for the thread path.) Do this all the way around the circle.

When you've made all of the rondels, join them by sewing the point bead of one rondel to a point bead of another rondel. Sew between these two beads several times to secure them, ending back at the first rondel. Weave down to the next point bead, but don't join it yet and don't cut the thread; a bead may have to be added at the second point to accommodate the increased circumference. (See Figure 5 on page 52.) Continue to join rondels at the upper points and then lay them on the macrame board right below the first row of chevron chain, curving them to fit the curve of the template. If the lower side points of the rondels are spread too far apart to be joined directly together, add a bead between these points. Sew all of these second rondel points together.

After positioning the rondel chain on the macrame board, fitting it to row 1, gently lift and sew all of the uppermost points of the rondels to the lower edge of row 1.

Row 3: Chevron Chain. Stitch the next row of chevron chain; Figure 6 on page 52 gives the pattern and color placement.

Note: The photo shows short bugle beads, but in the graph, beads 18 and 19 are shown as seed beads; either works well.

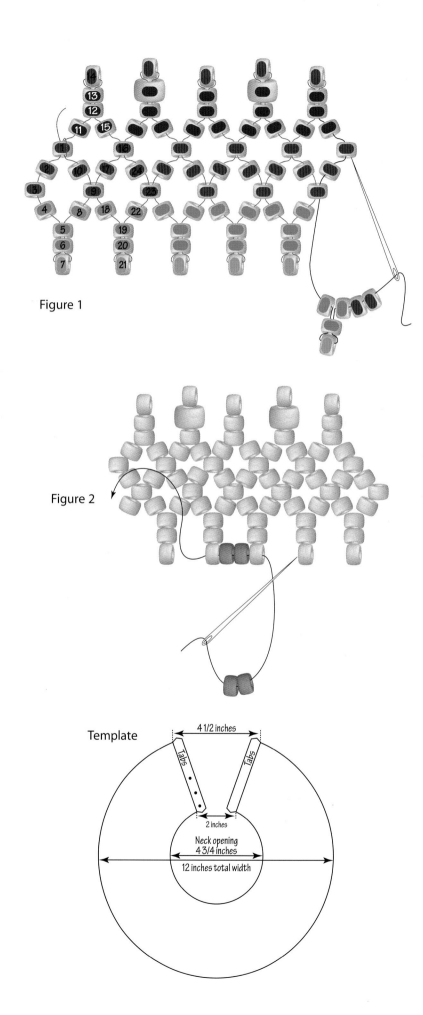

Figure 1

Figure 2

Template

4 1/2 inches

Tabs

Tabs

2 inches

Neck opening
4 3/4 inches

12 inches total width

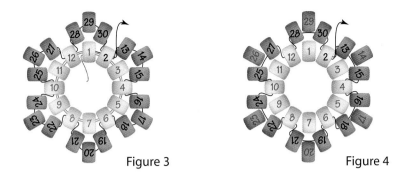

Figure 3   Figure 4

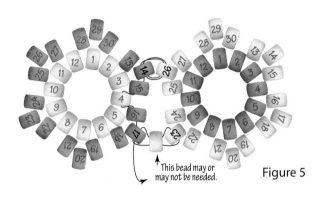

↑ This bead may or
may not be needed.   Figure 5

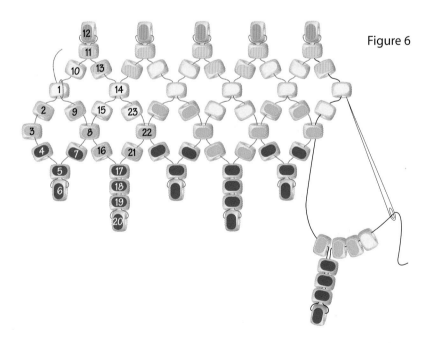

Figure 6

Pin the chain to the macrame board under row 2, being careful to follow the curve of the collar.

Working from the middle, add beads between the upper-end beads of the chevron chain, forming a solid line that lays flat and curves to match row 2. This is the same process shown in Figure 2, but on the upper edge instead. With that step completed, attach the lower points of each rondel in row 2 to the line of beads in row 3.

Row 4: Chevron Chain. Stitch the next row of chevron chain; Figure 7 on page 53 shows the pattern and color placement of the beads. Lay this strip on the board, and pin it into position, following the curve of the necklace.

The method used to join this row with the previous row is a bit different. Working from the middle, sew through the lower point bead of row 3, pick up a bead, sew through the upper point bead of row 4, pick up a bead, and sew through the next lower point bead of row 3. Continue in this manner until you reach the end, then stitch the other side. Remember that the work needs to stay flat and maintain the proper curve, so you may need more than one bead between points. Working from the middle, add beads between the end beads of the chevron chain, forming a solid curved line that lies flat. (See Figure 2.)

Row 5: Rondels. This row of rondels is made up of 15 with black centers and white points, 32 with white centers and black points, and 16 all-purple ones, for a total of 63 rondels. Stitch them together in the following pattern: white center, purple, white center, black center. After you join the rondels (at one point only) to form a chain, pin the chain to the macrame board, to see if any extra beads need to be added between the second points. Sew these points together, then attach this row of rondels to row 4 in the same way you attached row 2 to row 1.

Row 6: Chevron Chain. Stitch the last row of chevron chain. (See Figure 8.) Bugle beads could replace beads 6, 7, and 8. Pin this last strip to the macrame board, and adjust the length if necessary. Working from the middle, add beads between the upper points to form a solid line. Repeat on the other side. Attach the lower rondel points to this line of beads.

THE CLOSING

Make two peyote stitch tabs that measure seven beads wide and as long as the necklace is deep, decreasing them to points at both ends. Pin these tabs into position on your template. The opening will be reduced by about ½ inch (1.3 cm) on each side. Make any adjustments to the chevron chain and rondel rows by either lengthening or shortening them so that they butt up to the peyote tabs. Stitch each end of each row to its respective tab.

Sew the three buttons on the tab, weaving through beads to hide any threads. Make closing loops of beads on the edge of the other tab, lining them up with the buttons. Weave in and trim any loose threads.

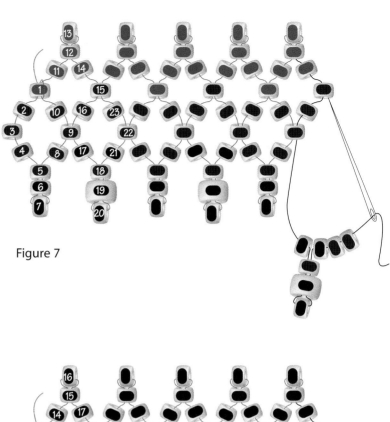

Figure 7

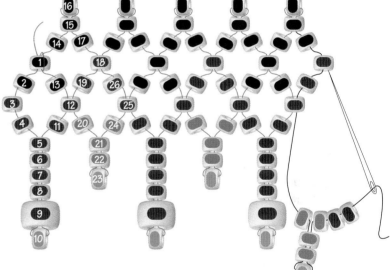

Figure 8

Peyote Spiral Bracelet

FINISHED SIZE
4 inches (10.2 cm) in diameter

MATERIALS
15/0 navy blue, orange, and green seed beads
14/0 yellow seed beads
11/0 dark blue seed beads
10/0 light blue seed beads
8/0 orange and red seed beads
Beading thread, size A, in color to blend with beads
Beading needle, size 12

Easy to make and wear, these bracelets are lightweight and flexible.

Note: This project starts with three dummy rows; these will be removed before closing the bracelet, but use the same beads and pattern for the dummy rows, too. Keep a tight tension throughout this project.

1. String on a stop bead (loop through an odd bead, and position it 6 inches [15.2 cm] from the end of the thread), then string these:
   2 – 8/0 orange
   2 – 8/0 red
   2 – 8/0 orange
   2 – 10/0 light blue
   2 – 11/0 dark blue
   2 – 14/0 yellow
   2 – 15/0 green
   2 – 15/0 red
   2 – 15/0 navy blue
   2 – 15/0 red
   2 – 15/0 green
   2 – 14/0 yellow
   2 – 11/0 dark blue
   2 – 10/0 light blue

2. Form a circle by passing the needle through the first orange bead, by-passing the stopper bead, then start this pattern:
   Add 1 – 8/0 orange bead, peyote into the next red bead.
   Add 1 – 8/0 red bead, peyote into the next orange bead.
   Add 1 – 8/0 orange bead, peyote into the next light blue bead.
   Add 1 – 10/0 light blue bead, peyote into the next dark blue bead.
   Add 1 – 11/0 dark blue bead, peyote into the next yellow bead.
   Add 1 – 14/0 yellow bead, peyote into the next green bead.
   Add 1 – 15/0 green bead, peyote into the next red bead.
   Add 1 – 15/0 red bead, peyote into the next navy blue bead.
   Add 1 – 15/0 navy blue bead, peyote into the next red bead.
   Add 1 – 15/0 red bead, peyote into the next green bead.
   Add 1 – 15/0 green bead, peyote into the next yellow bead.
   Add 1 – 14/0 yellow bead, peyote into the next dark blue bead.
   Add 1 – 11/0 dark blue bead, peyote into the next light blue bead.
   Add 1 – 10/0 light blue bead, and pass through (step-up) the next two orange beads. By passing through the two orange beads, you're ready for the next row of even count tubular peyote.

Note: From this point on, whatever bead size and color that you're exiting is the size and color that you'll pick up and stitch next. For example, if you're coming out of an 8/0 orange bead, pick up an 8/0 orange bead.

Repeat the pattern for at least 13 spirals. Adjust for personal fit.

FINISHING

3. Remove the stopper bead and the first three dummy rows. Close the bracelet by matching the pattern on each end, so that the beads interlock. You may have to add additional peyote rows on one end for the pattern to match. Weave the ends together by zigzagging back and forth with the thread and needle. Reinforce the closure by reweaving through the beads again.

Peyote Kaua'i Rings

FINISHED SIZE

1⅜ x ⅞ x ¾ inches
  (3.4 x 2.2 x 1.9 cm)

MATERIALS

11/0 seed beads or cylinder
  seed beads
Focal point bead (for center top)
Trim beads (to embellish sur-
  face—15/0's, crystals, drops,
  anything you like)
Beading thread, size B or D
Beading needle, size 12

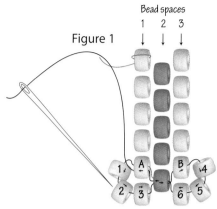

Figure 1

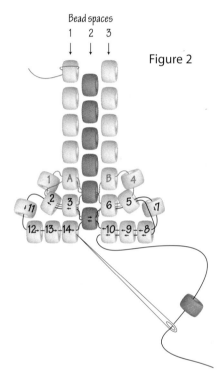

Figure 2

FIRST LAYER

Rows 1–10. Using a single thread, string on a stop bead, and loop back through it, leaving a 6-inch (15.2-cm) tail. Put three beads on your thread, and do odd count flat peyote stitch for a total of ten rows.

Note: To avoid losing your place, check off the rows as you work them.

Row 11. Increase the outside vertical rows (1 and 3) to three-drop peyote by putting three beads in the space of one. (See Figure 1.)

With the thread exiting bead A, pick up three beads, and pass through the center bead and bead B, heading right. Pick up three more beads (4, 5, and 6), and go back through the center bead and bead A, heading left. To set up for the next row, pass through beads 2 and 3, bypassing bead 1.

Row 12. Do a single peyote stitch, but pass the needle through beads 6 and 5, bypassing bead 4.

Row 13. Now you'll add four beads in vertical rows 3 and 1. (See Figure 2.)

Coming out of bead 5, pick up four beads (7–10), pass through the center bead (heading left) and beads 3 and 2 in row 11. Pick up four more beads (11–14), and pass through the center bead and beads 6 and 5 in row 11 (heading right). To set up for the next row, bypass bead 7, and weave through beads 8, 9, and 10.

Row 14–17. Continue doing flat peyote, using a regular three-drop in vertical rows 1 and 3 and single peyote in vertical row 2.

Row 18. Increase the center vertical row to two-drop peyote.

Rows 19–21. Continue doing flat peyote, using a regular three-drop in vertical rows 1 and 3 and two-drop peyote in vertical row 2.

Row 22. Decrease the center vertical row back to single peyote.

Rows 23–27. Continue peyote, using three-drop in vertical rows 1 and 3 and single peyote in the center.

Row 28. Add the bead in the center vertical row as usual, then begin to decrease by passing the needle through two of the three beads on the outside edge.

Row 29. Pick up two beads, and go through the center bead. Pass the needle through the first two beads in the outer vertical row. Pick up two beads, and finish the odd count turn through two beads on the outside edge.

Row 30. Add one bead in the center vertical row, and pass the needle through one bead in the outer vertical row.

Row 31. Now you'll decrease so that all vertical rows are single peyote.

Pick up a bead, and pass through the center bead and one of the beads in the outer vertical row. Turn, add one bead, and finish the odd count turn.

Rows 32–38. Continue doing single peyote.

EMBELLISHING

Weave a new thread through a few rows on the top of the ring; don't knot the thread. Place and attach the focal point embellishment bead. Add beads to the surface around the focal point bead and all over the top. Embellish the edges with tiny beads—at this point anything goes; be creative and have fun.

FINISHING

After the ring is encrusted, finish the band on the underside to fit your finger. Reinforce with a second layer to the band by adding beads over the center vertical row.

Zigzag Peyote Necklace

FINISHED SIZE

16¾ x 1⅝ inches
 (42.6 x 4.1 cm)

MATERIALS

11/0 cylinder seed beads
 23 grams semi-matte silver-
 lined green (7.5 grams
 weaves approximately 5½
 inches [14 cm])

11/0 seed beads
 5 grams matte blue iris
15/0 seed beads
 1 gram metallic blue iris
45 blue crystals, 4 mm
45 matte blue drop beads,
 3.4 mm
Single 10-mm bead, for
 closure
Blue beading thread, size D
Beading needle, size 12

Use the graph to help you visualize what your own patterns will look like before they're stitched.

Note: For this project, there are a few specialized term you will need to know:

Tweenie: *These are the 11/0 seed beads called "tweenie beads" because they are used to execute the short and long turns between the gemstone groups at the apexes of the zigzags.*

Long Turn: *The long turn has three elements: a main color pair, a tweenie bead, and another main color pair (the main color beads are the 11/0 cylinder seed beads). For the long turns between the apexes, string the three elements, then go back through the first of the main color pairs. The tweenie bead sits in a horizontal position.*

In order to keep the gemstone at the exact center, string the long turn at the apexes with three main colors, one 15/0, one gemstone, one 15/0, and one main color. After stringing, go back through the first two main color beads.

Short Turn: *Use one tweenie bead. For the basic short turn, string the 11/0 bead, then go back through the next available peyote pair. The tweenie bead sits in a horizontal position.*

For this project's short and long turns there are three beads in the tweenie bead space, rather than one. String on a 15/0, an 11/0, and a 15/0 for the tweenie bead, in the turns.

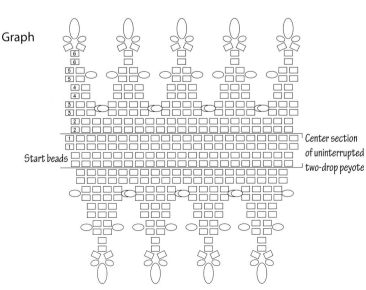

Graph

Start beads

Center section
of uninterrupted
two-drop peyote

1. Starting is slightly different than the established pattern. String on two cylinder seed beads, loop around, and go back through those beads to secure them, leaving an 8-inch (20.3-cm) tail. String on six pairs of main color beads (for a total of 12 main color beads) and the first apex unit, which consists of one main color, one 15/0, one trim bead, one 15/0, and one main color. (See Figure 1.)

   Turn and pass back through the beads numbered 6. Continue with two-drop peyote for three more stitches, with the third stitch going through the two starting cylinder beads. (See Figure 2.) The start-up is in place.

2. To create the zigzag, follow steps A through E.

   A. Do a long turn and three two-drop peyote stitches with the main color. (See Figure 3.)

   B. Do a short turn and three two-drop peyote stitches with the main color. (See Figure 4.) Repeat steps A and B, so that there are two tweenie beads on the top side and two on the bottom side. (See Figure 5.) Do this repeat only once; from now on follow the steps in order without the repeat.

   C. Do a long turn with an apex unit and three two-drop peyote stitches with the main color. (See Figure 5.)

   D. Do a long turn and three two-drop peyote stitches with the main color.

   E. Do a short turn and three two-drop peyote stitches with the main color. Repeat steps A through E; continue this process until the desired length is reached. Figure 6 shows steps A, B, A, B, C, D, E, A, B, and C completed.

Note: When you're making a turn, the beads may twist; you'll need to turn them so you can go through the main color pairs.

3. When you have your desired length, make the clasp by adding a bead or button to one end of the necklace and a loop of beads at the other end (see photo). It's a good idea to reinforce your work by going through the beads at the inside edges, where the necklace gets the most stress.

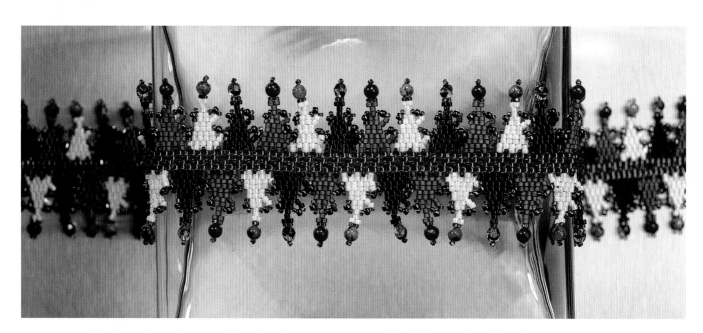

Another color scheme and bead choices creates an entirely different effect from the same pattern.

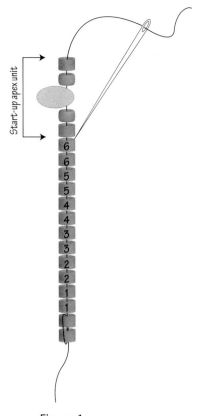

Figure 1

Figure 2

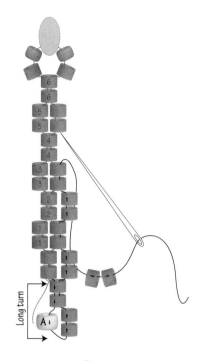

Figure 3

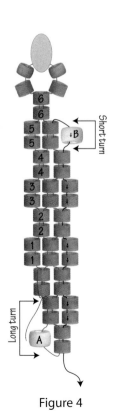

Figure 4

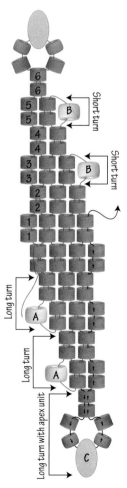

Figure 5

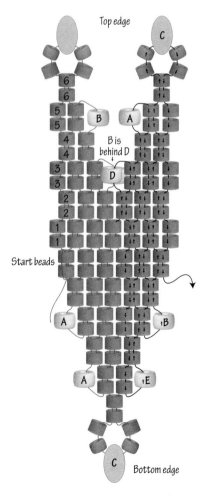

Figure 6

Ivy Leaf Peyote Stitch Bracelet

FINISHED SIZE

7 inches x ¾ inch

MATERIALS

Charlotte beads:
    4 grams navy blue
    4 grams translucent gray
    2 grams eggshell white
    2 grams translucent dark green
    2 grams translucent medium
      green
    2 grams light green
One accent bead, cobalt blue
   (for closure)
White nylon beading thread,
   size 00
Beading needle, size 15
Scissors

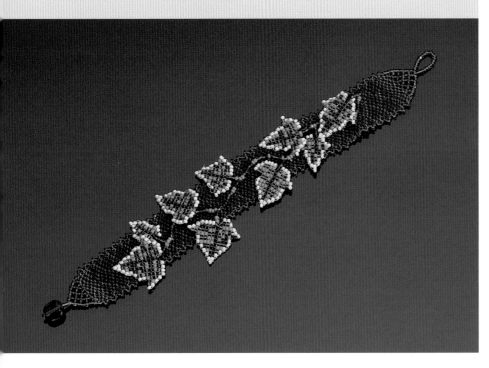

The body of this bracelet is done in peyote stitch and the leaves are made with the square stitch, which lends itself well to making free forms.

BODY OF BRACELET

Rows 1–3: Use about 6 feet of thread. String fourteen gray beads, leaving a tail about 1 foot long to use later for the end netting. String one gray bead. Skip the 14th gray bead strung. PNT next bead. ★String one gray bead. Skip next gray bead. PNT next gray bead.★ Repeat between asterisks until the last bead is passed through. Keep thread tension tight so the beads stack one upon the other. (See Figure 1.) This one row will form Rows 1–3. You will now have seven beads per row.

Rows 4–7: Use gray beads. String one bead. PNT first bead that is extended farther up than the one next to it. ★String one bead. PNT next bead from previous row (the first bead sticking up farther than the other two around it).★ Repeat between asterisks until the end of the row. Rows 5–7 are the same, using gray beads and the flat peyote stitch.

Row 8: Work the same as the other rows, but you must start changing colors between the blue and gray beads according to Design Chart 1 to create the latticework look.

Rows 9–165: Same as Row 8.

Rows 166–172: Work in the peyote stitch using only gray beads.

END NETTING

Working in netting stitch with gray beads, decrease one stitch on each end for five rows.

Row 1: PNT first bead of previous row. String three beads. ★PNT next bead. String three beads.★ Repeat between asterisks three more times (total of five stitches). On last stitch, PNT last two beads of previous row. (See Figure 2.)

Row 2: PNT top bead of last netting stitch. ★String three beads. PNT top bead of next netting stitch.★ Repeat between asterisks three more times (total of four stitches).

Row 3: Same as Row 2, except total of three stitches.

Row 4: Make two netting stitches.

Row 5: Make one netting stitch. Weave in end or, if it's long enough, use for closure. Repeat Rows 1–5 on other end of the bracelet.

LOOP CLOSURE

Work the thread so that it is coming out of the top bead of the end netting. String twenty-three gray beads. PNBT the top bead in the opposite direction of the thread that came out of it. (See Figure 3.) Weave in end, making it secure.

To form large bead clasp on the other end of the bracelet, work thread so that it is coming out of the top bead of end netting. String three gray beads, one octagonal accent bead, one gray bead. (Charlotte beads are so small that you have to pick your accent bead carefully so that the charlotte will not go through the accent bead hole.) PNBT accent bead and then the three gray beads. PNBT the top netting bead in the opposite direction of the thread that came out of it. (See Figure 4.) Weave in end.

Design Chart 1

■ Navy blue
■ Translucent gray

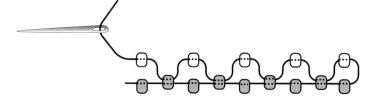

Figure 1

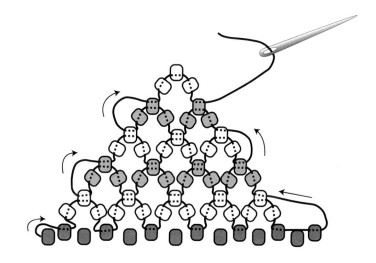

Figure 2

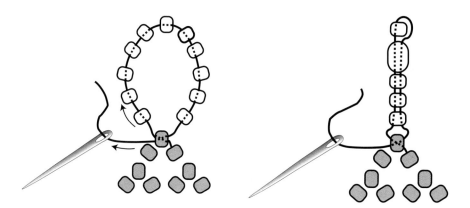

Figure 3   Figure 4

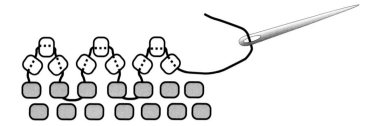

Figure 5

Design Chart 2

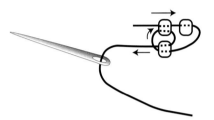

Figure 6

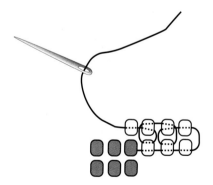

Figure 7

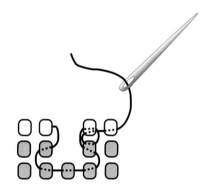

Figure 10

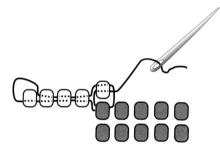

Figure 8

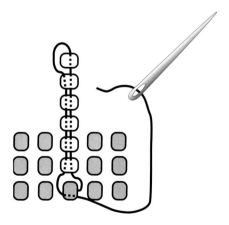

Figure 11

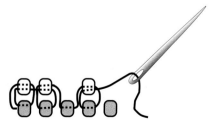

Figure 9

SIDE EDGE NETTING

Secure thread so it is coming out of the first bead of peyote stitch on the side edge of the bracelet. *String three gray beads. PNDT next bead of bracelet edge. PNUT the next bead.* Repeat between asterisks all along the edge of the bracelet. (See Figure 5.) Repeat on other side edge.

LEAVES

Leaves are done in the square stitch. All the leaves start the same way but vary in size and shape the way real leaves do. Vary the color of the leaves with all three greens, making sure that one shade of green goes in a line up the leaf for the vein. Use the white beads to outline the leaves. Feel free to vary the number of leaves, as desired.

Rows 1–2: Start at the tip of the leaf by making a small white triangle. String two white beads (these will be the second row). String one white bead. PNT the first white bead strung in the opposite direction of the row. PNBT the third bead strung. (See Figure 6.) PNT the two white beads on the second row. This will form the triangle.

Row 3: This row is worked in the regular square stitch with increases of one bead on each side. String one white and one dark green bead. PNT (in the opposite direction as the row) first bead on second row. PNBT (in the same direction as the row) the green bead just strung on. String one green bead. PNT (in opposite direction) second bead on second row. PNBT (in same direction) green bead that was just strung on. String one white bead (this is the increased bead). Go on to the next row using last strung white bead as last bead in Row 3. The row ends with a total of four beads (two green in the middle and two white on ends).

Rows 4–8: Work same as Row 3, increasing one bead at the beginning and end of the row. The increased beads are white to ensure that the leaves are outlined in white. The rest of the row consists of random greens except for one dark green (or shade of your choice) bead in the middle of the row for the vein. (See Design Chart 2 for guidance.) On some leaves, don't increase every row so that you have some narrow leaves and some wide ones. For shorter and longer leaves, make six rows on some, eight rows on others before you go to the next step.

Row 6 or 9: Depending on the leaf size, increase two to three beads at the beginning and end of the row. Keep white beads on the ends of the row and greens in the middle.

To increase more than one bead at the beginning of the row, string two or three beads, depending on leaf size. Skip last bead strung and PNBT the other bead or beads strung. Then start row as normal. (See Figure 7.)

It is easier to add beads on the end of the row. String two or three beads. Keep thread tension tight. Go to next row using strung beads as if they were part of row beneath. (See Figure 8.)

Row 7 or 10: Decrease one bead at the beginning and end of each row. Make sure the first and last beads are white.

To decrease one bead at the beginning of the row, simply PNBT second bead from the end and then begin your first stitch. To decrease at the end of the row, simply stop where the row ends.

Repeat Row 7 one or two more times, depending on size of leaf. On the second-to-last row (on most of the leaves this would be the third row after the large increase row), the middle bead (the dark green vein bead) is skipped to leave a space. (See Figure 9.) This leaves room for the stem of the leaf.

The next row is the last row and all white beads are used. When you get to the space, PNT bead on row beneath and then through three beads directly below the space. PNT bead above the last of the three beads, bring thread up, and finish row. (See Figure 10.)

STEM OF LEAF

After the leaf is done, weave thread in so that it is coming out of the bead at the bottom of the space on top of the leaf. String from five to eight beads of random green colors. Skip last bead strung and PNBT all the other stem beads. (See Figure 11.) Weave in end.

VINE

When all leaves are finished, they must be strung together on a vine. Start with 2 feet of thread. Use random green colors. String two beads.

Leave a 6 inch tail to weave into body of bracelet later. PNT top bead of one leaf stem. String twenty-two beads. PNT top bead of next leaf stem. String one bead. PNT top bead of third leaf stem. String twelve beads. PNT top two beads of fourth leaf stem. String seventeen beads. PNT top two beads of fifth leaf stem. String twelve beads. PNT top bead of sixth leaf stem. String ten beads. PNT top two beads of seventh leaf stem. String fourteen beads. PNT top bead of eighth leaf stem. String one green bead. PNT top bead of ninth leaf stem.

Once the vine is finished, attach it to the bracelet. Place the vine in a wavy line on the bracelet so that the leaves can fall in a natural way.

PNBT three beads of the vine. Attach to bracelet by PNT one bead of the bracelet. *PNT next five beads of vine and then attach to bracelet as before.* Make sure the vine lays flat. Repeat between the asterisks until the entire vine is attached. Weave in the end.

Dainty Violets Teacup and Saucer

FINISHED SIZES

Cup—1 inch high x ¾ inch wide; saucer—1 ⅜ inch in diameter.

MATERIALS

Delica Japanese tubular beads:
 7 grams Ceylon light yellow (off-white), #203
 4 grams lined gold, #042
 16 silver-lined violet, #610
 9 lined lime green, #274
 4 lavender, #73
 1 opaque yellow, #721
White nylon beading thread size D
Beading needle size 11 or 12
Scissors

CUP

Round 1: Using doubled thread so that cup will be stiff, string fifty gold beads. Do not make a knot. Weave in the ends later. PNBT all fifty beads to form a ring.

Round 2: This round is done with Ceylon light yellow beads (off-white) in the tubular double drop peyote stitch. String two beads. Skip next two gold beads from Round 1. PNT next two gold beads. (See Figure 1.) Repeat this stitch all the way around ring. Make sure ring of beads stays tight.

Round 3: Same as Round 2. Keep beads tight and make sure they go down, and not out, from the ring.

Round 4: PNT the first two beads from Round 3. String two beads, skip two beads, and PNT next two beads. By Round 4, you will know which two beads to PNT because they will be the ones from the round beneath and they will be sticking up higher than the two beads you skipped from two rounds before. On every other round at the beginning of the round, you must PNT the first two beads from the round below before stringing the two beads.

Round 5: Same as Round 3, except start colored beads according to the design chart. The colored beads can be started just about anywhere on this round.

Keep working in the double drop peyote stitch, adding colored beads as shown on design chart, until Round 21.

Round 21: Decrease one bead every third stitch for a total of three decreases. Decrease by stringing one bead instead of two. (See Figure 2.)

Round 22: Do not decrease. Work in double drop peyote.

Round 23: String one bead in the three decreases from Round 21 and decrease three more times in between the three other decrease stitches.

Round 24: Same as Round 22.

Round 25: String one bead for every one stitch instead of two (peyote stitch).

Rounds 26–28: Same as Round 25.

Round 29: This round starts the foot of the cup. String two gold beads for every stitch (double drop peyote).

Round 30: String one gold bead for every stitch (peyote stitch). When you are finished with the round, PNT the gold beads of both Round 29 and 30. This will form one stiff, straight round of gold beads.

Round 31: This round starts filling up the bottom of the cup. You must work with the cup upside down. PNT until thread is coming out of one of the Ceylon light yellow beads (off-white) along bottom edge. (See Figure 3.) String one bead for each stitch (peyote stitch). This round is hard and awkward.

Rounds 32–33: Work as for Round 31 (these will not be as awkward).

Round 34: Decrease every other stitch. For the decreases on this round, do not string a bead, just PNT.

Round 35: Do not decrease. There will only be one or two stitches left on this round. PNT last beads. Tighten thread and close up hole. Weave in end.

HANDLE

Using doubled thread, string eighteen gold beads. Skip last bead strung and PNBT all seventeen beads. To attach top of handle to cup, PNT the bead on the 6th round down from the top of the cup and five stitches (each stitch is a group of two beads) away from violet. Then PNBT the beads of the handle. Attach bottom of the handle to the bead on the 12th round directly below top of handle. Pull thread tight. Handle should bend into proper shape and be very stiff. Weave in end.

SAUCER

The saucer is done in the flat circular peyote stitch. Be careful not to pull the thread too tight, and don't get discouraged. Sometimes the flat circular peyote stitch doesn't want to stay flat, especially after about the 5th round. Just keep at it and eventually you'll have a flat saucer. The saucer is done in the Ceylon light yellow (off-white) bead, except for the last two rounds.

Round 1: Use doubled thread about 3 feet long. String three beads. PNBT first bead strung and pull tight to make a circle.

Round 2: String two beads. PNT second bead of Round 1. String two beads. PNT next bead of Round 1. String two beads. PNT last bead of Round 1. (See Figure 4.)

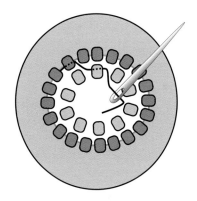

Figure 1

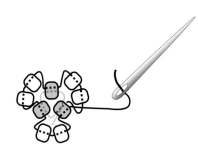

Figure 2

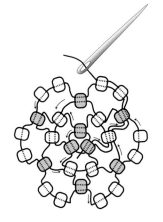

Figure 3

Figure 4

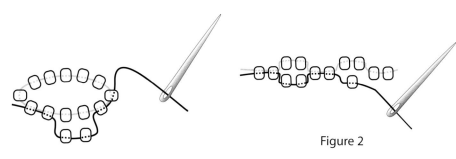

Figure 5

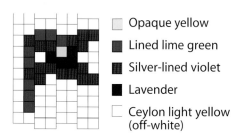

Detail of Dainty Violets
Teacup and Saucer

☐	Opaque yellow
■	Lined lime green
▨	Silver-lined violet
■	Lavender
☐	Ceylon light yellow (off-white)

Design Chart

Round 3: PNT first bead of Round 2. String one bead and PNT the next bead. Repeat until the end of the round by putting one bead between every bead of Round 2 (total of six beads).

Round 4: String two beads. PNT next bead of Round 3. Repeat until end of round. There will be two beads between each bead of Round 3 (total of twelve beads). (See Figure 5, page 67.)

Round 5: PNT first two beads of Round 4. ★String one bead. PNT next two beads of Round 4★. Repeat between asterisks until end of round (total of six beads). On every other round you will have to PNT first bead or beads of previous round before you begin round.

Round 6: String two beads. PNT next bead of previous round. Repeat until end of round.

Round 7: PNT first two beads of previous round. ★String one bead. PNT next two beads.★ Repeat between asterisks until end of round.

Round 8: ★String one bead. PNT next bead of previous round. String two beads. PNT next bead of previous round.★ Repeat between asterisks until the end of round.

Round 9: Same as Round 7.

Round 10: Same as Round 6.

Round 11: Same as Round 7.

Round 12: ★String one bead. PNT next bead or beads of previous round.★ Repeat between asterisks until end of round.

Round 13: Same as Round 12.

Round 14: Same as Round 8.

Round 15: Same as Round 12.

Round 16: ★String two gold beads. PNT next bead of previous round.★ Repeat between asterisks until end of round.

Round 17: PNT first two beads of Round 16. ★String one gold bead. PNT next two beads of previous round.★ Repeat between asterisks until end of round.

Round 18: PNBT rounds 16 and 17 all at once to create one round of gold beads. Weave in end.

Miniature Picnic Basket, Wine Bottle, Loaf of Bread, and Tablecloth

FINISHED SIZES

Bottle—1 ½ inches tall x ⅜ inch at its widest point.
Loaf—1 ½ inches long x ½ inch wide x ¼ inch tall.
Tablecloth—2 inches x 1 ⅝ inches.
Basket—2 inches long x 1 ¼ inches wide x 2 ¼ inches tall including handle.

MATERIALS

Delica Japanese tubular beads:

Bottle

2 grams, dyed matte transparent Kelly green, #776
31 Ceylon light yellow (off-white), #203
18 matte light brown, #853

Loaf

4 grams matte cantaloupe, #852

15 Ceylon light yellow (off-white), #203

Tablecloth

4 grams dyed matte transparent red, #774
4 grams Ceylon light yellow (off-white), #203

Basket

10 grams dyed opaque matte chestnut, #794
4 grams matte emerald, #859
2 greenish beads, ³⁄₁₆ inch long, for basket closures

Black or brown nylon beading thread, size D
White nylon beading thread, size D
Beading needle, size 12
Scissors

The bottle and bread are done in peyote stitch, the tablecloth and basket are in herringbone stitch.

WINE BOTTLE

Detail of wine bottle

Round 1: Begin with the cork at the top of the bottle.

Using about 3 feet of black or brown thread, string three brown beads. PNBT first bead strung to form a circle.

Round 2: ★String one brown bead. PNT next bead of previous round.★ Repeat between asterisks two times for a total of three brown beads. (See Figure 1.)

Round 3: This round is done in brown beads. PNT first bead of Round 2 and next bead from Round 1. ★String one bead. PNT next bead from Round 1, making sure that the strung bead is on top of the bead from Round 2.★ (See Figure 2.) Repeat between asterisks twice more.

Round 4: This round is also done in brown beads. PNT first bead of Round 3. ★String one bead. PNT next bead.★ Repeat between asterisks twice more.

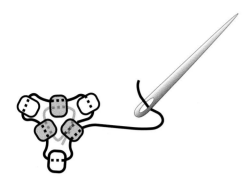

Figure 1

Figure 2

Round 5: PNT first bead of Round 4. Using brown beads, ★string 2 beads. PNT next bead of Round 4.★ Repeat between asterisks twice more, making sure the thread tension is kept tight.

Round 6: PNT first two beads of Round 5. ★String one green bead. PNT next two beads.★ Repeat between asterisks twice more.

Round 7: PNT first bead of Round 6. ★String two green beads. PNT next bead.★ Repeat between asterisks twice more.

Repeat Rounds 6 and 7 with green beads until Round 20 (total of fourteen rounds of green beads). It is important to tighten the thread tension after every round.

Round 20: This is the increase round that flares out the base of the bottle. PNT first two beads of Round 19. ★String one green bead. PNT first bead of next two-bead set. String one green bead. PNT last bead of two-bead set.★ Repeat between asterisks twice more for a total of six green beads on this round.

Round 21: PNT first bead from Round 20. ★String two green beads. PNT next bead from Round 20.★ Repeat between asterisks until the end of the round.

Round 22: PNT first two beads from Round 21. ★String one green bead. PNT next two beads from Round 21.★ Repeat between asterisks until the end of the round.

Repeat Rounds 21 and 22 for ten rounds until Round 31.

Round 31: This is the starting round for the white label. PNT first two beads of Round 30. ★String one white bead. PNT next two-bead set.★ Repeat between asterisks twice more. String one green bead. PNT next two-bead set. Finish round using green beads.

Round 32: ★PNT first white bead. String two white beads. PNT next white bead.★ Repeat between asterisks once more. String two green beads. PNT next bead. Repeat, using green beads until the end of the round.

Continue using white beads for the label. Keep the label square for a total of nine rounds.

Rounds 40–44: Work the same as the rest of the bottle using only green beads. Round 44 will be the foot of the bottle.

Round 45: This round is the start of the flat bottom of the bottle. Don't PNT the first two beads from Round 44 as you normally do. Instead, string one green bead. PNT next bead from Round 43. String one green bead. PNT next bead from Round 43. Continue in this manner until the end of the round.

Round 46: PNT first bead from Round 45. String one green bead. ★PNT next two beads from Round 45 (decrease).★ Repeat between asterisks two more times (total of three beads).

Round 47: Finishing round. String one green bead. PNT first bead of previous round. Repeat two more times. PNBT first bead of Round 47 and pull thread tight. Weave in loose ends.

LOAF OF BREAD

Detail of loaf of bread

Rows 1–3: String twenty-four tan beads. String one tan bead. PNT second tan bead. String one tan bead. Skip a bead and then PNT next bead. String one tan bead. Skip a bead, then PNT next bead. Repeat until the end of the row. (See Figure 1.)

Row 4: String one tan bead. PNT first bead that is sticking up (Row 3). String one tan bead. PNT next bead from Row 3 (sticking up). Repeat until the end of the row using tan beads (total of twelve beads).

Row 5: Increase one tan bead at beginning of row by stringing two beads and then PNT first bead strung. (See Figure 2.) Follow peyote stitch with tan beads until the end of the row.

Row 6: Same as Row 5.

Row 7–8: Do not increase. Work tan beads in peyote stitch.

Row 9: Decrease one bead at the beginning of row by PNT first bead. Then string one tan bead. Work the rest of row in peyote stitch.

Row 10–12: Same as Row 9.

Row 13: This row starts the rounded top of the loaf of bread. It is worked on the top of the flat

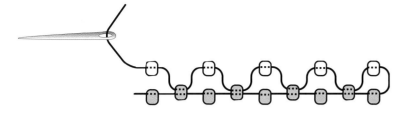

Figure 1

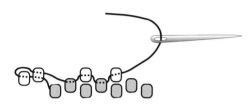

Figure 2

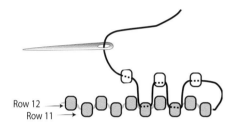

Figure 3

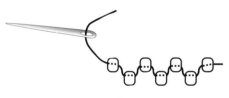

Figure 4

bottom you just completed. String one tan bead. PNT second bead of Row 11, making sure that you keep the flat bottom of the loaf horizontal and bead just strung on on top of the Row 11 beads. String one tan bead and PNT next bead of Row 11. (See Figure 3.)

Repeat in this manner until you get to the last bead of Row 11. PNT last bead of Row 11. To begin the curve around the end of the loaf, string one tan bead, then PNT first bead of Row 9. String one tan bead and PNT first bead of Row 7. String one tan bead.

PNT first bead of Row 4. String one tan bead. PNT second bead of Row 2. To finish Row 13, work with the beads of Row 2 in peyote stitch, repeating what you did on the beads of Row 11. To begin the curve around the end of the loaf, string one tan bead. PNT first bead of Row 4. String one tan bead. PNT first bead of Row 7. String one tan bead. PNT first bead of Row 9. Now you have formed a row of beads on top of the bottom part of the loaf.

Row 14: PNT first bead of Row 13. String one tan bead. PNT next bead of Row 13. Work the tan beads in peyote stitch for the rest of the row, which goes all around the loaf.

Row 15: Same as 14, except decrease one bead at each end of the loaf. To decrease, PNT two beads at the ends of the loaf, instead of one bead.

Row 16: PNT first bead of Row 15. String one white bead. PNT next bead. String one tan bead. PNT next bead. String one tan bead. PNT next bead. String one white bead. PNT next bead. String tan beads for next three stitches, then string one white bead. Use tan beads for next three stitches, then PNT next two beads. String one tan bead. PNT next bead. String one white bead. PNT next bead. String tan beads for next three stitches, then string one white bead. String tan beads for the next two stitches, and then one white bead. String tan beads for the next three stitches, then PNT

for next two beads. String tan beads for the last two stitches.

Row 17: PNT white bead. String one white bead for next stitch. String tan beads for next two stitches. String one white bead for next stitch. String tan beads for next three stitches. String one white bead for next stitch. String tan beads for next two stitches. PNT next bead from Row 15 and then the next bead from Row 16. String one tan bead. PNT next bead. String one white bead for next stitch. String tan beads for next three stitches. Then string one white bead. String tan beads for next two stitches. Then string one white bead. String tan beads for next two stitches. Then PNT next bead from Row 15 and the next bead from Row 16. String tan beads for next two stitches.

Row 18: Finishing. Sew sides of loaf together to form a solid top. This is accomplished by PNT interlocking beads from each side and pulling tight. This will close up the top of the loaf and the seam will be invisible. (See Figure 4.)

CHECKERED TABLECLOTH

Detail of tablecloth

Using about 4 feet of white thread, string twenty-four beads in this pattern: one white bead, ★two red beads, two white beads.★ Repeat between asterisks until last bead, which is one white bead. Leave a 6-inch tail of thread and hold tight so that the beads won't slip off the end before you finish the first row.

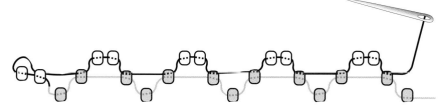

Figure 1

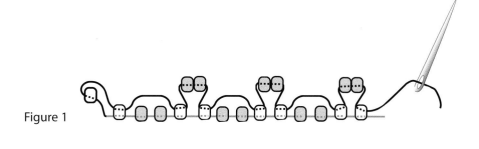

Figure 2

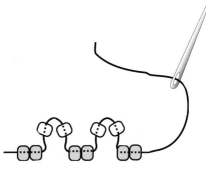

Figure 3

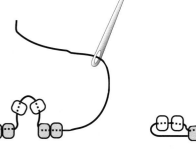

Figure 4

asterisks until the end of the row. PNT last bead of row. As you have probably noticed by now, the beads of each row are not in a straight line in the herringbone stitch. Each group of two makes an inverted U shape. When pulling your stitches tight, especially with the matte Japanese tubular beads, make sure one bead is on one side of the U and one is on the other. (See Figure 3.)

Row 5: Same as Row 4.

Rows 6–7: Same as Row 3.

Now follow the red-and-white checkered pattern for a total of thirty-two rows.

Row 33: Work in all red beads.

Ending row: String two white beads. PNT first red bead. String one white bead. ★PNT next two red beads. String one white bead.★ Repeat between asterisks until the end of the row. (See Figure 4.) Weave in the ends until they are secure.

BASKET

Detail of Miniature Picnic Basket

This is basically five flat rectangles sewn together (with two flat rectangles attached as the flip lids) and, of course, a handle.

Long sides of the basket

Using doubled thread, string twenty-four beads in this pattern:

Row 1: String one white bead. PNT next white bead. Skip two red beads. PNT next white bead. String two red beads. PNT next white bead. ★Skip two red beads, then PNT next white bead. String two red beads. PNT next white bead.★ Repeat until last white bead, which you PNT. (See Figure 1.)

Row 2: String two white beads. PNBT first white bead strung. Skip one bead, then PNT first bead of next two-bead set. String two red beads. PNT second bead of two-bead set. ★Skip one bead, then PNT next white bead. String two white beads. PNT other white bead. Skip one bead. PNT next red bead. String on two red beads. PNT next red bead.★ Repeat between asterisks until the end of the row. PNT last bead of row. This row is awkward, but once you get past it, the rest is

much easier. You might have to adjust the thread tension by loosening the row. (See Figure 2.)

Row 3: String two red beads. PNBT first red bead strung. ★PNT first bead of next two-bead set. String two white beads. PNT last bead of two-bead set. PNT first bead of next two-bead set. String on two red beads. PNT last bead of two-bead set.★ Repeat between asterisks until the end of the row. PNT last bead of row.

Row 4: String two white beads. PNBT first white bead strung. ★PNT first bead of next two-bead set.

String on two red beads. PNT last bead of two-bead set. PNT first bead of next two-bead set. String two white beads. PNT last bead of two-bead set.★ Repeat between

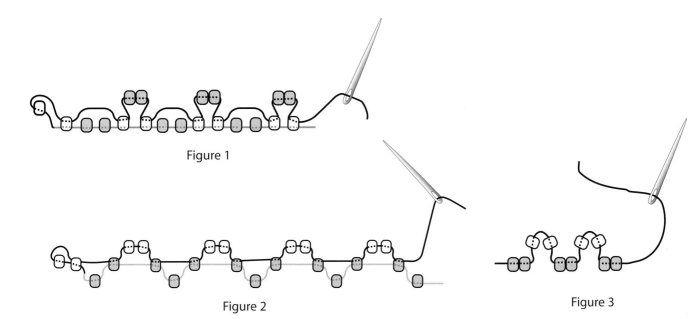

Figure 1

Figure 2

Figure 3

one green bead ★ two brown beads, two green beads.★ Repeat between asterisks four more times, string two more brown beads and one green bead.

Row 1: String one brown bead. PNT green bead. Skip the next two brown beads. PNT first green bead of two-bead set. String two brown beads. PNT second green bead of two-bead set. ★Skip two brown beads. PNT first green bead of two-bead set. String two brown beads. PNT second green bead of two-bead set.★ Repeat between asterisks until the end of the row. (See Figure 1.)

Row 2: String one brown and one green bead. PNBT brown bead. ★PNT first brown bead of next two-bead set. String on two green beads. PNT second brown bead of two-bead set. Skip one green bead.★ Repeat between asterisks until the end of the row. Every other two-bead set will be hanging down on this row. Therefore, you have to scoot the beads so that they are on top of the thread and ready to have the needle pass through them. This only happens on Row 2. (See Figure 2.)

Row 3: String one green bead and one brown bead. PNBT green bead. ★PNT the first bead of the next two-bead set. String two brown beads. PNT second bead of the two-bead set.★ Repeat between the asterisks until the end of the row.

As you have probably noticed by now, the beads of each row are not in a straight line in the herringbone stitch. Each group of two makes an inverted U shape. When pulling your stitches tight, especially with the matte Japanese tubular beads, make sure one bead is on one side of the U and one is on the other. (See Figure 3.)

Row 4: String on one brown bead and then one green bead. PNBT brown bead. ★PNT the first bead of the next two-bead set. String two green beads. PNT second bead of two-bead set.★ Repeat between asterisks until the end of the row.

Row 5: String one green bead and one brown bead. PNBT green bead. ★PNT first bead of next two-bead set. String two brown beads. PNT second bead of two-bead set.★ Repeat between asterisks until the end of the row.

Rows 6–13: Work with brown beads in herringbone stitch.

Finishing edge: To form an even edge for the bottom of the basket, string one brown bead. PNT next two-bead set. ★String one brown bead. PNT next two-bead set.★ Repeat between asterisks until the end of the row. (See Figure 4.) Leave thread end long for sewing the sides together.

Make two of these long sides. After you have finished the two long sides, complete the two shorter sides.

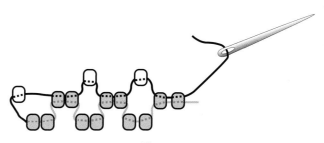

Figure 4

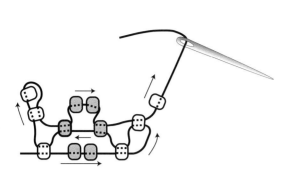

Figure 5

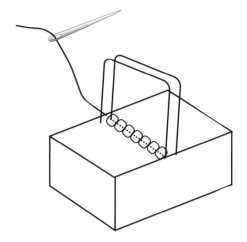

Figure 6

Short sides of the basket

Double the thread. String sixteen beads in the one green, two brown, two green, etc., pattern. Last bead is one green. Follow same instructions as for the long sides for thirteen rows. Make two.

Bottom of Basket

Using doubled thread, string sixteen brown beads. Work in herringbone stitch with brown beads for thirty-four rows.

Sew the sides and bottom together by weaving thread through every other bead back and forth from one edge to the other of the two pieces you're sewing together. The piece seems wobbly at this point, but it will be sturdier as you finish.

Handle of Basket

Using doubled thread, string four beads in this pattern: one green bead, one brown bead, one brown bead, one green bead.

Row 1: String one green bead. PNT last green bead strung. String two brown beads. PNT next green bead.

Row 2: String two green beads. PNBT first green bead strung. PNT first brown bead. String two brown beads. PNT next brown bead. PNT last green bead.

Row 3: Same as Row 2. (See Figure 5.) Repeat Row 2 for a total of fifty-two rows.

Using doubled thread about 6' long, find the middle of one long side of basket. Sew basket handle on top edge of side. PNT all the green beads on one side of the handle, then sew handle to top edge of middle of other long side. When secure, PNT all the green beads on the other side of the handle. This will help reinforce the handle. At this point, you can also reinforce the top edge of the basket by PNT all the top edge beads. With the same thread, come out on the inside of the basket under the middle of the handle. String twenty-two brown beads to make the bar for anchoring the flaps. (See Figure 6.) Sew the twenty-two-bead strand to the opposite side of the basket, making sure it's in the middle of the side. PNBT the twenty-two beads two more times so that the strand is somewhat stiff. Weave in the end.

Basket Flaps

Using doubled black thread, string sixteen brown beads.

Row 1: String one brown bead. PNBT the sixteenth bead strung. ★Skip two beads and PNT next bead. String two brown beads. PNT next bead.★ Repeat between asterisks to finish row.

Row 2: String two brown beads. PNBT first bead strung. ★Skip one bead and PNT next bead. String two green beads. PNT next bead.★ Repeat between asterisks until the end of the row.

Row 3: String two brown beads. PNBT first bead strung. PNT first bead of next two-bead set. String one green bead and one brown bead. PNT second bead of two-bead set. ★PNT first bead of next two-bead set. String two brown beads. PNT second bead of two-bead set.★ Repeat between asterisks until last stitch, then string one brown and one green bead. PNT last bead. The green beads form the stripe around the edge of the flap.

Repeat Row 3 twelve more times for a total of fifteen rows.

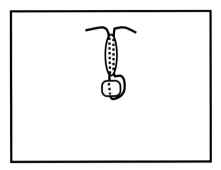

Figure 7

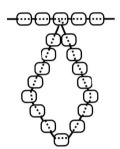

Figure 8

Row 16: Decrease one bead at the beginning of the row. To do this, do not string on two beads; just PNT first green bead. Work the rest of the row the same as Row 3.

Rows 17–18: Same as Row 16.

Row 19: Finishing edge. PNT first two beads. ★String one brown bead. PNT next two beads.★ Repeat between asterisks until the end of the row. Make two flaps.

Using double thread, reinforce edges of flaps by PNT all edge beads. Now sew flaps to the bar of beads in the middle of the basket. PNT two edge beads of flap. Then PNT two beads of middle bar. Skip two beads on flap and then PNT next two beads. Skip two beads on bar, then PNT next two beads. Repeat until entire edge of flap is connected. Do the same for other flap on opposite side of bar.

Basket Clasp

Do not double-thread for this step. Secure one end of the thread on the short side of the basket by bringing the needle out of the middle bead in the top brown stripe of the basket side. String green clasp bead and one green bead. PNBT clasp bead. PNT other brown middle bead and then weave in the end. (See Figure 7.)

On the flap, secure the thread and come out of the bead on the front edge in the middle of the flap. String fifteen brown beads. PNT other brown middle bead and then weave in the end. (See Figure 8.) Repeat on other side.

Herringbone Stitch Moon Maiden

FINISHED SIZE
18 inches (45.7 cm) long

MATERIALS
11/0 alabaster silver-lined round
 seed beads:
 15 grams Montana blue
 2 grams antique white
 3 grams gold
 3 grams apricot
 1 gram peach
 1 gram rust
 1 gram dove gray
 1 gram antique rose
 1 gram antique mauve
 8 beads sky blue
 6 beads pale pink
 2 beads strawberry

It is very important to use the same size beads throughout the project. It is recommended that you use beads all made by the same manufacturer.

MAIN GRAPH

Row 1–2. Thread the needle with a long piece of thread, add a stop bead, and position it 12 inches (30.5 cm) away from the tail (this will be used later). String on 28 beads, following Graph 1 for color and bead placement. Those beads are numbered on the graph and they'll make up rows 1 and 2 when they're stitched. All rows following the first two are read straight across from right to left and then left to right.

Row 3. Turn and stitch row 3. This row puts the strung beads in their proper herringbone positions, and it may be awkward to hold onto. At the end of row 3 the needle exits bead 1, which is the bead marked with a black dot. With this turn you'll increase one vertical row. Pick up three beads (numbered in red on the left side of Graph 1). The graph also shows their positions after they're stitched.

Row 4. Complete the turn, and stitch row 4. This row ends with the needle exiting another bead marked with a black dot, to indicate that another increase begins now. The beads that you'll pick up for the increase are numbered in red, to the left of the dot.

Row 5. Do the increase, and stitch row 5, following the graph for color placement. With the increases on both sides, you're now stitching with eight full spines across the working edge. Don't add beads when making the turns.

Rows 6–10. Follow the graph for color placement.

Row 11. This row begins with the bead marked with the black dot on the right-hand side of the graph. You'll be stitching from right to

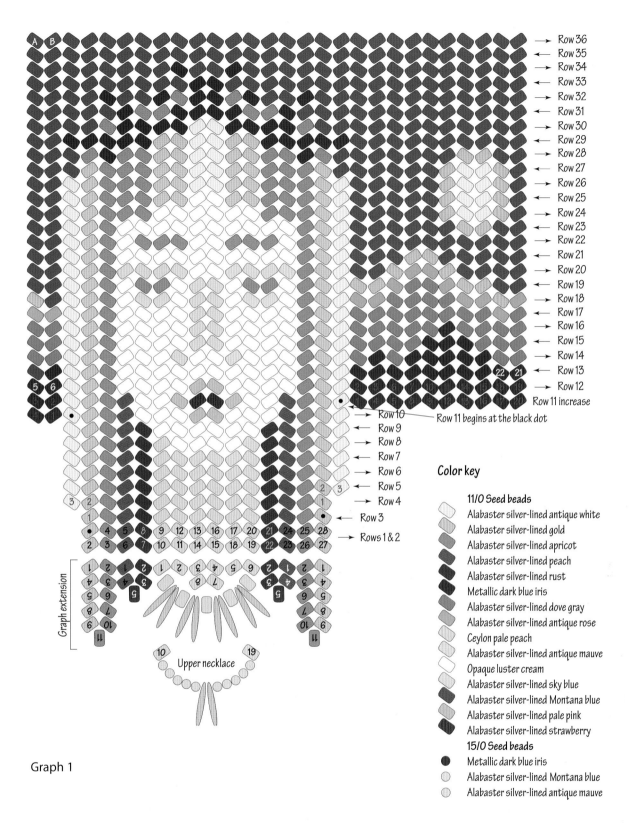

Graph 1

Color key

11/0 Seed beads
- Alabaster silver-lined antique white
- Alabaster silver-lined gold
- Alabaster silver-lined apricot
- Alabaster silver-lined peach
- Alabaster silver-lined rust
- Metallic dark blue iris
- Alabaster silver-lined dove gray
- Alabaster silver-lined antique rose
- Ceylon pale peach
- Alabaster silver-lined antique mauve
- Opaque luster cream
- Alabaster silver-lined sky blue
- Alabaster silver-lined Montana blue
- Alabaster silver-lined pale pink
- Alabaster silver-lined strawberry

15/0 Seed beads
- Metallic dark blue iris
- Alabaster silver-lined Montana blue
- Alabaster silver-lined antique mauve

left. The portion of the graph that sits to the right of the black dot is an increase that begins at the end of row 12, when the needle exits the bead with the black dot, heading right. Stitch row 11.

When you've completed the first part of row 11, there's an increase

on the left side of two vertical rows. The needle will be coming out of the bead marked with the black dot (on row 10 at the left-hand side of graph). Pick up the beads numbered 1, 2, 3, and 4, pass the needle back through bead 3, and pick up beads 5 and 6. Now

weave down through bead 2, and up through the neighboring bead on the right, above the black dot.

Rows 12–13. This row begins with beads 5 and 6; continue stitching across row 12 until the needle (heading right) exits the bead with the black dot, in row 11.

Now for the increase of 10 vertical rows. String on 20 beads (half of these beads are an increase to row 11 and half of them will finish row 12), following the graph for color placement, and position them next to the work. Turn, and pass the needle back through bead 19, pick up two beads (21 and 22), and weave through beads 18 and 15. This is the same process as beginning the herringbone stitch. Leave a little slack in the thread to start, and don't push the strung beads too tightly against the work. This next part may be tricky. After the beads are added for the increased portion of row 13 (they won't look like the graph just yet), carefully shape them into a scalloped shape. (See Figure 1.) This will take a little patience. When the beads line up properly, tighten the thread and stitch the rest of the row.

Rows 14–36. Stitch following Graph 1 for color placement. Tie off all threads except for the tail thread.

GRAPH EXTENSION AND SURFACE EMBELLISHING

1. Unloop the stop bead, and thread the needle with the tail thread. Turn the work and the graph upside down so that the beginning edge is on the top and pass the needle up through bead 2. For the hair, stitch a herringbone section that is two beads wide and 5 rows long. When the last stitch is completed, pass the needle back up through bead 10, pick up bead 11, and weave straight down through beads 9–2. Move over a row, and pass the needle down through bead 4 of the main graph, then turn, and pass the needle up through beads 5 and 6 of the main graph. Now stitch the next short section of hair.
2. The neck should have a gentle curve that's accented by the double strand necklace. Stitch the

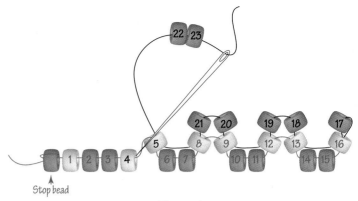

Figure 1

neck extension. Add the under-section of the necklace, which is made up of 11/0 beads and gold stars and hangs from beads 1 and 6. The upper necklace, made with 15/0 beads and gold stars, hangs from beads 10 and 19; see Graph 1 for color and bead placement. End the thread. If the thread is long enough, stitch the other two hair extensions; if not, add a new thread, and complete the weaving.

3. Add beads to the surface of the work for the eyes and nose. Begin by adding a new thread, coming in from the back of the work, and weave straight down towards the eye on the left side. Exit the dark blue bead, pick up a 15/0 bead, and weave up the two neighboring beads. Now weave across, add the other eye bead, and exit the dark blue bead on the back side of the work. On the back side, pass the needle down into the light blue bead, then weave across towards the nose. Add the 15/0 beads for the nose, and tie off both thread ends.

THE STRAPS

4. Add a new thread to the work and have it coming out of the bead marked with a B on row 36. (See Graph 1.) String on a blue crystal trim bead and two 11/0 Montana blue seed beads, pass the needle back through the crystal trim bead, and into the

bead marked A. Weave across and back up bead B and the crystal, and pick up two more blue seed beads. Again weave down into the body of the work, but a little farther this time, and then back up, exiting the crystal bead.

5. You're now ready to begin tubular herringbone from these four seed beads. Pass the needle into one of the seed beads, pick up two beads, pass the needle down into the neighboring seed bead, and up the next. Pick up two beads, pass down into the last seed bead of the original four, and up two in the next row. Continue adding beads for 122 rows or the desired length of chain.

6. Put the jump rings on the clasp. At the end of the herringbone chain weave through the last four beads, joining them together. String on a blue crystal bead and pass the needle through one of the jump rings, back through the crystal bead and into the next seed bead in the chain. Continue weaving up through the jump ring and down into the herringbone chain, until you've passed through all four seed beads on the end of the chain twice, and it all feels secure.

7. Repeat this on the other side of the work for the other half of the chain.

Twisted Ribbon Ndebele Necklace

FINISHED SIZE

18 inches (45.7 cm) long

MATERIALS

11/0 round seed beads:
  15 grams silver-lined matte
    pearl gray
11/0 cylinder seed beads:
  5 grams matte gray iris
  5 grams burgundy iris

Trim beads:
  2 pale amethyst crystals, 4 mm
  2 pale amethyst crystals, 8 mm
Variety of smaller seed beads,
  pearls, semiprecious chips,
  crystals, for center of twist
Beading thread, size D, in a color
  to match beads
Beading needle, size 12
6 inches (15.2 cm) 22-gauge wire

Used for over 200 years by the Ndebele (en-de-BEL-ay) women of South Africa, this variation of the tubular herringbone stitch gives a twisted ribbon effect that's emphasized by using two contrasting colors of cylinder seed beads. This necklace is made up of three parts, a non-twisted tube, a twisted center, and another, non-twisted tube. Two larger beads divide the three pieces.

The twist effect depends on the size of the round seed beads; a large round seed bead (such as 8/0) will create a strong twist, smaller round seed beads (such as 11/0) will twist less.

TWISTED SECTION ON NECKLACE

Rows 1–2. String on one 11/0 round seed bead, and loop back through it, leaving a 12-inch (30.5 cm) tail. Add another 11/0 round seed bead; six cylinder seed beads in the first color; and two 11/0 round seed beads and six cylinder seed beads in the second color. Make a double bead ladder, using the technique described below.

BEAD LADDER VARIATION

String sixteen beads, then weave back through beads 13 and 14. (See Figure 1.) This will make the last four beads sit vertically in two stacks of two. Continue to weave back through two beads at a time until all of the beads are sitting side by side in columns of two. (See Figure 2.) Unloop the first bead, and join the two ends together by stitching through beads 1, 2, 15, and 16. (See Figure 3.) Pass through these beads one more time to secure them.

Row 3. With the needle coming out of bead 2, pick up a round seed bead (17) and a cylinder seed bead (18). Pass the needle down through the neighboring set of cylinder seed beads (3 and 4) and up the next set (5 and 6), as shown. (See Figure 4.) Add two more cylinder beads in the same fashion, working your way around the tube, and keeping the same color pattern as the bead ladder.

When you reach the end of the row, pass the needle up through two beads only (2 and 17), as shown. (See Figure 5.) By not "stepping up," or passing through the first bead of the row, you'll now be making a spiral instead of concentric circles. It's the spiral and the larger round seed beads that cause the twist.

Rows 4–38. Continue adding beads by picking up two, passing down through two, and up through two, for a total of 38 stitches.

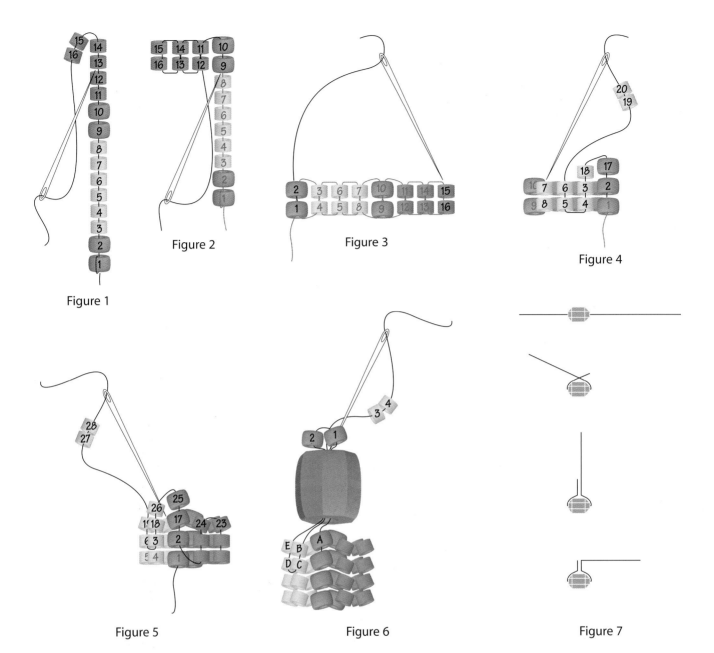

Figure 1

Figure 2

Figure 3

Figure 4

Figure 5

Figure 6

Figure 7

Note: After you weave 1 inch (2.5 cm), flatten the ribbon with the seed beads on the outer edges, and give it a twist. It should hold the twist by itself. If not, you may need to use larger seed beads, or replace the cylinder seed beads with 14/0 seed beads.

Rows 39–70. For the embellished part of the twist, weave down one bead and up three. This gives a different type of twist. It becomes a little awkward at the transition area, so embellishing over one of the colors with a variety of smaller seed beads, pearls, semiprecious chips, and crystals covers this and makes a perfect focal point.

Note: Embellish after the twisted section is done. Add the embellishment beads to one side only, randomly weaving to cover the area. Pick up three to five beads, with a larger bead centered between the smaller seed beads. Embellish until you have the effect you desire.

Rows 71–109. Begin the regular twist again, picking up two, passing down through two and up through two for 38 stitches.

ADDING LARGER BEAD BETWEEN SECTIONS

1. To add the 8-mm bead between the twisted herringbone section and the nontwisted section, you must first finish row 109. The needle should be coming out of the round seed bead marked A. (See Figure 6.) String on the large bead, and slide it to the work. Pick up two round seed beads (1 and 2), and pass the needle back down through the large bead and beads B and C.

2. Change direction, and weave up through beads D, E, and the large bead; snug up the thread.

Do this around the herringbone tube until there are eight beads on the top of the large bead and the large bead is secure to the other section.

Note: There's a slight change to the pattern of beads that sit on top of the large bead and create the base of the non-twisted section. Use two seed beads, two cylinder beads, two seed beads, and two cylinder beads. The needle should exit a seed bead; begin doing tubular herringbone from the eight beads, and continue for 75 stitches or the desired length.

3. Repeat steps 1 and 2 on the other side of the twisted section, using the long tail thread.

THE CLASP

4. Once the non-twisted tube is the desired length, add a 4-mm fire-polished bead across the opening at the end of the tube. With the needle coming out of a round seed bead, string on the 4-mm bead, and pass the needle through the round seed bead on the opposite side of the herringbone tube. Turn, and weave up the neighboring round seed bead and through the 4-mm bead again, then attach it to its opposite round seed bead. Repeat this process a few more times to secure the 4-mm bead, but leave enough room in the 4-mm bead for a wire to pass through it later. End off by weaving into the work.

5. Cut the 22-gauge wire into two 3-inch (7.6 cm) pieces. Insert one of the wires into the 4-mm, fire-polished bead on one end of the necklace so that ¾ inch (1.9 cm) of wire extends from the other side of the bead. (See Figure 7.) Using your finger and thumb, bend the two ends around the bead until they cross each other at the middle, forming an X. With chain nose pliers, uncross the wires and bend each one at a right angle, so they're parallel to each other and pointing away from the necklace. Trim the shortest wire to ⅛ inch (3 mm) from the bend. Bend the long piece of wire ⅛ inch (3 mm) up from the first bend, at a right angle. Use round nose pliers to make a loop that sits over the shorter piece of wire. Holding the loop with the chain nose pliers, wrap the excess wire around the two wires coming up from the bead. Repeat on the other side. Attach an S clasp to the loops.

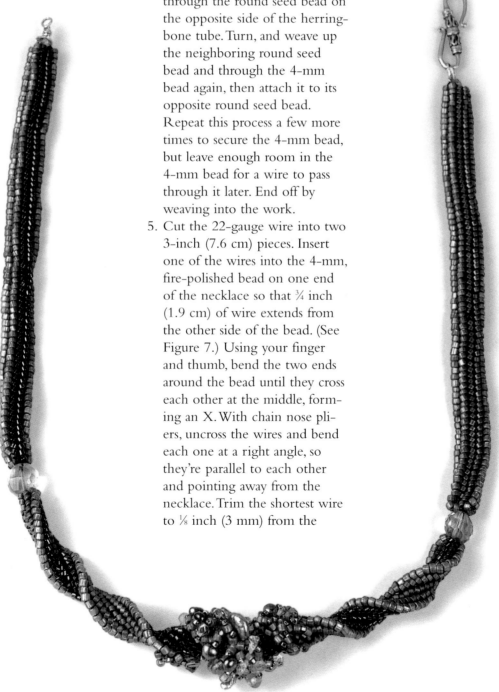

Brick Stitch Pin & Earrings

MATERIALS

6 mm aventurine flat beads with hole through length (5)

Delica beads:
   400 grams cream;
   50 grams galvanized gold;
   80 grams galvanized light green;
   75 grams galvanized dark pink;

160 grams galvanized light pink
2 ear wires
Embroidery needles, #9
Embroidery scissors
Pin back, 1½ inches
Needle-nosed pliers
2 rings (4 mm)
Off-white thread

1. Following pattern on opposite page, form foundation (top) row. (See Figure 1.) Review Brick Stitch technique on page 17, if needed.

   Note: This design uses the top row of the pin as the foundation row. The thread that would ordinarily be used to work upward will be used to sew the finished beadwork to the pin back, so do not cut it.

   Work consecutive rows until completing row 17. Weave thread through first and second bead on row 17 and bring needle out at bottom of third bead on row to begin row 18.

Continue working remaining rows until pattern is complete.

2. Using thread end at bottom of pattern, slip one galvanized dark pink delica bead, one aventurine bead, and one galvanized dark pink delica bead on needle. Run needle back through aventurine and first galvanized dark pink delica bead. (See Figure 2.)

3. Take needle up through cream delica beads on right side of woven piece. Bring needle out at bottom of second to last bead on row 17. Repeat Step 2 at base of row 17.

4. Take needle up through last cream delica bead on row 17.

Working from right to left, weave thread in and out of each bead on row 17 until reaching second bead on row. Bring needle out at bottom of bead and repeat Step 2. Bury excess thread in weave.

5. Using thread at top of pattern, whipstitch pin back onto back top edge of woven piece. (See Figure 3.)

6. Following Brick Stitch Earring Pattern, form foundation row. Work consecutive rows to complete one full pattern. Repeat for second full pattern. Repeat Step 2 for each. Bury excess thread in weave. (See Figure 4.)

7. Using thread end at top of each pattern, take needle through top two beads and sew on one 4 mm ring. Bury excess thread in weave. Using needle-nosed pliers, open loop on each ear wire. Slip ring on and close loop.

Brick Stitch Pin Pattern & Key

Foundation row

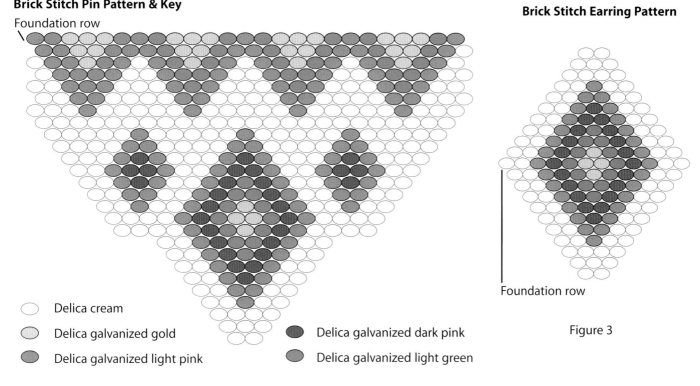

○ Delica cream

◐ Delica galvanized gold

● Delica galvanized light pink

● Delica galvanized dark pink

● Delica galvanized light green

Figure 1

Brick Stitch Earring Pattern

Foundation row

Figure 3

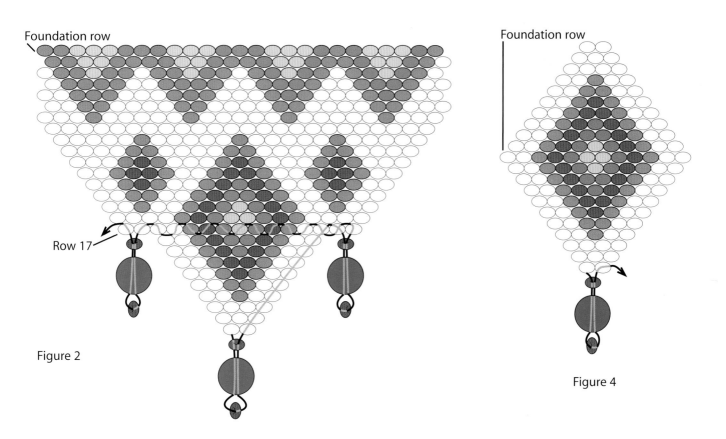

Foundation row

Row 17

Figure 2

Foundation row

Figure 4

Brick Stitch
Peacock Amulet Bag

FINISHED SIZE

2⅜ inches x 2¾ inches
(not including fringe)

MATERIALS

Delica Japanese tubular beads:
  20 grams silver-lined violet,
   #610
  10 grams semi-matte medium
   blue, #693
  7 grams lined lime green,
   #274
  7 grams dyed matte transparent
   Kelly green, #776
  5 grams silver-lined gold, #042
  4 grams lined topaz, #065
  1 black, #010
Black nylon beading thread,
  size D
Two beading needles, size 11
Scissors

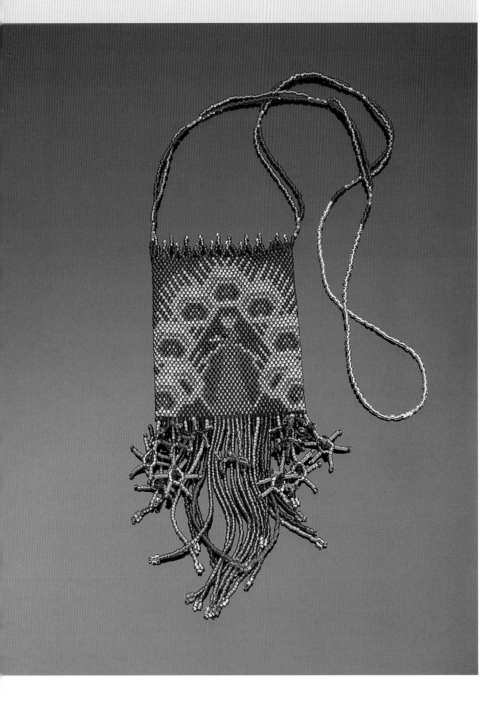

Thread two needles on either end
of a length of thread about 5 feet
long. Make a ladder stitch row, seventy-one blue beads long, as follows: String one bead and move it
to the middle of the thread. String
one bead with one needle, then
pass the other needle through the
same bead. Make sure the needles
pass in opposite directions. Pull
tight. (See Figure 1.) Repeat, using
all seventy-one beads. Connect the
first and last beads to make a ring.
This ring is the base from which
you will build the body of the bag.

Use one needle to make the body
of the bag and the other needle for
the edging around the top. Work
the bag from the top down by following the design chart from top to
bottom. It doesn't matter where you
place the design on the bag, because
you can position the bag so that the
design is in the center front when
you sew up the bottom of the bag.

BODY OF BAG

Round 1: Use the design chart to
determine what color beads to use.
String two beads. PNT the loop of
thread that connects the beads in
the previous row. PNBT the second
bead strung on and pull tight.
★String one bead. PNT the loop of
thread that connects the beads in the
previous round. PNBT the strung
bead and pull tight.★ (See Figure
2.) Repeat between asterisks until
the end of the round. Always start
the round with two beads instead
of one so the thread won't pass on
the outside of the first bead.

At the end of every round, PNDT
the first bead of the round and
PNUT the second bead. Now you
are ready to begin the next round.
(See Figure 3.)

Rounds 2–53: Same as Round 1,
changing colors of beads according
to the design chart.

Line up the design in the center
front of bag and flatten. If you have

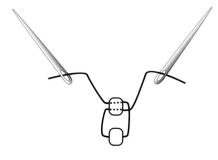

Figure 1

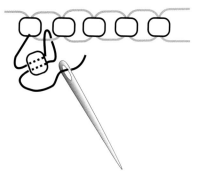

Figure 2

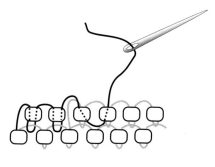

Figure 3

enough thread left over, use it to sew up the bottom. If not, anchor a new thread to the body of the bag. Work the thread to one of the bottom sides and sew. Pass needle under thread loop between the first two beads and then under the loop on the opposite side. Continue until the end. Then sew up one more time, going back over what you just sewed, to strengthen it. Leave thread end to use on fringe if it's long enough.

EDGING

Create the edging at the top of the bag using the second needle and thread. Start with front edging. (See Figure 4.) ★String three purple beads, two blue beads, and one gold. PNBT the two blue beads and then string on three purple beads. PNDT the third bead from the bead that the thread came out of on top round of the bag. PNUT the adjacent bead on top of bag.★ Repeat between asterisks until last bead at front of bag.

The back top edging is basically the same as the front top edging, except you use more beads to make a taller edging. (See Figure 5.) ★String five purple beads, two blue beads, and one gold bead. PNBT the two blue beads and then string five purple beads. PNDT third bead from where strung beads are coming out of and then PNUT adjacent bead.★ Repeat between asterisks until the end of the back of the bag. Weave end back through body of work.

■ Silver-lined violet
□ Semi-matte medium blue
□ Matte transparent Kelly green
□ Lined lime green
■ Lined topaz
□ Silver-lined gold
■ Black

Design Chart

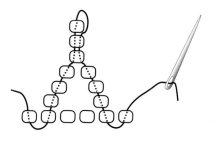

Figure 4

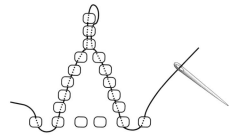

Figure 5

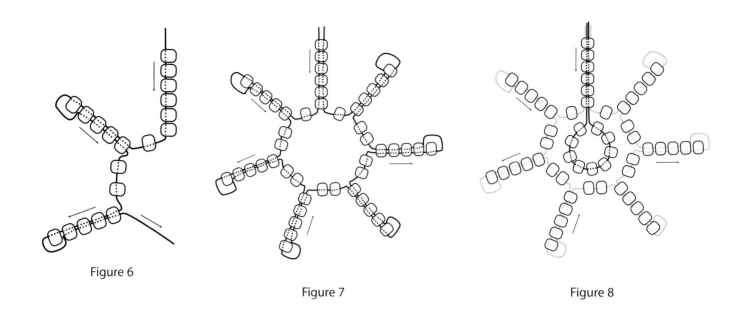

Figure 6

Figure 7

Figure 8

FRINGE

Thread needle with 5-foot length of thread. Weave through work to anchor it and bring needle out through bead at the bottom left edge of bag.

There are thirty-five strands of fringe, one for every bead along bottom of bag.

Strand 1: String three lime-green beads, one Kelly green, one blue, one Kelly green, three lime green, one gold, four lime green, and one blue. PNBT four lime-green beads. This forms one finger of feather fringe. ★String 2 gold beads, 4 lime green, 1 blue. PNBT 4 lime-green beads.★ (See Figure 6.) Repeat between asterisks four more times for a total of six fingers. PNBT three lime-green beads, one Kelly green, one blue, one Kelly green, and three lime-green beads. (See Figure 7.) PNUT bead on bottom of bag to the left of where strand came out and then PNDT the bead where the strand is coming out. PNBT strand of lime-green beads, Kelly green beads, and blue bead so that the needle is coming out of

the middle of the top of the circle of beads. String three purple beads, three blue beads, and three more purple beads. PNBT the strand of lime-green, Kelly green, and blue bead. PNUT bead on bottom of bag directly above the strand. PNDT the next bead on the bottom of the bag. (See Figure 8.)

This forms the peacock feather strand. There are six of them in the fringe, three on each side of the middle of the bag, with increasingly more beads in each strand as you move towards the middle.

Strand 2: ★String two blue beads, three Kelly green beads, one gold bead. PNBT three Kelly green beads.★ Repeat between asterisks two more times for a total of three fingers on strand. Then string two blue beads and one gold bead. PNBT all the blue beads. PNUT the bead on the body of bag directly on top of the strand. PNDT the next bead.

Strand 3: Same as Strand 2, but use purple for the blue beads and topaz for the green beads.

Strand 4: This is another peacock feather strand. Work same as Strand 1, except instead of stringing three lime-green beads on either side of Kelly green bead, blue bead, Kelly green bead, string on five lime-green beads (this is the part of the strand that is above the circular feather part) so that this feather strand is longer than Strand 1.

Strand 5: Same as Strand 2, except make five green fingers instead of three.

Strand 6: Same as Strand 3, except make five topaz fingers instead of three.

Strand 7: Same as Strand 4, except string eight lime-green beads on either side of Kelly green, blue, and Kelly green.

Strand 8: String twenty-six purple beads and five gold beads. This forms a small gold ring at the end of the strand. PNBT all purple beads and PNUT bead on bottom of body of bag. PNDT next bead on body of bag.

Strand 9: String thirty-five purple beads and five topaz beads. PNBT all purple beads. PNUT bead on bottom of body of bag. PNDT next bead on body of bag.

Strand 10: Same as Strand 8, except string thirty-nine purple beads instead of twenty-six.

Strand 11: Same as Strand 9, except string forty-five purple beads instead of thirty-five.

Strand 12: String forty-eight lime-green beads and five gold beads. PNBT all green beads, PNUT bead on body of bag that is directly above strand, and then PNDT next bead on body of bag.

Strand 13: Same as Strand 12, except string fifty Kelly green beads and five topaz.

Strand 14: Same as Strand 12, except string fifty-two blue beads and five gold beads.

Strand 15: String fifty-six blue beads and five topaz.

Strand 16: String fifty-nine blue beads and five gold.

Strand 17: This is the peacock foot strand. String three blue beads, twelve topaz beads, and one lime-green bead. PNBT three topaz beads. String four topaz beads and one lime-green bead. PNBT three topaz beads. String three topaz beads and one lime-green bead. PNBT three topaz beads. String

three topaz beads and one lime-green bead. PNBT three topaz beads. These are the four toes of the peacock. String forty-seven blue beads and five topaz. PNBT all forty-seven blue beads, topaz beads of leg (not toes), and three blue beads. PNUT bead on body of bag that is directly above strand and then PNDT next bead on body of bag.

Strand 18: Same as Strand 16, except string sixty-two blue beads.

Strand 19: Same as Strand 17.

Strand 20: Same as Strand 16.

Strand 21: Same as Strand 15.

Strand 22: Same as Strand 14.

Strand 23: Same as Strand 13.

Strand 24: Same as Strand 12.

Strand 25: Same as Strand 11.

Strand 26: Same as Strand 10.

Strand 27: Same as Strand 9.

Strand 28: Same as Strand 8.

Strand 29: Same as Strand 7.

Strand 30: Same as Strand 6.

Strand 31: Same as Strand 5.

Strand 32: Same as Strand 4.

Strand 33: Same as Strand 3.

Strand 34: Same as Strand 2.

Strand 35: Same as Strand 1.

Weave in ends.

NECKLACE

Use two strands of thread about 3 feet long. Thread a needle to each length of thread. Pass both needles up through the bead at the top edge where you want the necklace to start. Leave thread ends about 6 inches long to later separate and weave back into the work. String onto both needles ★★eight purple beads, ★one gold, one topaz, one Kelly green, one lime green, one Kelly green, one topaz, one gold. Now string forty purple beads on one needle and forty blue beads on the other needle.★ Repeat between single asterisks two more times. Then string onto both needles one gold, one topaz, one Kelly green, one lime green, one Kelly green, one topaz, one gold, eight purple beads.★★ String 160 gold beads to both needles for the back of the necklace. Repeat between double asterisks for the other side of the necklace. Pass both needles through bead at top of bag on other side. Weave in the four thread ends separately.

Square Stitch Rainforest Frog

FINISHED SIZE

4 inches x 2½ inches

MATERIALS

11/0 seed beads:
- 2 grams opaque red
- 2 grams lined translucent dark red
- 2 grams opaque orange
- 2 grams translucent bright yellow
- 2 grams translucent cobalt blue
- 2 grams lined translucent light blue
- 2 grams translucent mint green
- 2 grams opaque medium green
- 2 grams lined translucent dark green
- 43 black
- 17 white

White nylon beading thread, size D

Beading needle, size 12

Scissors

To make a barrette:

6-inch x 6-inch piece of ⅛-inch cowhide leather

1 yd of dark blue edging cord

One 3-inch long barrette finding

Leather matte knife

Leather glue

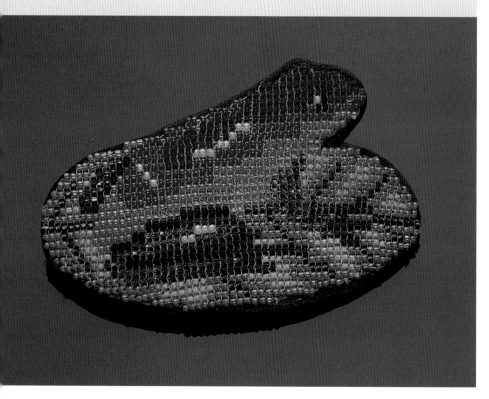

The versatile square stitch lends itself well to making free forms that can be made into pins, barrettes, or appliqué pieces. You may also choose to weave in a background of your choice, to make a larger piece.

As it is much easier to decrease, start beading on the widest row, Row 11, in order to have as few increases as possible. Work from Row 11 down to Row 1, (the bottom of the graph.) Then work up from Row 12 to 29.

Row 11: String fifty-seven beads according to the color scheme of the design chart from left to right. Leave a long tail of thread and hold securely it so that the beads won't slip off. Don't make a knot so that the first row can be adjusted.

Row 10: Work in square stitch, reading the design chart from right to left. String two beads. PNT second bead on first row with needle pointing in the opposite direction of the row. PNBT the second bead strung and pull tight. String on one bead. PNT next bead in first row with needle pointing the opposite way of the row. PNBT bead you just strung. Pull tight. Continue until the end of the row. (See Figure 1.)

Rows 9–1: Work in square stitch. Decrease according to design chart. Read the chart, switching from left to right and right to left every other row. Weave in end of thread .

Decrease: To decrease, PNBT second bead from the end and bring out the needle next to the bead that is directly under the first bead in the row you're starting. Then start row with the square stitch. (See Figure 2.) To decrease one bead at the beginning of the row, simply PNBT second bead from the end and then begin the first stitch. To decrease at the end of the row, simply stop where the row ends.

Turn piece around. Secure the thread in body of work by positioning thread so that it comes out of the second-to-last bead on right side of Row 11. (See Figure 3.)

Rows 12–29: Start on Row 12 of design chart, working in square stitch from right to left. Decrease on edges of every row except Rows 20–24, where you increase on right side edges for frog's nose.

Increase: To increase at end of row, string the desired number of beads and, on the next row, treat them as if they had been square-stitched. To increase at the beginning of the row, string on desired number of beads. PNBT the beads, skipping the last bead strung. Now start the row as normal. (See Figure 4.)

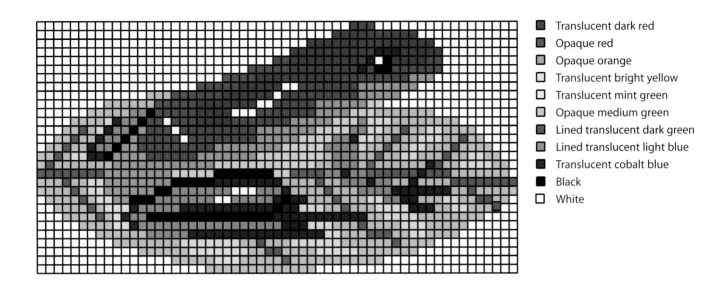

- Translucent dark red
- Opaque red
- Opaque orange
- Translucent bright yellow
- Translucent mint green
- Opaque medium green
- Lined translucent dark green
- Lined translucent light blue
- Translucent cobalt blue
- Black
- White

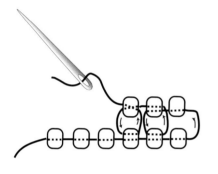

Figure 1

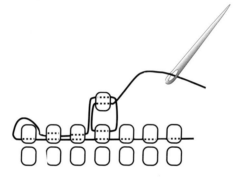

Figure 2

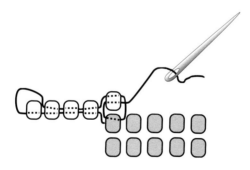

Figure 3

FINISHING

To make this design into a barrette:
Trace the outline of the finished
frog onto paper. Cut out and place
on leather. Using a leather matte
knife, cut the leather to the shape
of the frog. Glue beads to wrong
side of leather, so the back will be
smooth. Make sure the beads cover
the whole surface. Cut a piece of
the blue cord long enough to go
around the perimeter of the
leather. Glue onto the edge of
leather, starting and ending under
the frog's chin, cutting the cord at
an angle so that the ends fit
together. Glue barrette finding to
middle of back.

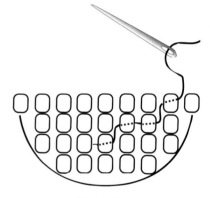

Figure 4

Squared Needle-Weaving Purse Necklace

MATERIALS

11/0 seed beads:
    5 grams matte aqua
    5 grams black
    2 grams metallic gold
    60 lime
    75 lavender
    30 light orange
    20 purple
    50 rose

Beading needle, size 12
Tan beading thread, size D, tan
Medium-weight cord, 18 inches
2 pressure crimps
2 rings (6 mm)
Clasp
Jewelry glue
Needle-nosed pliers
Scissors

1. Refer to page 14 for technique review. Following Design Chart and Key, weave entire piece. Work the flap as charted, adding and decreasing beads in length as indicated.

    Note: The pattern is not shown in its entirety; the body of the bag is made of alternating vertical rows or columns of black and matte aqua, each eighty-one beads long.

2. When entire piece has been woven, fold body of bag in half, allowing three horizontal rows between top edge of body and beginning of flap as space for attaching leather cord. Join sides of body by treating doubled rows as if each were now Row 1 and Row 2. Bury excess thread in weave.

3. Center leather cord on inside of bag just below flap over three horizontal rows. Whip-stitch cord onto inside of bag. Attach pressure crimps, securing firmly with glue. Using needle-nosed pliers, attach rings and clasp.

Design Chart and Key

Body of bag extends to 81 beads per column

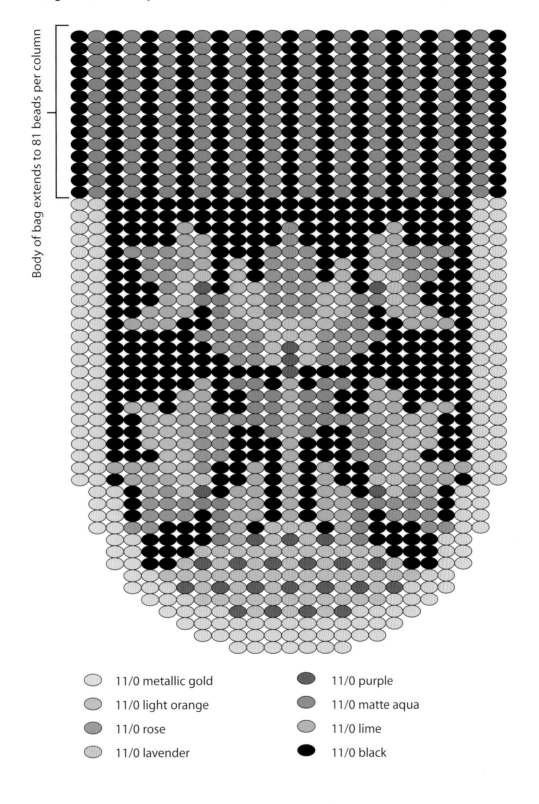

⬭ 11/0 metallic gold	⬤ 11/0 purple
⬭ 11/0 light orange	⬤ 11/0 matte aqua
⬭ 11/0 rose	⬭ 11/0 lime
⬭ 11/0 lavender	⬤ 11/0 black

Squared Floral Necklace

MATERIALS

Delica beads:
    7 grams dark blue-lavender
    2 grams metallic gold
    1 gram light green
    89 dark green
    1.5 grams ivory
    1.5 grams light blue-lavender
    1 gram light rose
    80 dark rose

6 mm faceted crystals:
    27 light blue
6/0 seed beads:
    37 lavender
Barrel clasp
Beading thread, size D, in a color
    to match beads
Beading needle, size 12
Scissors

1. Following Design Chart and Key, string beads for Row 1 from top to bottom. Skipping last bead, insert needle back through all beads. Note: The needle should emerge from the top bead of Row 1.

2. String beads for Row 2, from top to bottom. Add first fringe by continuing to string as charted from top to bottom. Skipping last bead, insert needle back through all beads on fringe. Insert needle into loop exposed at bottom of Row 1. Pull thread gently until entire second row is taut, but not tight, and beads rest against first row without puckering. (See Figure 1.)

Note: When forming fringes, the tension of the thread is important. Try to leave enough slack so that the fringes move freely, but not so much that there is a lot of visible thread. Part of the beauty of fringes is their motion.

3. Insert needle into last three beads of Row 2, and bring thread out until it is taut, but not tight. Loop thread around Row 1 so it is nestled between corresponding beads of Row 1. Insert needle into next three beads of Row 2, bringing needle out again between subsequent beads on Row 2. Again, thread should be taut, but not tight.

4. Loop thread around Row 1 so it is nestled between corresponding beads of Row 1. Insert needle into next three beads on Row 2 and continue this looping and inserting process until thread emerges from bead 1 of Row 2. Repeat Steps 1–4 for all subsequent rows of pattern and fringes.

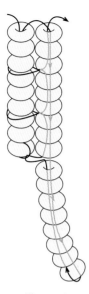

Figure 1

Design Chart and Key

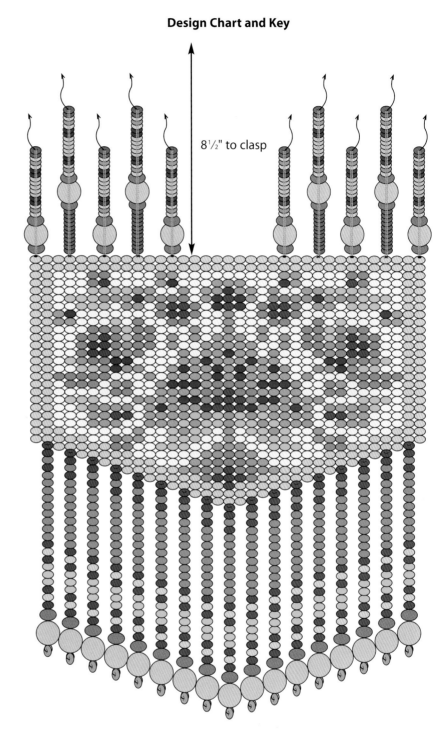

8½" to clasp

NECKLACE

5. Thread needle with a 24-inch length of thread. Attach thread at end of top row, at either side of foundation pattern by running it through several beads in the foundation until secure, or by tying it on the end of thread left from weaving.

6. Slip dark blue-lavender Delica beads on needle to 8½-inch length. From this point, here are two patterns of strands, "dots" and "Xs", which emanate from the top of rows marked on the foundation pattern. (See Design Chart.) Slip beads on needle as indicated.

7. Take needle through loop of one end of barrel clasp and then reinsert it into top bead of necklace strand. Run thread through all beads on strand until reaching foundation pattern. Run thread through beads in foundation pattern and bring out at next marker. Repeat until all strings are attached.

○ Delica ivory
◯ Delica metallic gold
● Delica light rose
● Delica dark rose
● Delica light blue-lavender
● Delica dark blue-lavender
◯ Delica light green

● Delica dark green
● 6/0 lavender
◯ 6 mm faceted crystal

Woven Southwest Tube Necklace

MATERIALS

#3 bugle beads:
  18 grams gold
11/0 seed beads:
  2.5 grams dark aqua
  4.5 grams light aqua
  2.5 grams metallic copper
  11 grams cream
  3.5 grams metallic gold

Turquoise carved drop
Barrel clasp
18 inch piece of ¼-inch
  clothesline
Craft scissors
2 beading needles, size 12
Tan beading thread, size D

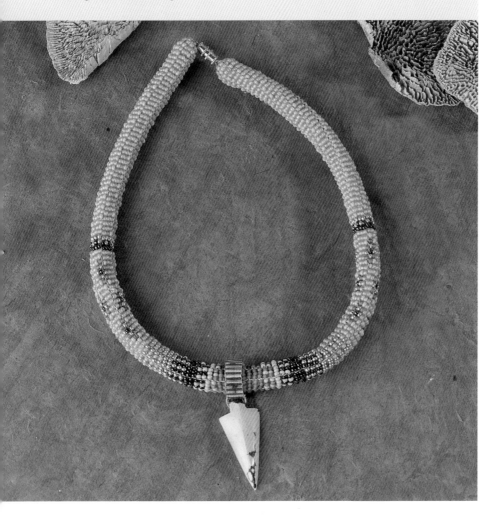

Note: An arrowhead-shaped drop was used to embellish this piece, but any shaped drop will work.

1. Refer to page 14 to review Squared Needle-Weaving. Following Woven Southwest Tube Necklace Pattern opposite, weave right half of piece, beginning at center row as indicated on pattern. Weave vertical rows as charted, repeating final section until length of half-strip is 8½ inches long.

2. Attach thread at center row (first woven row), rotate work piece 180° and repeat pattern until both ends are identical. *Note: As there is no front or back to the design, rotate or flip the work piece and complete the weave in a manner that is most comfortable for you.*

3. Wrap width of woven piece around clothesline, matching top and bottom beads of each vertical row.

4. Attach new thread at one end of weave. Take needle through last three beads on first row and continue through first three beads on same row. Take thread through first three beads on next row and continue through last three beads of same row. Continue weaving back and forth until entire length has been joined together. (See Figure 1.)

5. Trim each end of clothesline very close to end of weave.

6. Attach new thread at one end of weave. Take needle through three beads on last row of weave. Slip two cream 11/0 seed beads on needle and run needle back through first three and next three seed beads on woven row. Slip two more beads on needle and continue in this manner all around until twelve beads have been added onto weave. (See Figure 2.)

7. Take needle through first two beads on row of twelve. Slip one cream 11/0 seed bead on needle and run needle back through first two and next two seed beads on row. Slip one more bead on needle and continue in this manner all around until six beads have been added on. Run thread through last six beads and pull thread taut so gap closes.

8. Repeat Steps 6–7 for remaining end.

9. Sew one part of clasp onto each finished end, looping thread back through last few beads until clasp is secure. Bury thread in weave.

10. Using Ladder Stitch (page 17), weave eighteen bugle beads together in a strip. Join length together in a circle around center of tube necklace.

11. Sew turquoise drop onto one bugle bead in ring and bury excess thread in weave.

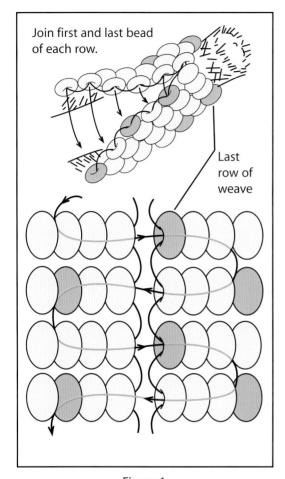

Join first and last bead of each row.

Last row of weave

Figure 1

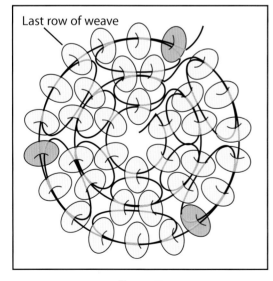

Last row of weave

Figure 2

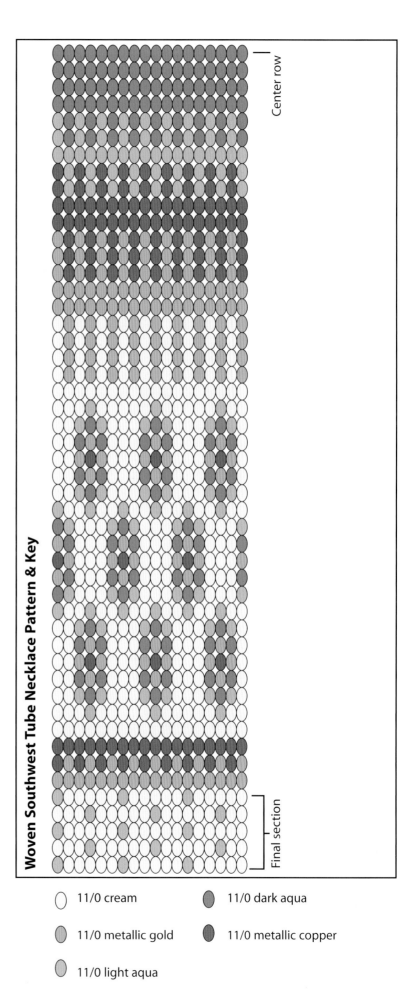

Woven Southwest Tube Necklace Pattern & Key

Center row

Final section

○ 11/0 cream ● 11/0 dark aqua

● 11/0 metallic gold ● 11/0 metallic copper

● 11/0 light aqua

Looming, Knitting & Crochet

Loomed Hat Bands

MATERIALS

11/0 seed beads:
- black
- light blue
- medium blue
- gold
- light green
- lime green
- medium green
- lavender
- orange
- pink
- turquoise
- yellow

Beading loom
Off-white beading thread
Beading needle
Scissors

1. Warp your loom with ten warp threads, following manufacturer's instructions.
   Note: In any loomed piece the warp will have one more thread than the number of beads across the width of the design.

2. Cut one 30-inch length of thread and thread needle. To start horizontal (or weft) thread, knot end of thread onto farthest left warp thread.
   Note: If you are left handed, knot the thread onto the farthest right warp thread. Review looming technique on pages 00-00.

3. Following one of the Design Charts on page 99, slip beads for top horizontal row on needle. Pass beaded thread under warp threads, positioning beads and threads so one bead falls between two warp threads.

4. After beads are seated into warp, pass needle back through beads so weft thread goes over warp threads. Repeat Steps 3 and 4 for remaining horizontal rows. Bury any excess thread in weave. (See Figure 01.)

5. To finish ends of band, separate warp threads into groups of two threads, beginning from each side of center weft bead.
   Note: Outermost warp threads will remain single. Trim each group of threads as one for a clean edge. Thread needle with these threads.

6. Slip twelve black and one of each remaining color 11/0 seed beads on needle (in order of rainbow). Skipping last bead, insert needle back through all beads of fringe. Bury excess thread in weave. Trim excess thread. Repeat for each remaining warp thread.

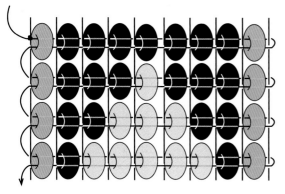

Figure 1

Alternate Design Patterns & Keys

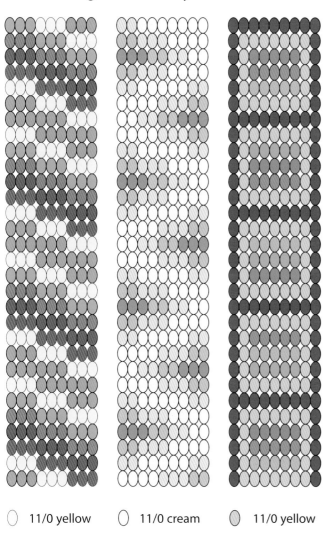

⬭ 11/0 yellow	⬭ 11/0 cream	⬭ 11/0 yellow
⬭ 11/0 orange	⬭ 11/0 tan	⬭ 11/0 red
⬭ 11/0 pink	⬭ 11/0 gold	⬭ 11/0 purple
⬭ 11/0 purple	⬭ 11/0 copper	⬭ 11/0 blue
⬭ 11/0 blue		⬭ 11/0 teal
⬭ 11/0 green		⬭ 11/0 green

Loom-woven Band Pattern & Key

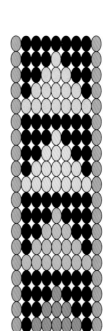

- ⬭ 11/0 black
- ⬭ 11/0 light green
- ⬭ 11/0 medium green
- ⬭ 11/0 yellow
- ⬭ 11/0 lavender
- ⬭ 11/0 orange
- ⬭ 11/0 gold
- ⬭ 11/0 pink
- ⬭ 11/0 light blue
- ⬭ 11/0 medium blue
- ⬭ 11/0 turquoise
- ⬭ 11/0 lime green

Sea Turtle Bookmark

FINISHED SIZE

2 inches x 7 inches

MATERIALS

11/0 Delica Japanese tubular
   beads:
   10 grams, lined crystal/yellow
      luster, #233
   7 grams lined crystal/green
      aqua luster, #238
   7 grams semi-matte silver-
      lined medium blue, #693
   4 grams lined green/lime,
      #027
   4 grams dyed matte transparent
      Kelly green, #776
   4 grams Japanese tubular
      beads, dyed opaque jade
      green, #656

2 grams blue iris, #002
2 grams lined topaz AB, #065
2 grams dyed opaque turquoise
   green, #658
2 grams silver-lined smoked
   topaz, #612
2 grams lined topaz/olive,
   #273
2 beads black, #010
6/0 seed bead:
   1 royal blue bead
½-inch transparent crystal bead:
   1 green oblong
Black nylon beading thread,
   size D
1 long beading needle, size 12
Loom
Scissors
Pliers (optional)
1 Charm

1. Warp the loom with 34 warp
   threads, each 40 inches long.
   Follow the design chart for fifty-
   five rows. Read the chart from
   bottom to top and right to left.
   Turn to pages 20–22 for technique review if needed.

2. For the next row, decrease one
   bead at each end. To decrease in
   loom work: after PNT last bead
   on the row before you wish to
   decrease, pass the weft thread
   under the outermost warp
   thread and PNBT the last bead.
   (See Figure 1.) After pulling
   thread tight, make sure needle
   and thread are at the back of the
   work.

3. String beads for the next row.
   Push the beads up into the
   spaces between the warp threads
   as usual and PNBT the beads
   above the warp threads, skipping
   the outermost warp thread on
   the right. (See Figure 2.)
   Decrease one bead at each end
   of a row, following the design
   chart to the end.

4. Remove from loom and thread
   two warp threads from the center top onto the needle. String 4
   inches of green aqua beads and
   tie a knot to hold beads in
   place. (See Figure 3.) Thread the
   next two warp threads onto a
   needle, string 4 inches of
   medium blue beads, and tie a
   knot to hold beads in place. Take
   the next two warp threads from
   the opposite side of the strand
   of green aqua beads and thread
   onto a needle. String 4 inches of
   yellow luster beads and tie a
   knot. (See Figure 4.) Braid the
   three strands together. Tie the
   strands together with a knot at
   the top.

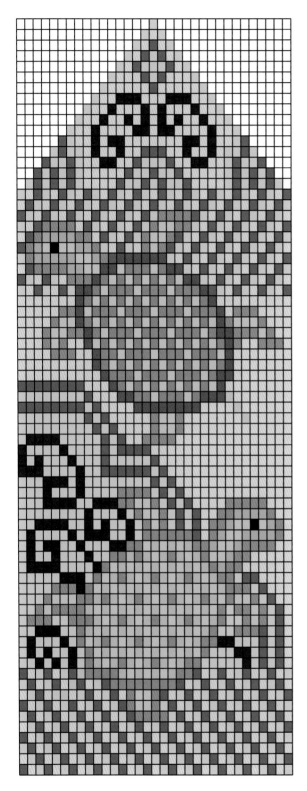

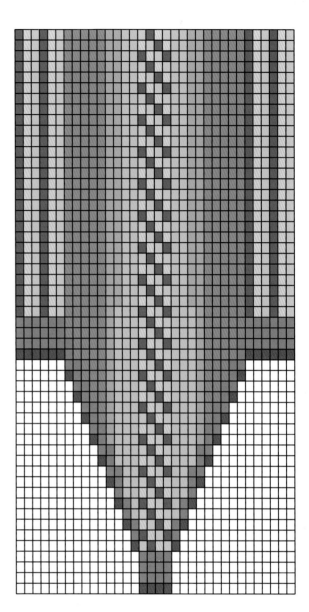

□ Lined crystal/yellow luster
□ Lined crystal/green aqua luster
■ Semi-matte silver-lined meduim blue
■ Dyed matte transparent Kelly green
□ Dyed opaque jade green
□ Lined green/lime
■ Lined topaz
■ Silver-lined smoked topaz

Fringe Chart

□ Lined crystal/yellow luster   □ Lined green/lime
■ Semi-matte silver-lined medium blue □ Lined topaz/olive
■ Blue iris   ■ Silver-lined smoked topaz
□ Lined crystal/green aqua luster   ■ Lined topaz
■ Dyed matte transparent Kelly green   ■ Dyed opaque turquoise
□ Dyed opaque jade green   □ green
                                       ■ Black

Design chart

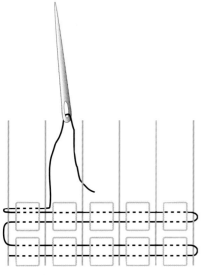

Figure 1

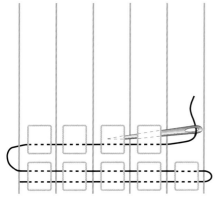

Figure 2

5. String the ½-inch green bead and the size 6 blue seed bead onto all six threads. Bring the threads back through the green bead and tie another knot at the bottom of the bead. (See Figure 05.) Weave excess thread through the strands of beads and cut. Weave the remaining warp threads at the top of the bookmark back into the beads in the body of the work.

6. Use the warp threads at the bottom of the bookmark to create the fringe. Follow the fringe chart and refer to the instructions on making fringe in the technique review (see pages 21–22).

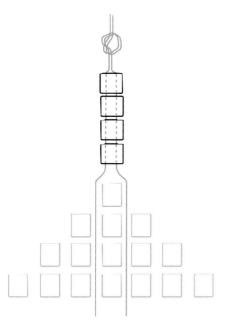

Figure 3

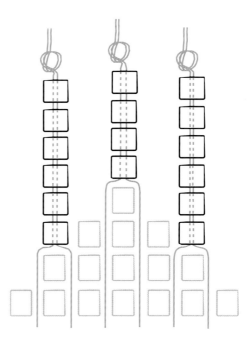

Figure 4

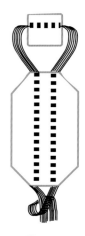

Figure 5

Loomed Egyptian Column Bracelet

FINISHED SIZE

7½ inches x ¾ inch

MATERIALS

11/0 Delica Japanese tubular beads:
  2 grams transparent dark tangerine, #704
  2 grams matte light blue, #862
  2 grams, dyed opaque squash, #651
1 oval amber bead, ⅜ inch
White nylon beading thread, size D
One beading needle, size 10
Loom
Scissors

1. Warp the loom with fourteen 19-inch-long warp threads. The first eleven rows will be worked later. Be sure to leave about 1 inch on the warp threads for these eleven rows before you start. Starting with Row 12 on the design chart, follow the chart for the next thirty-eight rows. Read the chart from left to right and from bottom to top. Refer to pages 20–22 for review of technique, if needed.
2. The next row is the loop row. For this row, string on four squash beads, ★one blue bead, five tangerine beads, one blue bead, nine squash beads.★ Repeat between asterisks eleven times. Then string on one blue bead, five tangerine beads, one blue bead, and five squash beads.
3. Working from right to left, push up the last bead into the first space created by the first and second warp threads and PNT bead to hold it in place. The loops will be formed at the back of the work. Go to the next fifth squash bead, push it up through the second space between warp threads, and PNT the bead. Continue in this manner until the end of the row. This work is awkward, but it will be over soon.

4. Work the next twenty-five rows on the design chart. On the next row, you will be decreasing one bead on each side.
5. To decrease: after PNT the last bead on the row before you want to decrease, pass the weft thread under the outermost warp thread and go back through the last bead. (See Figure 1.) After pulling the thread tight, make sure the needle and thread are at the back of the work. String the beads for the decreased row. Push the beads up into the spaces between the warp threads as usual and PNBT the beads above the warp threads, skipping the outermost warp thread. (See Figure 2.) Decrease according to chart for the next ten rows.
6. Remove needle from the thread, get a new strand of thread, and thread the needle. Turn the loom around and weave thread into the body of the work to anchor it. Make sure the needle is coming out on the first row worked on the left. Weave the first eleven rows following the chart from Row 11 to Row 1 and decrease as shown in Figures 1 and 2 to create the other end of the bracelet. Weave excess thread into the body of work and cut. Remove from the loom.

BUTTON AND LOOP CLOSURE

7. Begin with one end of the bracelet and weave in the warp threads, except for the center four threads. Thread the center two warp threads onto a needle, and string two squash beads and three tangerine beads; leave for now. Thread the warp thread to one side of the center strand onto a needle and string three squash beads and three tangerine beads. Repeat with opposite warp thread. String one blue bead onto all four threads. (See Figure 3.)

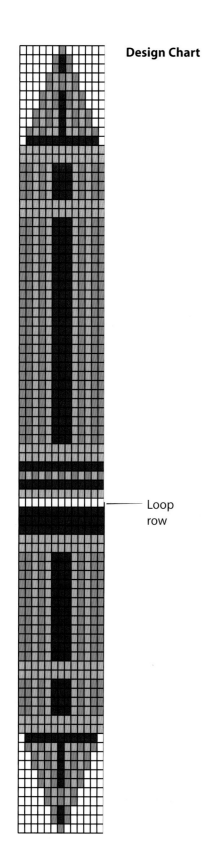

Design Chart

Loop
row

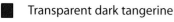
■ Transparent dark tangerine

Dyed opaque squash

Matte light blue

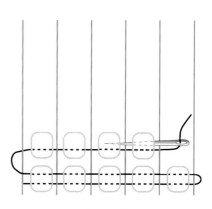

Figure 1

Figure 2

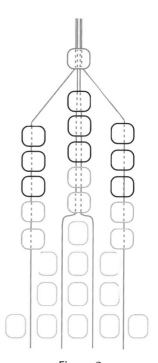

8. Next, string twenty-two squash beads (or enough to fit over the amber bead) onto the two warp threads on the left. Take the other two threads and PNT the twenty-two squash beads in the opposite direction. (See Figure 4.) Pull tight and tie a knot below the loop of beads. Hide the excess thread ends in the beads and cut.

9. Now begin work on the other end of the bracelet. Weave in the warp threads, leaving the center four threads. Thread the center two warp threads onto a needle and string three squash beads, five tangerine beads, and one blue bead; leave for now. Thread warp thread to one side of the center strand onto a needle and string three squash beads, five tangerine beads, and three blue beads. Repeat with opposite warp thread. Tie an overhand knot, using all four warp threads to secure beads. Thread all four warp threads through the amber bead and tie another knot under the bead. Weave excess thread back up through beads to hide ends.

Figure 3

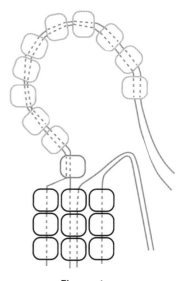

Figure 4

Water Lily Comb

FINISHED SIZE
8 inches x 1¼ inches

MATERIALS
11/0 seed beads:
- 3 grams transparent silver-lined royal blue
- 3 grams metallic light green
- 3 grams transparent iridescent light green
- 3 grams opaque white
- 3 grams turquoise white heart
- 1 gram transparent forest-green
- 0.5 gram iridescent opaque yellow

White nylon beading thread, size D
One beading needle, size 12
8-inch comb (with square ends)
Scissors
Glue

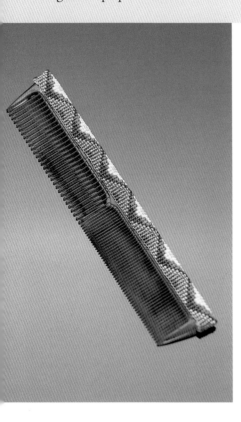

This project, with the Tri-Diamond Headband on the next page, and the Water Lily Mirror found on page 177 can make a nice set.

1. Warp your loom with seventeen warp threads, 20 inches long. Read the design chart from left to right and from bottom to top. If you are left-handed, read the chart from right to left. Attach the weft thread to left outermost warp thread (reverse, if left-handed) and weave according to design chart for ninety-six rows. End the work by weaving ten or more rows of thread cloth to the top of the work.

2. Turn the loom around and create a bit of thread cloth at the other end. This keeps the beads from moving along the warp threads and falling off. Remove from the loom and tie off all pairs of warp threads with surgeon's knots. Trim the ends and fold thread cloth to the back of the work and glue in place.

3. Next, glue work to the spine of the comb. Make sure that the design is lined up evenly along the spine. If necessary, temporarily sew the beadwork onto the comb to hold it in place while the glue dries. To sew it in place, catch the outer warp threads with your needle and take the thread back and forth between the teeth of the comb. Before the glue dries, sew the work together at both ends of the comb. After the glue dries, cut and remove the thread used to hold the beading in place.

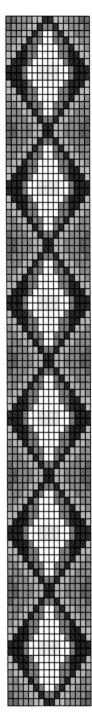

Design Chart

- ■ Transparent silver-lined royal blue
- ■ Turquoise white heart
- ■ Transparent forest green
- ■ Transparent iridescent light green
- ■ Metallic light green
- □ Iridescent opaque yellow
- □ Opaque white

Tri-Diamond Loomed Headband

FINISHED SIZE

11¼ inches x ½ inch

MATERIALS

11/0 seed beads:
  4.5 grams transparent silver-lined royal blue
  3 grams turquoise white heart
  2 grams opaque white
  2 grams metallic light green

29 iridescent opaque yellow beads
White nylon beading thread, size D
One beading needle, size 12
½-inch plastic headband
Loom
Scissors
Glue

1. Warp the loom with ten 24-inch-long warp threads. Read the design chart from left to right and from bottom to top. If you're left-handed, read the chart from right to left. Attach weft thread to the left outermost warp thread (reverse if left-handed) and weave according to the design chart for 131 rows. End by weaving ten or more rows of thread cloth to the top of the work.

2. Turn the loom around and create a bit of thread cloth at the other end. This keeps the beads from moving along the warp threads and falling off. Remove from the loom and tie off all pairs of warp threads with surgeon's knots. Trim the ends and fold the warp cloth to the back of the work and glue in place.

3. Glue finished beadwork to the headband. Align the center diamond with the center of the headband. If necessary, temporarily sew the beadwork in place by catching the outermost warp threads every ½ inch or so on either side, taking the thread back and forth underneath the headband. When the glue is dry, cut and remove the thread used to hold the beadwork in place.

Design Chart

☐ Opaque white
☐ Iridescent opaque yellow
▨ Metallic light green
▨ Turquoise white heart
■ Transparent silver-lined royal blue

Loom-Woven Parakeets

FINISHED SIZE

7½ inches x 3¾ inches

MATERIALS

11/0 seed beads:

- 41 grams transparent iridescent gold
- 14 grams opaque iridescent yellow
- 14 grams opaque light blue
- 14 grams silver-lined transparent royal blue
- 14 grams transparent Kelly green
- 14 grams silver-lined transparent dark red
- 5 grams opaque light green
- 5 grams opaque black
- 5 grams opaque light orange
- 5 grams opaque brown
- 5 grams opaque dark brown
- 5 grams pearl white
- 5 grams transparent off-white
- 5 grams transparent forest green
- 5 grams silver-lined transparent green
- 5 grams transparent dark green

One beading needle, size 12
White nylon beading thread, size D
Loom (wide enough for sixty-three warp threads)
Scissors

This design was inspired by a nineteenth century lithograph by H.C. Richter.

1. Warp the loom with sixty-three warp threads about 25 inches long. Thread the needle with a length of thread and attach this weft thread to the outer left warp thread with a half-hitch knot, leaving a tail of thread about 6 inches long.
2. String all the beads in the first row according to the design chart. Read the chart from left to right and from bottom to top. Count your beads correctly, because you won't know if you've made a mistake until you have finished the row. Because of the width of the design, you will have to work your needle through the beads in stages. Starting at the right edge, push up seven or eight beads at a time and then PNT. Continue to the end of the row. Work according to the design chart for eighty-nine rows.
3. When you have finished the design, weave several rows without beads to create a thread cloth of about ¼ inch. Turn loom around and, with a new weft thread, create a thread cloth on the other end. Remove from the loom and tie off pairs of warp threads with surgeon's knots. Trim ends, fold thread cloth to back of work on both ends, and sew in place.

This motif can be appliquéd onto a pillow, placed in a floating frame, or incorporated into an item of your choosing. It might also be adapted to the lampshade design that follows, using three panels instead of six and adding a few more warp threads at the sides of each.

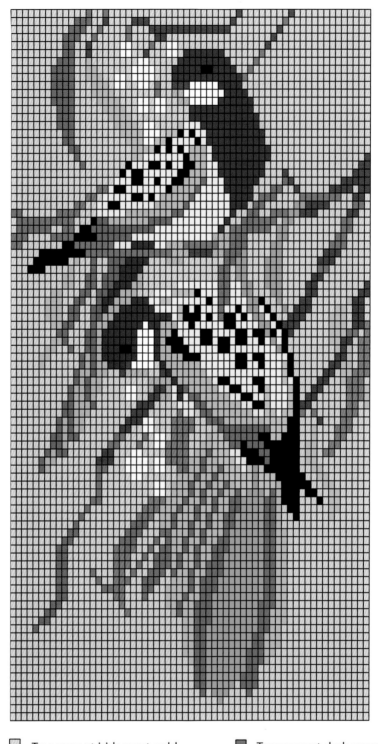

▨	Transparent iridescent gold	▨	Transparent dark green
▢	Opaque iridescent yellow	■	Opaque black
▨	Opaque light blue	▨	Opaque light orange
■	Silver-lined transparent royal blue	▨	Opaque brown
▨	Transparent Kelly green	■	Opaque dark brown
▨	Opaque light green	■	Silver-lined transparent dark red
▨	Transparent forest green	▢	Pearl white
Design Chart ▨	Silver-lined transparent green	▢	Transparent off-white

Loomed Mandarin Lamp Shade

MATERIALS

11/0 seed beads:
  2 hanks dark blue
  2 hanks dark medium blue
  3 hanks medium blue
  1 hank pale blue
  6 hanks white
6/0 seed beads:
  72 medium blue
6 mm x 10 mm teardrop crystals:
  36 light blue

Loom to accommodate 36 warp
  threads, each 20 inches long
Beading needles: long with very
  small eyes
Between needle, #10
Embroidery needle, #9
Jewelry glue
Lamp shade: 4-inch-diameter top,
  clamp-on style with paper
  removed
White beading thread

1. Following manufacturer's instructions, warp loom with thirty-six warp threads.
   Note: Roll the warp on one end if necessary, but make certain that the entire length of the warp is at least 20 inches.

2. Refer to pages 20–22 for review of looming technique, if needed. Allowing 4 inches of unloomed warp, work weft threads according to Mandarin Lamp Shade Pattern #1 until the point where rows begin to decrease in size.
   Note: Roll the loomed beadwork onto the starting end of the loom as necessary.

3. To decrease number of beads on rows, slip beads on needle and pass under warp threads, positioning beads and threads so each bead falls between two warp threads as charted and ignoring outer warp threads. After beads are seated into warp, pass needle back through beads so weft thread goes over warp threads.
   Note: As work continues, multiple warp threads will be ignored. All warp threads will eventually be worked into the finishing.

4. Remove panel from loom, leaving as much warp thread as possible. Repeat for two more panels, ending with three panels of Pattern #1.

5. Following Mandarin Lamp Shade Pattern #2, repeat Steps 1–4, making three panels in Pattern #2.

6. At top end of each panel, tie four consecutive warp threads together, positioning knot very close to weave. (See Figure 1.)

7. Apply dot of glue onto each knot and trim tied warp ends to less than 1 inch.
   Note: These ends and knots will eventually be hidden behind the beads when the top edge is sewn onto the shade frame.

Mandarin Lamp Shade Pattern #1   Mandarin Lamp Shade Pattern #2

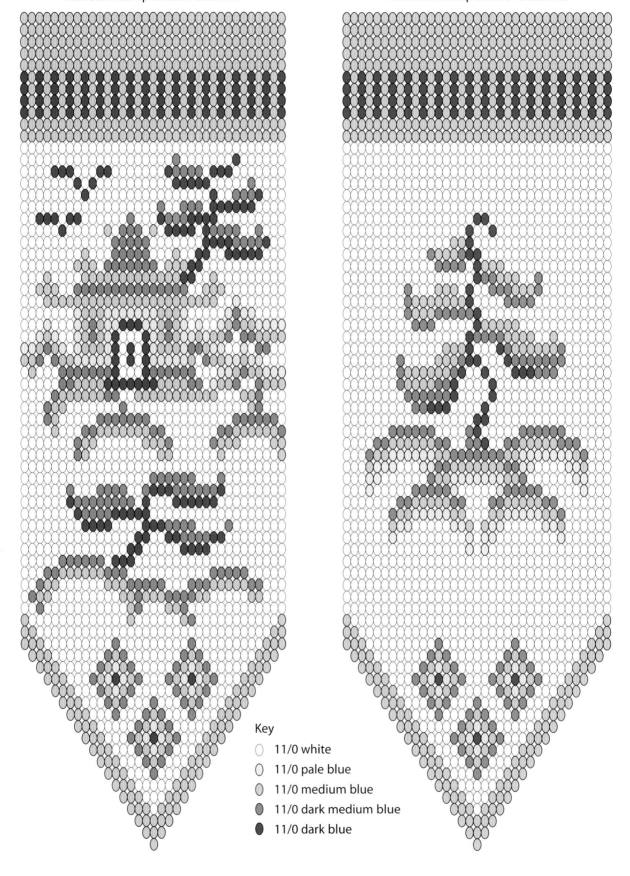

Key
○ 11/0 white
○ 11/0 pale blue
○ 11/0 medium blue
● 11/0 dark medium blue
● 11/0 dark blue

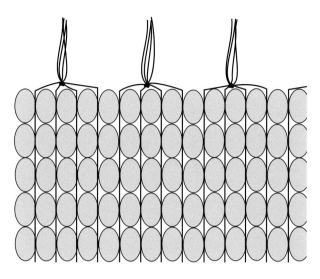

Figure 1

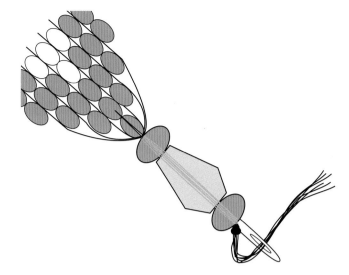

Figure 2

8. Join all six panels together—two at a time and alternating panels—taking needle through last three beads on first row of one panel and continuing through first three beads on same row of remaining panel. Weave thread back and forth until entire length has been joined together. Bury any excess joining thread in weave.

9. To finish bottom edge of shade, separate consecutive warp threads into groups of six threads, beginning with three threads from each side of each panel point. Trim all six threads as one for clean edge. Thread #9 embroidery needle with these threads. Slip one 6/0 bead, one crystal, and one 6/0 bead on needle. Knot threads, positioning beads very close to woven panel. Note: It may be necessary to knot over the first knot one or more times to make certain that the beads are secure.

10. Apply small dot of glue just beyond knot and take needle back through beads until only knot remains visible beyond beads. (See Figure 2.) Trim excess thread that was pulled through beads close to first 6/0 bead, taking care to avoid cutting any threads that secure beads. Repeat for each panel point.

11. Repeat Steps 9 and 10 for each group of six warp threads at the angle of the joined seams (three warp threads from each side); then for the remaining groups of six warp threads.

12. After all drops are in place, pin top edge of assembled piece onto shade frame.
Note: As this is a circular design, it makes no difference where the assembled panel is positioned on the frame.

13. Using #10 between needle and thread, sew panel onto frame by wrapping top three to four rows of beading around frame, tucking knots along top edge into sewing, and securing edge with in-and-out stitches through weave. Carefully trim excess threads.

Note: Each stitch that shows on the outside of the design should be no wider than one bead so it will not be noticeable.

Try a different color scheme for working this design, substituting shades of red or brown or yellow to accent the decor of your own home; or use a different design motif for the one that is charted. The Parakeets on page 107 or the Sea Turtle design on page 100 could be easily adapted. Cross-stitch and needlepoint books can also yield pleasing designs. Make certain the horizontal and vertical counts are the same as the original. Each charted square on the cross-stitch or needlepoint graph will represent one bead.

Bead–Knitted Jewelry Envelope

FINISHED SIZE WHEN CLOSED

4¾ inches x 3¾ inches

MATERIALS

8/0 seed beads:
  60 grams background color
  6 grams pale green
  3 grams pale pink
  3 grams pale lavender
  4 grams pink
Beading needle, size 10
One twisted wire beading needle

KNITTING SUPPLIES

Knitting needles, size 0
Cotton Cord (one of the following in a color that blends with
  your background beads):
2 balls DMC Cebelia, size 10
  (work double strand)
or
1 ball Mondial Cotone "Marea 5"
or
1 50-gram ball Coats Opera 5

A container to hold your ball of
  cotton when stringing beads
  down the cord.
Paper and paper scissors for cutting dividers between rows
Crochet hook to help correct
  errors

FINISHING SUPPLIES

11/0 seed beads:
  14 grams to match background
    bead color
Twenty fringe beads
¼ yard ultrasuede or pig suede
  (Measure your knitting before
  purchase to make sure the size
  is correct. The suede needs
  to be the same size as your
  knitting.)
¼ yard woven fusible interfacing
Sew-on snap, size 3
Nylon beading thread, size B, or
  quilting thread to match beads
Sewing needles
Thimble
Scissors

ABBREVIATIONS

KB: Knit bead

PB: Purl bead

K2tog: Knit 2 stitches together

P2tog: Purl 2 stitches together

Sl 1, K1, psso: Slip a stitch
  from the left needle to the
  right needle as if to knit but
  without working it, knit the
  next stitch, pass the slipped
  stitch over the knit stitch and
  off the right needle.

Sl 1, P1, psso: Slip a stitch
  from the left needle to the
  right needle as if to purl
  without working it, purl the
  next stitch, pass the slipped
  stitch over the purl stitch and
  off the right needle.

Detail of Envelope Jewelry Case

1. On Design Chart 1, beginning
   at Row 33, string size 8 beads
   and work down to Row 2, from
   either left to right or right to
   left (the design is symmetrical)
   onto the cotton cord. At the end
   of each row, string on a small
   piece of paper (about ⅜-inch
   square). This helps keep track of
   the rows. It is torn off as you get
   to it while knitting.
2. On size 0 needles, cast on thirty-
   nine stitches (simple cast on).

Row 1: Purl

Row 2: K2, KB36, K1

Row 3: P1, PB37, P1

Repeat Row 2 for all even rows through Row 32.

Repeat Row 3 for all odd rows through Row 33. Cut the cord leaving a 6" tail.

3. On Design Chart 2, beginning at Row 95, string size 8 beads and work down to Row 34 in the same manner as before.

4. Tie cord onto knitting at Row 33, and continue knitting odd and even rows as before through Row 68.

5. Row 69: P2, PB35, P2

Row 70: Sl 1, K1, psso, K1, KB34, K2

Row 71: Sl 1, P1, psso, P1, PB33, P2

Row 72: Sl 1, K1, psso, K1, KB32, K2

Row 73: Sl 1, P1, psso, P1, PB31, P2

Row 74: Sl 1, K1, psso, K1, KB30, K2

Row 75: Sl 1, P1, psso, P1, PB29, P2

Row 76: Sl 1, K1, psso, K1, KB28, K2

Row 77: Sl 1, P1, psso, P1, PB27, P2

Row 78: Sl 1, K1, psso, K1, KB26, K2

Row 79: Sl 1, P1, psso, P1, PB25, P2

Row 80: Sl 1, K1, psso, K1, KB24, K2

Row 81: Sl 1, P1, psso, P1, PB23, P2

Row 82: Sl 1, K1, psso, K1, KB22, K2

Row 83: Sl 1, P1, psso, P1, PB21, P2

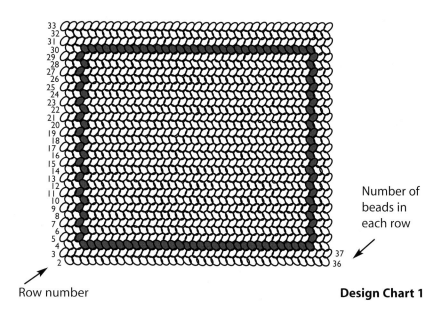

Number of beads in each row

Row number

Design Chart 1

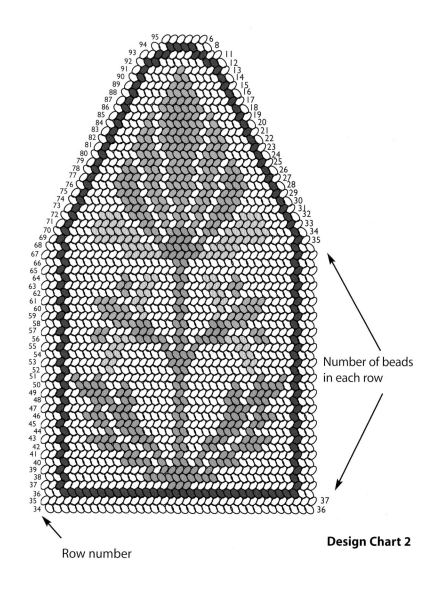

Number of beads in each row

Row number

Design Chart 2

113

Figure 1

Blocking Template

Row 84: Sl 1, K1, psso, K1, KB20, K2

Row 85: Sl 1, P1, psso, P1, PB19, P2

Row 86: Sl 1, K1, psso, K1, KB18, K2

Row 87: Sl 1, P1, psso, P1, PB17, P2

Row 88: Sl 1, K1, psso, K1, KB16, K2

Row 89: Sl 1, P1, psso, P1, PB15, P2

Row 90: Sl 1, K1, psso, K1, KB14, K2

Row 91: Sl 1, P1, psso, P1, PB13, P2

Row 92: Sl 1, K1, psso, K1, KB12, K2

Row 93: Sl 1, P1, psso, P1, PB11, P2

Row 94: Sl 1, K1, psso, K2, KB8, K3

Row 95: Sl 1, P1, psso, P2, PB6, P2, P2tog

Row 96: Sl 1, K1, psso, K8, K2tog

Cast off in purl.

6. See blocking instructions for beaded knitting on page 30. When the piece is laid flat, check that all the beads are on the front of the piece and adjust as needed. When piece has dried thoroughly, sew in all loose thread tails.

LINING & FINISHING

7. Lay your knitted piece on top of Figure 1 to be sure that the lining fits your piece. The lining should be about ⅛ inch to ¼ inch smaller all around. Adjust the guide if necessary, then cut the interfacing. It should cover the back side of the beads, but not the back side of the selvedge. Iron on to the wrong side of your knitting.

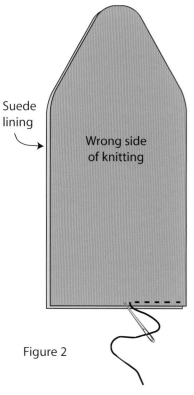

Suede lining

Wrong side of knitting

Figure 2

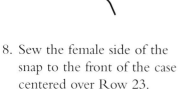

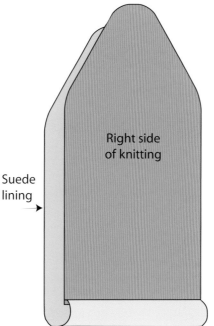

Suede lining

Right side of knitting

Figure 3

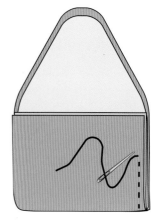

Figure 4

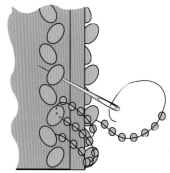

Figure 5

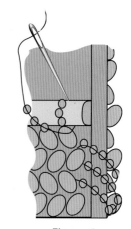

Figure 6

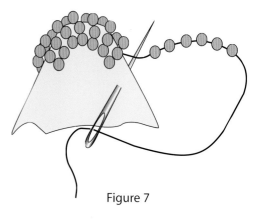

Figure 7

8. Sew the female side of the snap to the front of the case centered over Row 23.

9. Cut the ultrasuede the same size as the knitting. Place the right sides of the ultrasuede on the knitting together. Using a running stitch, join as close as possible to the first row of beads. (See Figure 2.) Turn the ultrasuede to the wrong side of the case. (See Figure 3.)

10. Fold up the bottom of the case at the fold line, smoothing out the ultrasuede and lining it up with the edges of the case. Pin in place. Use a matching color thread (quilting thread or beading thread) to stitch the sides in place with a running stitch close to the first column of beads and catching the suede in each stitch. (See Figure 4.)

11. Overcast stitch around the sides of the case by stringing seven size 11/0 seed beads for each stitch and passing through the size 8/0 beads at the edge of the knitting. (See Figure 5.)

12. At the sides of the opening, cover the raw edges of the suede by making three vertical stitches, each with three beads per stitch. (See Figure 6.)

13. Cover the edge of the knitting and the edge of the suede all along the flap with six size 11° seed beads on each stitch around the edge. (See Figure 7.)

14. Sew the fringe by passing through one size 8° bead on Row 33 of the knitting. String two size 11/0 seed beads, one fringe bead, and two size 11/0 seed beads. Then skip the next bead on the knitting and pass through the third bead on the knitting. Continue in this pattern all across Row 33, always stitching through the beads on the knitting in the same direction (i.e., either from the back to the front or the front to the back).

15. Sew the male side of the snap to the flap, being careful to line it up with the female side of the snap when the case is closed.

Wild Rose Clasp Purse

FINISHED SIZE, WITH FRINGE

3½" x 5½" on a 10" chain.

MATERIALS

11/0 seed beads:
  56 grams light blue
    (for background)
  42 grams light green
    (for leaves)
  42 grams medium green
    (for leaves)
  42 grams dark green
    (for leaves)
  42 grams pale pink
    (for flower petals)
  42 grams pink
    (for flower petals)
  42 grams salmon-pink
    (for flower petals)
  42 grams salmon-red
    (for flower petals)
  29 purple (for flower center)
  18 yellow (for bee and flower
    center)
  8 black (for bee)
  12 light gray (for bee's wings)
  4 dark gray (for bee's wings)
  20 clear AB finish (for chain)
11/0 delica Japanese tubular beads:
  8 silver lined, #41 (for chain)
15/0 seed beads:
  5 grams clear AB (for clasp
    lining, fringe, and chain)
8/0 seed beads:
  20 pale blue-lined, clear AB
    finish, (for chain)
6/0 seed beads:
  8 clear AB finish, (for chain)

5/0 seed beads:
  2 faceted, (for chain)
1 small teardrop bead (for inside
  clasp lining)
14 small dagger drop beads (for
  fringe)

KNITTING SUPPLIES

Knitting needles, size 0000
1 ball perle cotton, size 8, in
  color to match background
  bead color
Beading needles, size 10 or 12
  and size 13 or 15
Beading thread, size 0, in color to
  match background beads, or
  size 15 seed beads
Sewing thread to match clasp or
  lining
Two 4" x 5" pieces of silk (for
  lining)
Pins to hold lining in place while
  stitching
Container to hold the ball of
  thread and beads when moving them down the thread.

TOOLS & FINDINGS

2½ inch clasp
*Note: You will need to use the same
  shaped clasp as in the photo, since
  this design will not fit a 2½ inch
  clasp with a different shape at the
  top, such as a square-top clasp.*
Thin wire
Ultrasuede
Tacky glue
Toothpicks

ABBREVIATIONS

KB: Knit bead

PB: Purl bead

K2tog: Knit two stitches
  together

P2tog: Purl two stitches
  together

Inc1: Increase by knitting or
  purling (corresponding to the
  row) into the front and back
  of the stitch. Slip the stitch
  off the left needle.

Psso: Pick up the second stitch
  on the RIGHT needle and
  pull it over the first stitch on
  the needle and off the needle.
  This is a decrease.

Add 2 stitches: Place two
  loops on the end of the row
  as in a simple cast on.

1. Beginning at Row 59 on the design chart, string beads onto #8 perle cotton, always starting on the side with the black row number. The magenta number indicates the number of beads in the row, so count your beads after each row to make sure the number is the same as the magenta number for each row. At the end of each row, string on a small piece of paper (about ⅜-inch square). This helps keep track of the rows. It is torn off as you get to it while knitting.

2. On size 0000 needles, cast on 22 stitches (two-handed cast on).

Row 1: Knit
Row 2: Inc1, P20, inc1
Row 3: Inc1, K22, inc1
Row 4: P4, PB18, P4
Row 5: Inc1, K2, KB21, K1, inc1
Row 6: Inc1, P1, PB24, P1, inc1
Row 7: Inc1, K1, KB27, inc1
Row 8: Inc1, PB30, inc1
Row 9: Inc1, KB33, add 2 stitches
Row 10: Inc1, P1, PB34, inc1
Row 11: Inc1, K37, inc1
Row 12: P2, PB38, inc1
Row 13: K2, KB39, inc1
Row 14: P2, PB40, inc1
Row 15: K2, KB41, inc1
Row 16: Inc1, P1, PB41, P1, inc1
Row 17: K2, KB43, K2
Row 18: P3, PB42, P2
Row 19: K2, KB43, K2
Row 20: P3, PB42, P2
Row 21: K2, KB43, K2
Row 22: P3, PB42, P2
Row 23: K3, KB41, K1, K2tog
Row 24: P2, PB42, P2
Row 25: K3, KB41, K2
Row 26: P3, PB40, P3
Row 27: K2tog, K2, KB39, K3
Row 28: P2tog, P2, PB38, P3
Row 29: K3, KB39, K2
Row 30: P3, PB38, P1, P2tog
Row 31: K3, KB37, K1, K2tog
Row 32: P2, PB38, P2
Row 33: K3, KB37, K2
Row 34: P3, PB36, P3
Row 35: K2tog, K2, KB35, K3

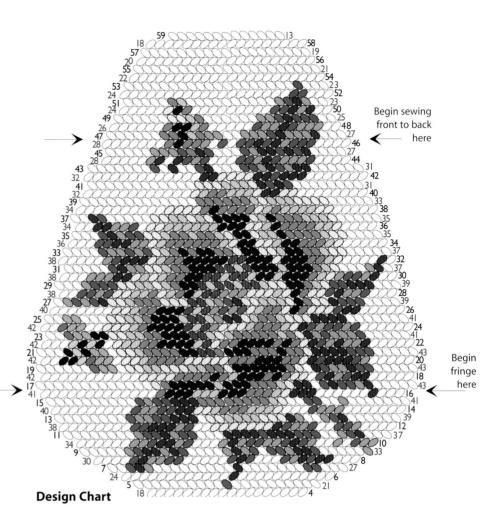

Design Chart

Begin sewing front to back here

Begin fringe here

Row 36: P2tog, P2, PB34, P3
Row 37: K3, KB35, K2
Row 38: P3, PB34, P3
Row 39: K2tog, K2, KB33, K3
Row 40: P2tog, P2, PB32, P3
Row 41: K2tog, K2, KB31, K3
Row 42: P3, PB32, P2
Row 43: K3, KB31, K3
Row 44: P2, psso, P1, psso, P1, psso, P1, PB28, P4
Row 45: K2, psso, K1, psso, K1, psso, K1, KB27, K2
Row 46: P2, PB28, P1
Row 47: K2, KB27, K2
Row 48: P2, psso, P1, PB26, P2
Row 49: K2, psso, K1, KB25, K2
Row 50: P2, psso, P1, PB24, P2
Row 51: K2, psso, K1, KB23, K2
Row 52: P2, PB24, P1
Row 53: K2 KB23, K2
Row 54: P2, psso, P1, PB22, P2
Row 55: K2, psso, K1, KB21, K2

Row 56: P2, psso, P1, PB20, P2
Row 57: K2, psso, K1, KB19, K2
Row 58: P2, psso, P1, PB18, P2
Row 59: K2, psso, K3, KB13, K2, K2tog
Row 60: P2, psso, P16, P2tog
Row 61: Cast off

3. For the back, transfer six strands from a hank of light blue size 11/0 seed beads onto #8 DMC perle cotton. Knit the same as for the front, counting the proper number of beads for each row before knitting each row.

4. See blocking instructions for beaded knitting on page 27. When the piece is laid flat, check that all the beads are on the front of the piece and adjust as needed. When piece has dried thoroughly, sew in all loose thread tails.

5. Pin front to back with the right sides together. Backstitch seam, beginning at Row 47 and continuing around the bottom of the bag and back to Row 47 on the other side. Be careful to leave no gap of beads in the seam. Turn to front and backstitch again, closing seam completely.

6. To sew the bag to the clasp, thread a piece of thin wire through the top center of each side of the bag and temporarily attach to the centers of the clasp. Beginning at one side of the clasp, backstitch bag to clasp through clasp holes. Hold the bag so that the beaded edges are flush with edge of clasp. Repeat for other side of bag. Remove wires.

LINING & FINISHING

7. Lay bag on Lining Pattern. (See Figure 1.) Check to be sure that the lining is about the same size as the knitted bag. Adjust if necessary, then cut two silk lining pieces from the Lining Pattern. Use a small running stitch to join the lining sides and bottom together. Fit into bag. Turn under and pin top of lining flush with the edge of the bag. Stitch lining in place through clasp holes.

8. Cut two ultra suede pieces using Figure 2 pattern. Tie a small knot in size 0 beading thread and anchor it on the wrong side of the suede. Stitch beads in a picot edging on the inside curve of one of the suede pieces. (See Figure 3.) Be careful not to straighten out the curve of the suede as you stitch on the beads.

9. On the other suede piece, begin in the same manner by stitching the small picot edging up to the curve, then gradually increase the number of beads in each picot to the center drop bead. (See Figure 4.) Decrease on the other side exactly the same as the increases.

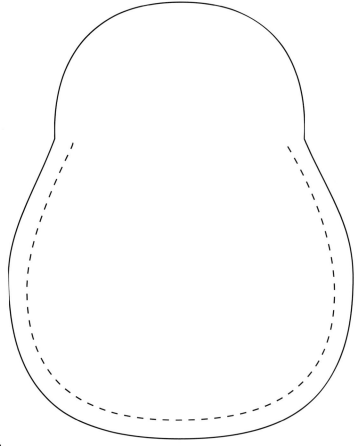

Figure 1

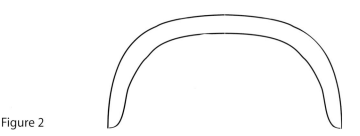

Figure 2

10. Using a toothpick, carefully cover the inside of the clasp with tacky glue and press beaded suede in place.

FRINGE & CHAIN

11. Attach 6 feet of beading thread at Row 16 of the knitting in the seam.

Row 1: String seven 15/0 seed beads. Take a small stitch in the seam of the knitting, three beads away. Repeat sixteen more times or to the other side of Row 16 of the knitting.

Row 2: PNBT the last four beads in Row 1. (See Figure 5.) ★String seven size 15/0 beads, PNT the middle bead in the next loop of Row 1.★ Repeat between asterisks to the end of the row.

Row 3: PNBT the three beads in Row 1 up to the knitting. Take a small stitch in the seam and PNBT the same three beads and through the next bead in Row 1 and the next four beads in Row 2. ★String seven size 15/0 beads and PNT the center bead in the next loop of Row 2.★ Repeat between asterisks to the end of the row.

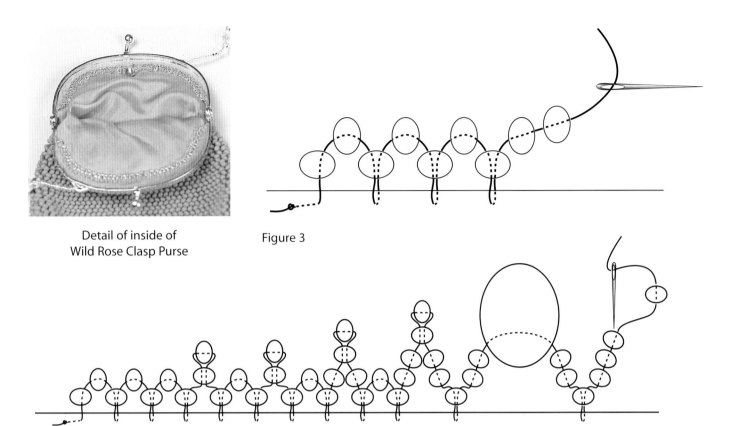

Detail of inside of
Wild Rose Clasp Purse

Figure 3

Figure 4

Row 4: Repeat in the same method as for Row 3. String four size 15/0 beads, one dagger, and four size 15/0 beads for each loop in the row. Knot and weave in end.

12. Knot a 3-foot strand of bead-ing thread to one loop on the clasp. String the beads for the chain. (See Figure 6.) Knot thread through other loop of clasp. Weave in ends.

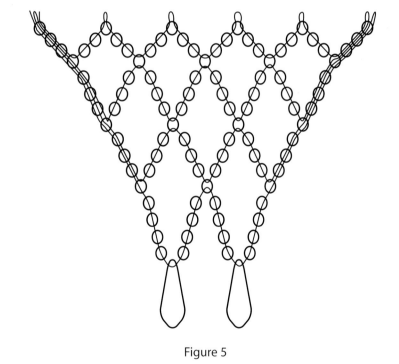

Figure 5

String once:

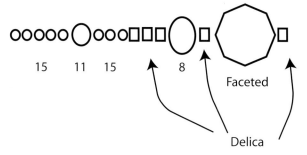

15   11   15

8

Faceted

Delica

String eight times, then string above pattern once more:

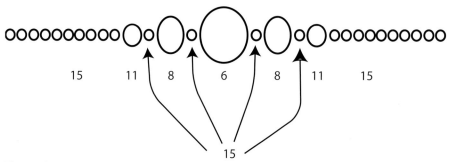

15   11   8   6   8   11   15

15

Figure 6

Tubular Crochet Pattern Families

MATERIALS

10/0 Seed Beads in assorted colors
Silk thread in colors to blend with beads, size E
Crochet hook, size US8/1.25mm

Dots

Little Diamonds

Flowers and Line

Sawteeth

Eyebeads

The inspiration for many of these patterns comes from motifs and patterns found in traditional crocheted beadwork from Bulgaria and other parts of the Balkans.

The five pattern families given here include Dots, Diamonds, Flowers and Line, Sawteeth, and Eye Beads. Within each family are ideas for variations. All of the patterns shown were worked right-handed. If you are working left-handed, use the exact same stringing sequences, but your work will look like a mirror image.

Note: The stringing sequences are given as text and also as a graph that shows the pattern in a visual format.

DOTS

Close-Spaced Dots

Crochet this 12-bead sequence on either five or six beads around. (Graph 1 has four repeats on six beads around.) Work it in two colors as shown, or use more colors for the dots, such as A X B X C X 7X.

Far-Spaced Dots

Do this 9-bead sequence on either five or six beads around. There are four repeats on six beads around. (See Graph 2.)

LITTLE DIAMONDS

This pattern is found in traditional Bulgarian beadwork. It's an 18-bead sequence (three rows of six beads each), crocheted on six beads around; Graph 3 shows two repeats.

This elegantly simple pattern can be used to produce many different effects, depending on color choice and arrangement. Some ideas follow:
• Make A and C the same color, then try reversing the foreground and background colors to make, for example, white diamonds on black, and black diamonds on white.

Graph 1

Stringing sequence

A X A X A 7X

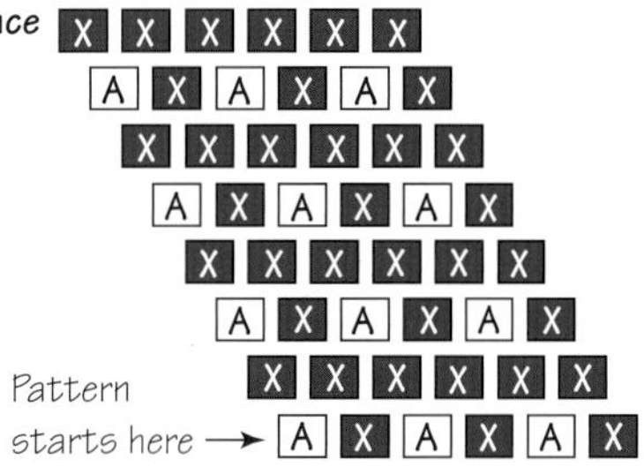

Pattern starts here →

Graph 2

Stringing sequence

A 8X

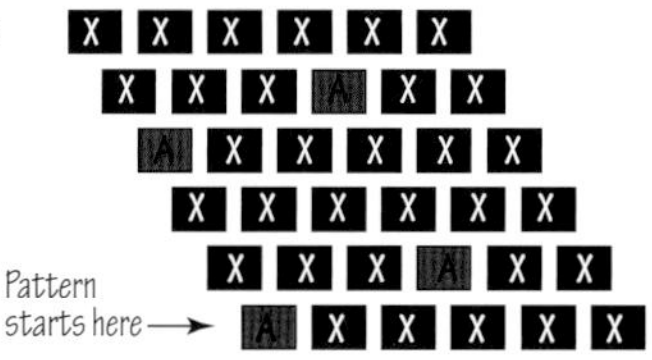

Pattern starts here →

Graph 3

Stringing sequence

A B B C B B
A A B C C B
B A B B C B

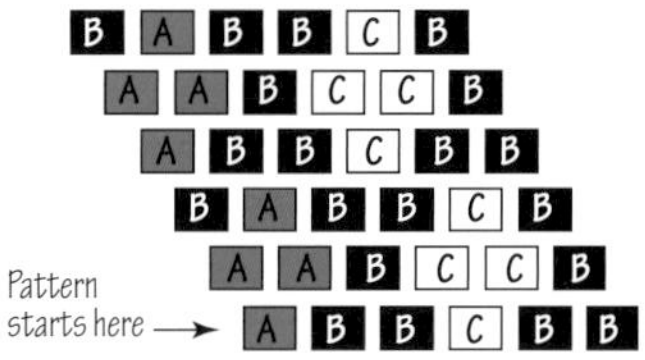

Pattern starts here →

Graph 4

Stringing sequence

A 5B
A B 2F 2B
A B F C F B
A 2B 2F B

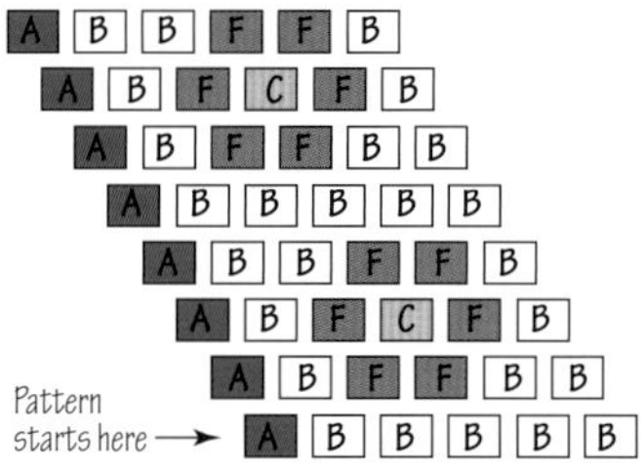

Pattern starts here →

Graph 5

Stringing sequence

A 5B
2A 4B
3A 3B
4A 2B
5A B

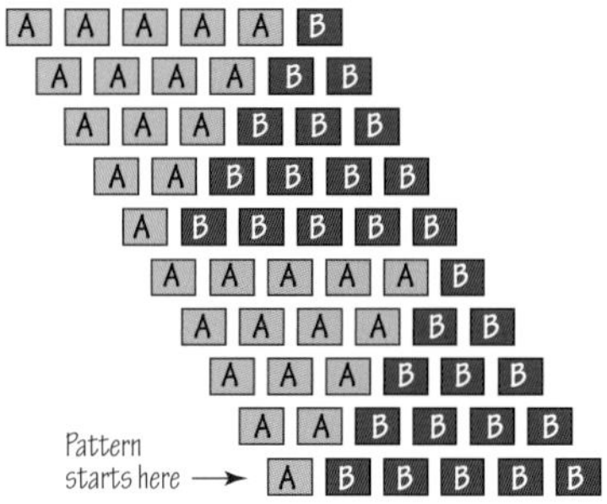

Pattern starts here →

Graph 6

Stringing sequence

A 4B C
2A 3B C
3A 2B C
4A B C

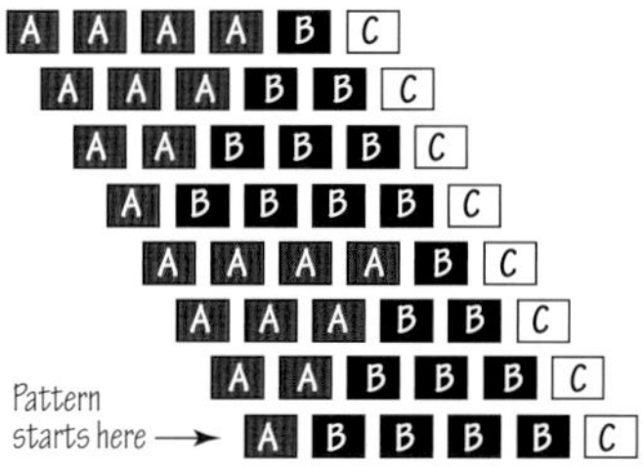

Pattern starts here →

Graph 7

Stringing sequence

5A B C
4A 2B C
3A 3B C
2A 4B C
A 5B C

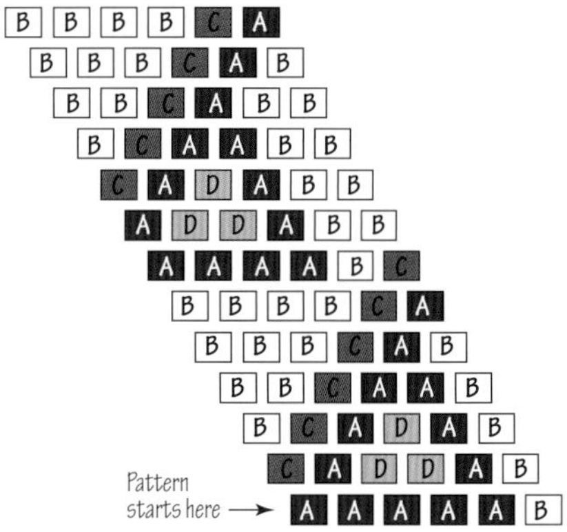

Pattern starts here →

Graph 8

Stringing sequence

4A B C D
3A 2B C D
2A 3B C D
A 4B C D

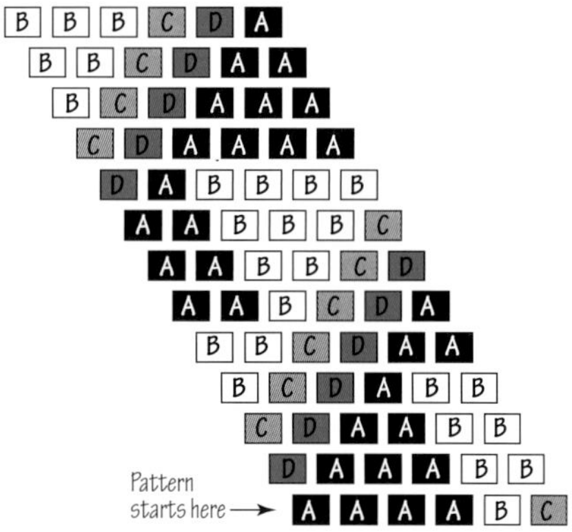

Pattern starts here →

Graph 9

Stringing Sequence

X A B C B A
2 X A 2B A
X D X A B A
X 2D X 2A
X D E D X A
X D 2E D X   ←— Middle of stringing sequence —→
X D E F E D
2X D 2E D
X A X D E D
X 2A X 2D
X A B A X D

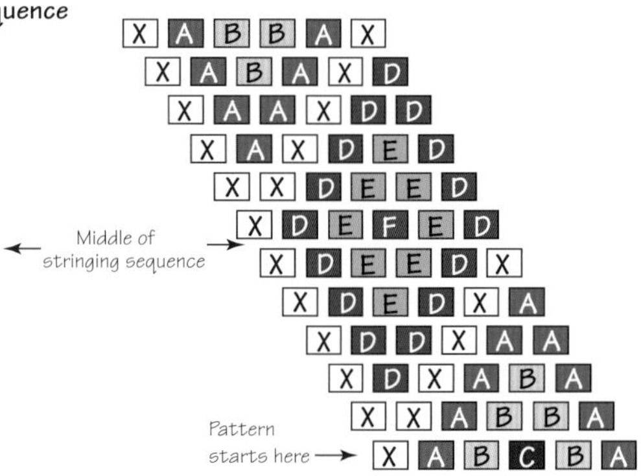

Pattern starts here →

122

- For another look, make A and C the same color in one sequence and a different color in the next sequence. Keep alternating these sequences throughout the piece.
- Place colors randomly for a flower garden effect—just be sure that all four beads in each diamond are the same color.

FLOWERS AND LINE

Flowers are actually a minor variation of diamonds. The basic pattern has a single spiral line and one row of background between each pair of flowers. Graph 4 shows two repeats. It's a 24-bead sequence (four rows of six beads each), worked on six beads around.

Flowers can be made all the same color or varied, either randomly or in a controlled sequence of colors. Leave out the first row (A 5B) if you want to butt the flowers up next to each other, or increase the spacing between the flowers by adding one or more rows between them.

SAWTEETH

The sawtooth pattern and its variations are found in Balkan crocheted beadwork. The pattern family falls into two groups, based on the number of beads in a row.

These first two patterns are multiples of six-bead rows that are crocheted on six beads around, with continuous spiral lines, or spines (moving up to the left if you're right-handed).

Sawteeth #1

This 30-bead sequence (five rows of six beads each), crocheted on six beads around, uses two colors of sawteeth, A and B, and no additional spine; Graph 5 shows two repeats.

Variation

You can fill one or both of the sets of triangles with a different color. Here the A triangles were filled with color C. The stringing sequence is A 5B, 2A 4B, A C A 3B, A 2C A 2B, 5A B.

Sawteeth #2

This 24-bead sequence (four rows of six beads each), crocheted on six beads around, uses two colors of sawteeth, A and B, and an additional spine line, C. See Graph 6 for the two-repeat pattern.

Variation

Again, you can fill the triangles or not, and you can add more spine lines if you like. As more spines are added, the sawtooth triangles will become smaller.

These two patterns are multiples of seven-bead rows, crocheted on six beads around. The spiral lines in these will go in the opposite direction (up to the right if you're right-handed).

Sawteeth #3

At first glance this pattern appears to be a mirror image of Sawteeth #2. The 35-bead sequence of five seven-bead rows, crocheted on six beads around, has two colors of sawteeth, A and B, and an additional spine line, C. Graph 7 shows a two-plus repeat.

Variation

As with the previous Sawteeth patterns, you can fill one or both of the sets of the triangles with another color, following the model given as a variation for Sawteeth #1.

Sawteeth #4

This 28-bead sequence of four seven-bead rows, crocheted on six beads around, has two colors of sawteeth, A and B, and a double spine line, C and D. (See Graph 8.)

Variation

This pattern also works nicely using only two colors, A = C and B = D.

EYE BEADS

This is an advanced pattern, a variant of the diamond motif that's found in most cultures, in beadwork and beyond. The pattern is a 72-bead sequence (twelve rows of six beads each), worked on six beads around. See Graph 9 for a single repeat. It's a concentric diamond pattern with a single dividing row of beads between the diamonds (with colors A, B, and C on one side of the piece and colors D, E, and F on the other side). The divider bead color is shown as X.

Note: Each half of the pattern begins and ends with an X—this isn't a mistake! You'll be stringing X X D E F E D X X and X X A B C B A X X.

There are many ways to vary your color placement. Try making all the diamonds the same color, such as A = D, B = E, C = F. If you're brave, do it in only two colors, where A = C and B = F. Or (this is also tricky) make the colors of the diamonds vary randomly throughout the piece.

Whirligig Crocheted Choker

FINISHED SIZE

17 ½ inches (44.5 cm) long

MATERIALS

8/0 seed beads:
    10 grams opaque light green
    10 grams dark green iris
    7 grams plum lined with green
10/0 triangle beads:
    56 opaque turquoise daggers,
      8 x 5 mm

48 matte transparent pale blue
    iris drops, 3.4 mm
2 turquoise faceted crystals, 10 mm
Green silk thread, size E
Beading needle, size 10, or
    twisted-wire needles
Crochet hook, size US 8/1.25 mm
1 clasp, 10 mm
2 clamshell bead tips

CROCHETED ROPE SECTION

1. Thread the needle with the silk, and string on eight repeats plus one without the DE sequence. Don't cut the thread. Leaving an 8-inch (20.3 cm) tail, make a slip knot; do six chain stitches, with one bead in each stitch. The chain needs to be loose enough to produce a comma-shaped section of beads and thread. Join the ends with a beaded slip stitch. Crochet all beads.

2. With this pattern, whichever bead color you bring down is the bead color you should crochet into. For example: if the bead on the thread nearest the work is light green, then you'll stitch under a light green bead. Use this tip to build your confidence; it will also alert you if you've made a mistake. If you'd like the choker to be longer, increase it to the desired length by adding another repeat or two of beads.

3. Do six more stitches without beads. Cut the thread 8 inches (20.3 cm) from the work, and pull the thread through the loop on the crochet hook. This closes the end and secures the beads.

THE CLASP

4. Put a beading needle on one of the tail threads. String on a 10-mm crystal bead, a bead tip, and a bead that's small enough to fit inside the bead tip. Pass the needle back through the bead tip, the 10-mm bead, and into the crocheted rope. Turn and go back through all the beads again, and weave back down to the rope, securing the group to the end of the necklace.

5. Attach one end of the clasp to the bead tip. Bend the hook so that the tip is inside the walls of the clamshell, and close the two sides over the small bead and the tip of the hook. Repeat on the other side of the necklace.

Graph 1

Note: The graph shows one full repeat of the pattern.

Stringing sequence
A A B B C C (repeat 21 times)
D E D E D E D E D E D

8/0 Seed beads
A Opaque light green
B Dark green iris

10/0 Triangle beads
C Green lined with plum

Trim beads
D Opaque turquoise dagger
E Matte transparent pale blue drop

Pattern starts here ⟶

Primarily Texture

FINISHED SIZE

24 inches (61 cm) long

MATERIALS

11/0 seed beads:
    10 grams opaque black
8/0 seed beads:
    2 grams opaque red
    2 grams opaque orange
    2 grams opaque green
    2 grams opaque light blue
    2 grams opaque cobalt blue
    1 gram opaque black

18 black onyx beads, 4 mm
9 lace net beads without embel-
    lishment, 14 mm, painted in
    primary colors, and netted in
    opaque black 15/0 seed beads
    (see pages 136-137 for instruc-
    tions on how to make them).
Black silk thread, size E
Beading needle, size 10, or
    twisted-wire needles
Crochet hook, size US 8/1.25 mm
1 clasp, 10-mm
2 clamshell bead tips

CROCHETED ROPE SECTION

1. Thread the size 10 needle with
   the silk, and string 54 repeats of
   beads (if you want to crochet
   one section at a time, string six
   repeats instead). Don't cut the
   thread from the spool. You will
   be making eight 1½-inch (3.8
   cm) sections and two ¾-inch (1.9
   cm) sections of crocheted rope.

2. Leaving an 8-inch (20.3 cm) tail
   thread, make a slip knot. Do six
   bead chain stitches. Join the ends
   together with a beaded slip
   stitch, and crochet six repeats of
   beads. Do six more slip stitches
   without beads.

3. Cut the thread 8 inches (20.3
   cm) from the work, and pull the
   thread through the loop on the
   hook to secure the beads. It's
   important to have long tail
   threads because they'll be used
   to put the necklace together.
   Repeat the stitching until there
   are eight full segments, then
   make two half-segments.

PUTTING THE NECKLACE TOGETHER

4. Put a needle on one tail thread
   of a ¾-inch (1.9 cm) section and
   a needle on one tail thread of a
   full section. String an 8/0 black
   bead and a 4-mm onyx bead
   onto each thread. Pick up one
   of the lace net beads with one
   of the needles, push it to the
   work, passing into the 4-mm
   onyx and 8/0 seed beads of the
   other section and into the crocheted rope as well. Pull the
   thread to pull the work
   together. Now, using the other
   needle, pass through the lace net
   bead and the opposite 4-mm
   onyx and 8/0 seed beads and
   into the other segment of rope.

Graph 1

Stringing sequence
3A B1 A
3A B2 A
3A B3 A
3A B4 A
3A B5 A

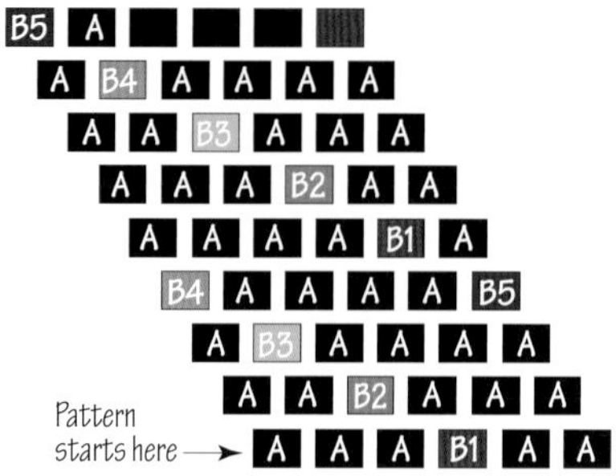

B5 A ■ ■ ■ ▦
A B4 A A A A
A A B3 A A A
A A A B2 A A
A A A A B1 A
B4 A A A A B5
A B3 A A A A
A A B2 A A A

Pattern
starts here ➤ A A A B1 A A

11/0 Seed beads
A Opaque black
8/0 Seed beads
B1 Opaque red
B2 Opaque orange
B3 Opaque green
B4 Opaque light blue
B5 Opaque cobalt blue

Pull both opposing threads to join the segments together. Don't tie off any threads yet; instead, wait until you've completed this process with every section (you may want to make some changes).

5. With the half-segments on the ends of the necklace, put together all crocheted sections with lace net beads and the other trim beads between them. Tie off all threads into the crocheted sections, making sure that everything is joined well and is secure.

6. To add the clasp, put a needle on one of the tail threads at the end of the necklace. String on an 8/0 bead, a bead tip, and a small seed bead. Weave back down through the tip, the 8/0 bead, and into the rope. Turn, and pass through all the beads again; turn and work back to the rope. If everything feels secure, tie off the thread, weave through the rope, and cut.

7. Add the bead tip to the other side of the necklace in the same manner, then attach the clasp ends to the bead tips.

Crocheted Spiral Bracelet

FINISHED SIZE

7¼ inches (18.4 cm) long

MATERIALS

15/0 seed beads
  1 gram matte cream
  0.5 gram transparent gold
    luster rose
11/0 seed beads
  2 grams matte cream
8/0 seed beads
  2 grams matte blue iris
2 stick pearls, 17 x 7 x 2 mm
2 natural apricot pearls, 8 x 7 mm
12 gold pearls, 6 mm

2 raku beads, 12 x 12 x 6 mm
*Note: If you can't find these beads,
replace them with beads that you
love, adjusting the length of the
crochet section to accommodate
them.*
Ecru/cream silk thread, size E
Gold beading thread, size D
Beading needles, size 12, or
  twisted-wire needles
Crochet hook, size US 9/1.15 mm
6-mm gold-filled clasp
2 gold-filled bead tips
4 gold-filled jump rings
2 gold-filled head pins

See the graph for the stringing
sequence and color key.

CROCHETED ROPE SECTION

1. Following the basic instructions
   for beaded crocheted ropes on
   page 25, thread the needle with
   the silk, and string on enough
   beads to crochet 4 inches (10.2
   cm). Don't cut the thread.
   Leaving an 8-inch (20.3 cm)
   tail, make a slip knot, and do
   five chain stitches with one bead
   in each stitch. The chain should
   be loose enough to produce a
   comma-shaped section of beads
   and thread. Join the ends with a
   beaded slip stitch. Crochet a
   total of 4 inches (10.2 cm). If
   you'd like the bracelet to be
   longer, increase the crochet section to the desired length.

2. Do five more stitches without
   beads, cut the thread 8 inches
   (20.3 cm) from the work, and
   pull the thread through the loop
   on the crochet hook. This closes
   the end and secures the beads.

3. Add the rose 15/0 beads that
   twist around the rope now.
   Thread a beading needle with
   16 inches (40.6 cm) of beading
   thread, weave into the crocheted
   rope ½ inch (1.3 cm) from one
   end, pass through a few beads
   and make a knot around a silk
   thread between beads, then
   weave into the rope again to
   hide the knot. Weave through
   the rope exiting the end near
   the center 15/0 bead on the
   end. Change direction, and pass
   the needle through the center
   15/0 bead on the end. String on
   enough rose seed beads to wind
   around the rope, then pass the
   needle through the center 15/0
   bead on this end, and weave
   back into the crocheted rope to
   secure it. Knot, weave, and cut
   the thread ends.

STRUNG SECTION

4. Put a needle onto one of the silk thread ends, and string on one stick pearl, one 8/0 bead, one apricot pearl, one 8/0 bead, the bead tip, and one 15/0 bead. Pass back through the bead tip, all the beads you just strung, and into the end of the rope. Weave in 1 inch (2.5 cm), and pull the thread tight, snugging up the beads strung to the end of the rope. Don't knot or tie off the thread yet; wait until all the components are put together and the bracelet is the correct size.

5. Put a needle on the other tail thread, and string on the same set of beads and the bead tip, weaving back through all the beads and into the rope.

6. The raku beads are very rough and would eventually wear away the silk thread, so cut off the head from a headpin and bend the headpin at a right angle, ¼ inch (6 mm) away from the end. Use round nose pliers to roll the ¼ inch (6 mm) piece of wire into an eye. Slide the raku bead

onto the headpin. Make the other eye as close to the bead as possible. Repeat for the other raku bead.

7. Attach one bead tip to the eye of one raku bead and the clasp to the other eye. Repeat the process for the second raku bead.

8. Check the size of the bracelet and, if it's correct, tie off the silk threads into the crocheted rope.

PEARL CLUSTERS

9. Attach one jump ring to each of the four eyes on either side of the raku beads. Cut a 12-inch (30.5 cm) piece of beading thread, and put a needle on each end. String on three 15/0 beads, a gold pearl, two 15/0 beads, and one 8/0 bead. Push them to the center of the thread, and use the other needle to pass back through the pearl, the two 15/0 beads, and the 8/0 bead. This creates a picot on the bottom of the pearl.

10. Pass the needle through one of the jump rings and back down through the 8/0 bead. Pick up two 15/0 beads, a gold pearl, and three 15/0 beads, and go back through the pearl, the two 15/0 beads, and the 8/0 bead. Pass through the jump ring and back down through the 8/0 bead. Pick up two 15/0 beads, a gold pearl, and three 15/0 beads, and go back through the pearl, the two 15/0 beads, and the 8/0 bead. Weave down into one of the three pearl stems, knot the thread, and weave into the pearl; cut the thread. Pass the other needle through the jump ring and into a pearl stem, then knot, weave, and cut as before.

11. Repeat this process of making pearl clusters on the other three jump rings.

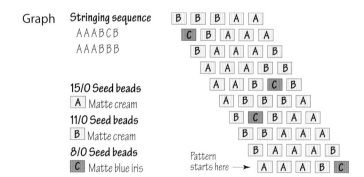

Graph

Stringing sequence
AAABCB
AAABBB

15/0 Seed beads
[A] Matte cream
11/0 Seed beads
[B] Matte cream
8/0 Seed beads
[C] Matte blue iris

B B B A A
C B A A A
B A A A B
A A A B B
A A B C B
A B B B A
B C B A A
B B A A A
B A A A B
Pattern starts here → A A A B C

Beads, Cords & Tassels

Black and Blue Spoke Beads

FINISHED SIZES

Small round bead, 11.5 mm
  diameter
Large oval bead, 20 x 16 mm

MATERIALS

15/0 seed beads:
  2 grams opaque black
11/0 cylinder seed beads:
  4 grams opaque black cut
  2 grams opaque periwinkle
    blue
  2 grams lined Ceylon pale blue
    gray

Wooden beads
  4 round, ⁵⁄₁₆ inch (8 mm)
    diameter
  5 oval, ½ x ¾ inch
    (1.3 x 1.9 cm)
Gesso primer
Sandpaper (very fine grit)
Straws, drink-stirrer type and
  regular plastic
Black liquid acrylic paint
High gloss acrylic varnish
Paintbrushes, sizes 0, 2
Polystyrene foam block
Black beading thread, size B
Beading needles, sizes 12 and 13
Scissors

PREPARING WOODEN BEADS

The preparation process may seem
overdone, but everything matters
and needs to be done well if the
work is to succeed. If you have
several projects in mind, paint lots
of the wooden beads with the
gesso and sand them.

1. Pour a small amount of gesso
   onto a glass dish and, using the
   small paintbrush, paint the inside
   openings of the beads at both
   ends. Let them dry.

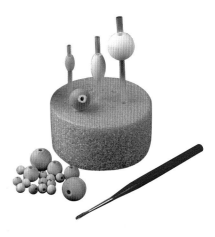

2. Cut a straw lengthwise. Roll it
   tightly, and slide it into the bead.
   The re-expansion of the straw
   will hold the bead on the straw.
   Do this for each of the beads.
   Use a regular-size straw for a
   larger bead, and a smaller straw
   for the small bead. Paint the
   outside of the beads with the
   gesso. As you finish each one,
   stand it up in the styrene block
   to dry. Take care to get an even
   application of paint.

3. Gesso pulls up the grain of the wood, so the beads must be sanded. Take the bead off the straw and, using the fine sandpaper, sand each bead until it's very smooth. Don't forget to sand the interior as well; it isn't critical, but if you use a silk cord to hang the beads, a smooth channel will keep the cord from fraying. Roll up a small piece of the sandpaper and put it through the bead, pulling it back and forth a few times. Remove the dust from the beads with a soft cloth.

4. Paint the interior openings with the acrylic paint. When they're dry, put the beads back on the straws. Now paint the outside of the beads with a thin coat of paint. Let them dry, then paint them all again. Several thin coats of paint are better than one thick one; they'll dry faster and will be smoother. If you want the bead to have a shiny look, put on several coats of varnish, letting each coat dry before adding the next. Let the painted beads dry overnight to a hard finish.

BEADING ROUND WOODEN BEADS

Note: You may need to adjust the bead counts as beads may vary in size and change the count in the ring of beads and in the spokes.

5. Thread the needle with 60 inches (1.5 m) of thread, and string on ten seed beads. Slide them to within 6 inches (15.2 cm) of the tail end of the thread, then pass the needle back through all of the beads (See Figure 1.) Tie the thread ends together using a square knot, and cut the working thread about 6 inches (15.2 cm) away from the bead. The tails will be woven in later.

6. Make a second ring of beads in the same manner. Tie the ends together, but don't cut the working thread; it will be used for making the spokes.

7. Put a painted bead on a clean straw. Slide a bead ring on each end of the straw. Position them so that each ring is touching the painted bead and the working thread is coming from the top ring of beads. Pass the needle into bead A (at the left of the knot), and pick up nine 15/0 seed beads. Pass the needle into bead B in the bottom ring of beads, heading to the right, and pull the thread tight, to fit the beads to the curve of the wooden bead. Now carefully weave the needle back up through all nine beads and through the beads marked A and C. (See Figure 2.)

8. Tighten the thread and check the beads for fit. If they look loose or don't lie against the wooden bead tightly, you may need to make adjustments to the count you're using. Continue making the spokes by coming out of an upper ring bead, picking up nine beads, attaching the spoke to the corresponding bead in the bottom ring, and passing back up through them all.

9. The spoke beads won't cover the full surface of the round painted wooden bead. This allows us to add a horizontal line of periwinkle blue cylinder beads that will separate the spokes. When the last spoke is finished, bring the needle out of bead A, pass it down through the first spoke, and out bead 5. Pick up a periwinkle blue bead and pass the needle down through the corresponding middle bead of the second spoke (See Figure 3, page 134.) Add a cylinder bead between each spoke. They'll sit a little crooked, so straighten them by passing the needle and thread through each of the beads in the opposite direction (See Figure 4, page 134.)

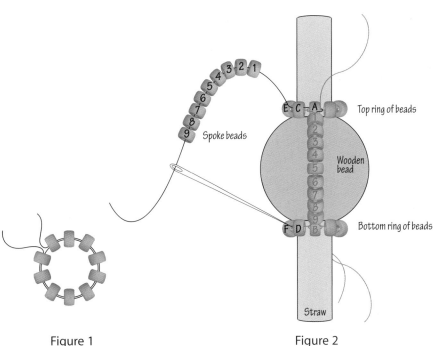

Figure 1

Figure 2

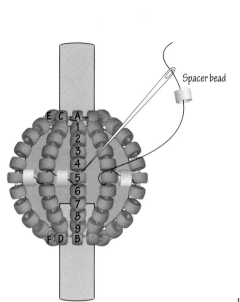

Spacer bead

Figure 3

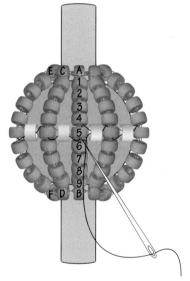

Figure 4

10. There will be a lot of thread passing through each of the 15/0 beads, making the job of ending the threads a little more difficult, however it can and must be done. Weave the tail ends into the spokes, knot and weave them a bit more, then clip the threads as close to the beads as possible. Repeat the beading process three more times for a total of four round beaded spoke beads.

BEADING OVAL WOODEN BEADS

There are five oval spoke beads in this project, and each has a different pattern of cylinder seed beads. Follow the Graphs 1 through 5 for color placement. Oval beads aren't worked on a straw. To get an oval spoke bead that is almost totally covered with beads, the upper and lower rings must be bigger than the hole of the wooden bead. The rings sit lower on the wooden bead, at its edges, and must be held there, between your fingers, while you stitch the spokes. They're harder to make but worth the effort.

11. Following a graph for color placement, string on 18 cylinder seed beads for the first ring, then pass through them again, and tie them with a square knot. Repeat for the other side, leaving the working thread to use for making the spokes.

12. Place a ring of beads on each end of the painted oval wooden bead. Hold them tightly in place, between your thumb and forefinger. Pick up the beads for the first spoke, and pass the needle through the correct bead in the lower ring.

13. Continue adding the spokes, making sure that everything remains tight (this is the hard part because as you pull the spokes tight, the upper and lower rings tend to come off the wooden bead—tight is the operative word here). If the spokes aren't pulled tight, they won't hold the wooden bead in place when you're done stitching. Once you've started stitching the spokes you can't stop making the bead—it must be completed before you can put it down.

14. Make all five beads, following their respective patterns, as shown in graphs 1–5. When the beads are completed, thread them all onto a cord or chain.

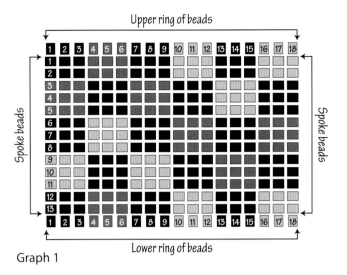

Graph 1

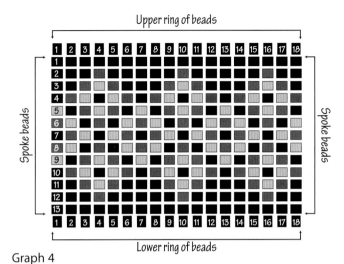

Graph 4

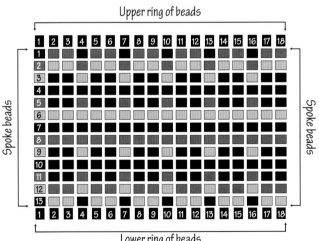

Graph 2

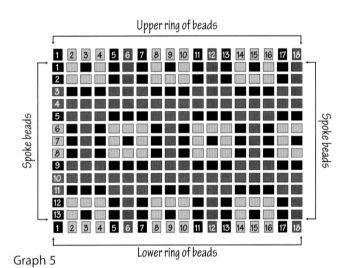

Graph 5

Graph 3

Lace Net Beads

FINISHED SIZE

17 mm diameter

**MATERIALS TO
MAKE ONE BEAD**

*(Multiply according to your
project needs.)*

15/0 seed beads:
  0.5 gram dark blue iris

14 sterling silver beads, 3 mm
14 sterling silver beads, 4 mm
Round wooden bead, 14 mm
Dark blue liquid acrylic paint
Black beading thread, size B
Beading needles, sizes 12 and 13
Scissors

1. Prepare wooden bead following instructions on page 132.
2. Thread a size-12 beading needle with a long piece of thread. Pick up 14 seed beads, and push them to the end of the thread, leaving a 6-inch (15.2-cm) tail. Pass through all of them again, and tie the ends together with a square knot, pulling the beads into a tight circle. (See Figure 1.)

Figure 1

Note: Keep the tension snug throughout this project. The wooden beads and the seed beads may vary in size and you may need to make adjustments to the number of beads used in the loops of the lace net, or add beads when stitching the two sides together. Different sizes of wooden beads can be used by adjusting the counts in the netting.

3. Pass the needle to the left, through bead N. Pick up 17 seed beads, and pass the needle to the left, through beads C and B. (See Figure 2.) For clarity, the illustration shows the circle of beads spaced apart, but they should be touching each other.
4. Pick up four beads, and pass the needle to the right, through bead 13. Pick up 12 more beads, and pass the needle to the left, through beads E and D.
5. Repeat step 4 four more times (bead 13 is now bead 8), moving around the initial ring of 14 beads.

6. Coming out of bead L, pick up four beads and pass the needle through bead 8. Pick up seven beads, and pass through bead 5 in the first loop, then pick up four more beads and pass through beads A and N.

7. Weave the working thread through a couple of beads and knot it, then weave it again and clip the thread. Tie off the tail thread as well.

8. Make another lace cap by repeating steps 2 through 6, but don't tie off the working thread.

9. Center the painted wooden bead on a straw. Slide a beaded cap on each end of the straw, and push them to the painted bead.

10. Weave the thread down through beads 1–9. Pick up four beads, and pass through the center bead on side 2. Pick up four more beads and pass through the center bead on side 1. (See Figure 3.) Continue around, pulling the thread tight. When you've finished adding all the beads, pass through all of them again to make sure both sides are securely attached and the threads aren't showing.

EMBELLISHMENT

11. To add the trim beads to the surface of the wooden bead, have the needle coming out of bead 13. Pick up a 3-mm silver bead, and pass the needle through the opposite bead (8); the dotted line shows the thread path. Continue adding silver beads in each open section of the netting. When you have finished the first row, weave through the 15/0 beads, and stitch the next row, adding 4-mm silver beads. Embellish the rest of the netted bead, following figure 2, filling each open section with a trim bead. Tie off the thread, and remove the bead from the straw.

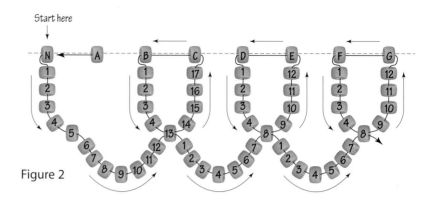

Figure 2

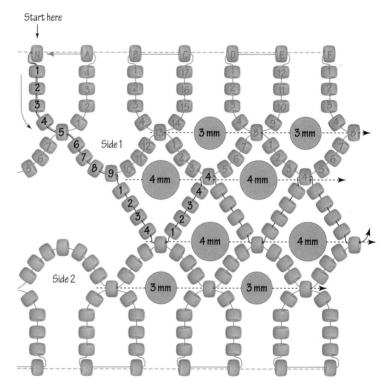

Figure 3

Caged Bead

FINISHED SIZE

½ inch x 1½ inches (1.3 x 3.8 cm)

MATERIALS

15/0 seed beads:
  0.1 gram Color A, transparent gold luster moss
  0.5 gram Color B, transparent gold luster light amber
  0.3 gram Color C, metallic bronze iris
11/0 cylinder seed beads
  1.5 grams Color D, metallic olive

1 gram Color E, 24K gold-lined cream opal
0.5 gram Color F, silver-lined gold ocher
0.1 gram Color G, silver-lined cerulean blue
0.1 gram Color H, silver-lined orange
6 x 3 mm teardrop beads:
  19 frosted green
Beading thread, size B, in color to blend with beads
Beading needles Sizes 12 and 13
Sharps needles, size 12

This bead is made up of odd and even count peyote stitch and horizontal netting.

Note: Keep a very tight tension throughout this project. Create the base tube, then add both the second and third layers to one end before adding them to the other end.

THE BASE

1. Using the cylinder seed beads and odd count flat peyote stitch (review on page 13), weave a piece 21 beads wide by 16 rows deep, following the graph on page 140 for color placement. Weave the tail thread into the flat piece, then trim close to work.

2. Roll the flat piece into a tube, and stitch the edges together with the working thread. (See Figure 1.) Add 15/0 edging beads to the side the thread is on. (See Figure 2.)

SECOND LAYER

3. The second layer is done in two parts. Begin a strip four beads wide on the base tube at the outer edge. Referring to Figures 3a and 3b, pick up bead A, and pass the needle through bead 1 in the base. Pick up bead B, and pass through bead 2 in the base; pick up bead C, pass through bead B; pick up bead D, pass through bead A. Beads A and B are the only beads that attach to the base tube. Continue stitching until the strip is 28 rows long, following the graph on page 140.

4. Wrap the strip around the base tube and attach it to itself in the same manner used for closing the base tube. Weave back to the outer edge. The peyote strip needs to fit tightly around the base tube; you can't adjust the number of beads to make it fit because this strip controls the size of the outer layer. The outer layer must be 40 rows long so the netting can be properly spaced.

5. Stitch the two layers together with a size-12 sharps needle. (See Figure 4.) The needle exits from a second layer outside edge bead (bead A). Put the tip of the needle into a neighboring base edge bead. Angle the needle upward and on a diagonal, pushing the needle through the bead and up through beads in the second layer (the dotted line in the illustration shows the thread path through the two layers). Come out through bead B, at the second layer's inner edge, then put the needle into a neighboring base bead. Angle it up and pass it through the second layer, coming out of bead C. Put the needle into the next base bead, angle it up, and stitch across to D. Continue attaching the second layer to the base; try to have a thread going into every base bead.

Note: For clarity, Figure 4 has no edge beads. The bead you're making will have beads along the edges of the base tube and it will be a little

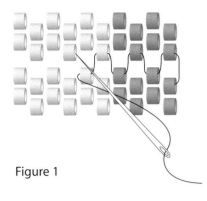

Figure 1

Figure 2

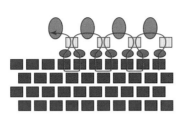

Figure 4

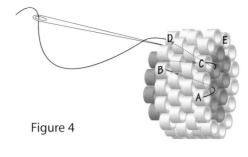

Figure 5

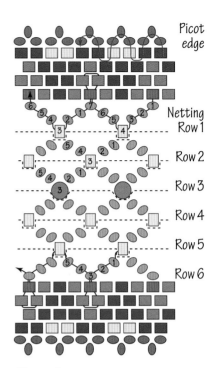

Figure 6

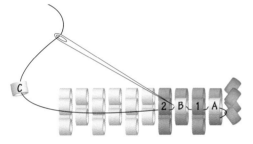

Figure 3a

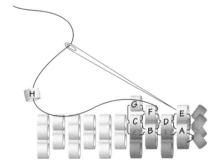

Figure 3b

harder to see where you're stitching, but the goal is to attach the second layer securely without any threads showing.

6. Add the edge beads to the second layer; Figure 5 shows the thread path and bead placement. Pick up one 15/0 seed bead, one cylinder bead, one trim bead, one cylinder bead, and another 15/0 bead. Pass the needle down into the next bead in the second layer and up the neighboring one. Pick up one

15/0 seed bead, pass the needle through the cylinder bead you just put on, pick up a trim bead, a cylinder bead, and one 15/0 bead, and weave into the second layer. Continue adding beads to the edge; when you're done, weave to the outside edge.

THIRD LAYER

7. The third layer is done the same way as the second layer, but each strip will be 40 rows long. This layer has a color pattern and a picot edge. The pattern at the two inner edges of this layer will need to match up perfectly when you add this layer on the other side of the bead. You'll have to figure out where on the bead to begin so that the orange beads on one edge are opposite the orange beads on the other edge. You'll attach the netting to these orange beads.

Referring again to the Graph on page 140, stitch the third layer, wrap it around the second layer, and join it to itself. Now stitch the two layers together.

8. After attaching the third layer to the second layer, add the picot edging. Figure 6 shows the thread path and the bead and color placement. Tie off the thread when you've finished.

9. Add a new long thread to the base tube so that it exits at the outer edge. Add the edge beads to the other side of the base layer. To add the second and third layers to the other end of the bead, repeat steps 3 through 8. Don't tie off or cut your working thread.

NETTING

10. The horizontal netting is made with 15/0, cylinder, and trim beads. There are six rows of netting; the first and last are attached to the third layer of the bead. The graph shows the full netting, but see Figure 6 for more detail. With the needle exiting an orange bead, pick up three 15/0 beads (beads 1–3), one cylinder (bead 4), and three more 15/0's (beads 5–7), then pass the needle up

139

into the next orange bead. To
make the turn, weave up into
one of the beads above the
orange bead and then down
through its neighbor, the
orange bead, and seed bead 7.
Pick up six beads (refer to the
graph), and weave into the
next orange bead as before.
Continue in this manner,
adding loops of beads to the
inner edge of the third layer.
The last loop has five beads,
and the sixth bead is bead 1
from the first loop. Make the
turn, and weave down through
beads 1–4, in position to stitch
row 2 of the netting. Pick up
five beads and pass the needle
through the center bead of the
next loop in the previous row.
When you get to the end of
the row, pass through the center bead of the previous row
and down the first three beads
of the row you're finishing.
Stitch rows 3–5; the center bead
of row 3 is a teardrop bead.

11. Row 6 of the netting attaches
to the third layer on the opposite side. With the needle exiting
a center bead in row 5, pick up
three 15/0 seed beads. Pass the
needle into an orange bead,
make the turn as you did in
row 1, and pass through the
orange bead and the 15/0 seed
bead. Pick up two 15/0 beads
and pass through the next center bead in row 5. Continue
adding beads and weaving into
the third layer, pulling the
thread as you go to stretch out
the netting. When the netting is
complete, tie off and cut the
thread.

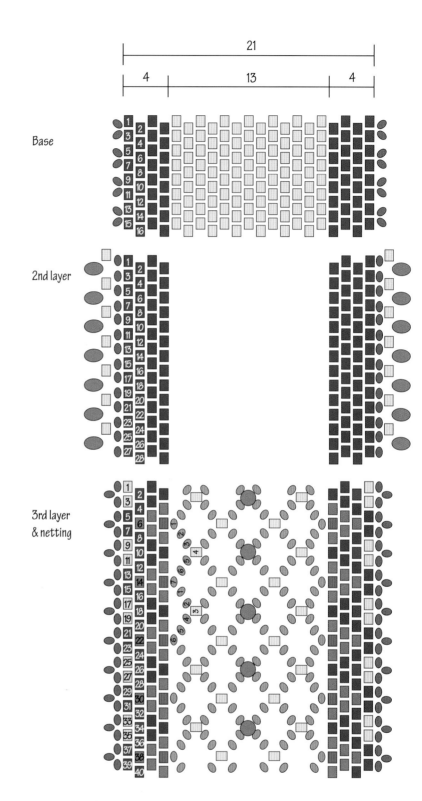

Base

2nd layer

3rd layer
& netting

Graph

Fringed Caged Bead

FINISHED SIZE

2¾ inches long x 1¼ inches wide
    x ½ inch thick
(6.8 x 3.1 x 1.3 cm)

MATERIALS

15/0 seed beads:
    2 grams opaque black
    1 gram matte black
11/0 cylinder seed beads:
    2 grams opaque black
    0.1 gram cut opaque black
    2 grams matte black

21 fire-polished black, 3 mm
21 fire-polished black, 4 mm
Black beading thread, size B
Beading needles, sizes 12, 13
Sharps needles, size 12

SECOND LAYER

2. Starting at the outer edge of the base tube, make a strip four beads wide and 28 rows long (for reference, see figures 3a and 3b on page 139 of the Caged Bead project). Wrap the strip around the base tube, and attach it to itself in the same manner used for closing the base tube. Weave back to the outer edge.

   The peyote strip needs to fit tightly around the base tube. Don't add or remove beads, because the second layer controls the size of the outer layer. The outer layer has to be 40 rows long so the netting can be spaced properly. Stitch the two layers together. (See Figure 4, page 142.)

3. Add a picot edge to the second layer. (See Graph, page 142, for color and placement.)

THIRD LAYER

4. The third layer is done the same way as the second layer except that each strip is 40 rows long, there's a color pattern, and the picot edge is spaced apart. Stitch the third layer, wrap it around the second layer, join it to itself, and stitch to the second layer. After attaching the third layer to the second layer, add the picot edging. Tie off the thread.

5. Add a new long thread to the base tube and have it exit the outer edge. Add the edge beads to the other side of the base layer. Now repeat steps 2 through 4 on the other end of the base tube. Don't tie off or cut your working thread; it will be used for the netting.

For a Caged Bead that has a little more presence—one that would be the centerpiece of a necklace and have more visual weight—make a small front panel that folds over a larger one. You can add short and/or long fringes to each panel. You'll use odd and even count peyote stitch and horizontal netting to make this bead.

Note: Keep a very tight tension throughout this project.

THE BASE

1. Using the cylinder seed beads and odd count flat peyote stitch, weave a piece 21 beads wide by 16 rows deep, following the Graph, page 142. Weave the tail thread into the flat piece, then cut it away. Roll the flat piece into a tube, and stitch the edges together with the working thread.

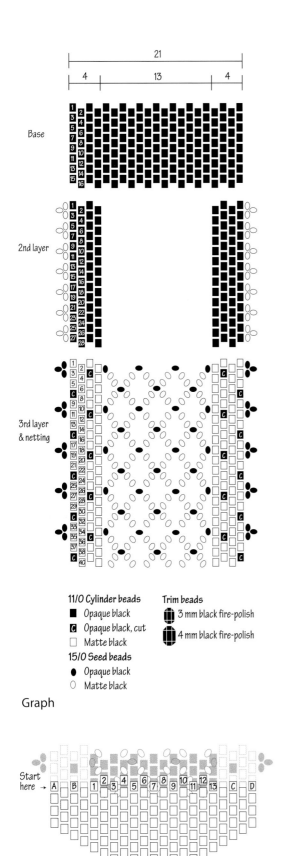

Base

2nd layer

3rd layer
& netting

Graph

11/0 Cylinder beads
■ Opaque black
C Opaque black, cut
□ Matte black

15/0 Seed beads
● Opaque black
○ Matte black

Trim beads
● 3 mm black fire-polish
● 4 mm black fire-polish

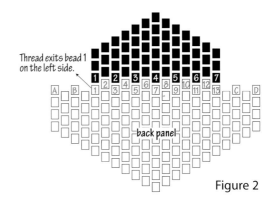

Thread exits bead 1
on the left side.

back panel

Figure 2

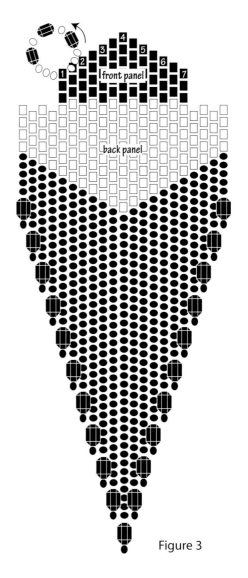

front panel

back panel

Figure 3

Start
here →

D is added with
an odd count turn.

Figure 1

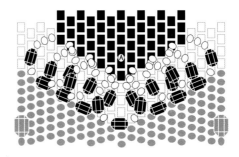

Figure 4

NETTING

6. The horizontal netting is made with 15/0 beads. There are six rows of netting; the first and last are attached to the third layer of the bead. See the Graph for the full netting and color placement of beads. Stitch the netting.

ADDING THE PANELS

7. If the thread is long enough use it; if not, add a new thread now. Referring to Figure 1, have the thread exiting an outside edge bead on the third layer, then add two cylinder beads (A and B) to the surface, the way you would start another layer. (See Figure 3a on page 139.) Pick up 13 more cylinder beads, and pass into the opposite cylinder bead on the other side in the third layer. Now add beads C and D. (See Figure 1.) Doing peyote stitch, turn and stitch the back panel to the size shown in Figure 1.

8. To add the front panel, weave up to bead 1 and have the thread exiting this bead on the left side. (See Figure 2.) Pick up a bead, turn, and stitch across, adding seven beads. Stitch the front panel to the size shown on the graph. The front panel is a different color than the back panel, and is a little awkward to stitch, but it's worth the effort.

Different effects can be achieved with different color beads

THE FRINGE

9. The fringe for the back panel is made up of 15/0 seed beads and 4-mm fire-polished beads. Add a straight fringe to every lower edge bead on the back panel. (See Figure 3 for placement, length, bead size, and color.)

The front panel has a circular type of fringe that's made up of 15/0 seed beads and 3-mm fire-polished beads. These are positioned at beads 1–7 on the front panel (See Figure 3.)

10. After the fringes have been completed, fold the front panel down and over the back panel. Attach the two together by stitching from the back panel up through the front panel in the center, pick up a 15/0 bead, A, and stitch through to the back again. (See Figure 4.) Tie off and clip the threads.

Dimensional Right-Angle Weave Beads

FINISHED SIZE

½ inch x ½ inch (1.3 x 1.3 cm)

MATERIALS

11/0 seed beads in several colors
Mandrel, dowel, pencil or straw, used as support
Beading thread, size B, to match the beads
Beading needles, sizes 12 and 13

These little beads show you how to work tubular right-angle weave in a dimensional manner. They can be large, with lots of embellishment, or small and plain and used as spacers. Weave around a mandrel, changing the size of the mandrel to change the size of the bead's hole.

Note: Make the basic bead by doing three layers of right-angle weave; the first and third layers are horizontal, and the second layer is vertical, standing perpendicular to the other two layers.

BASE

1. The base of the bead is made up of eight right-angle weave units, five rows deep. (See Figure 1.) Review right-angle weave technique on page 15–16, if needed.) Stitch the base layer in tubular right-angle weave, then put it on the mandrel.

SECOND LAYER

2. The second layer of right-angle weave is stitched perpendicular to the base layer in rows, working off the beads with the white dots. (See Figure 2.). Work from one end of the bead to the other, then weave over to the next row of beads with white dots and stitch that row. Stitch every row of white dotted beads (eight rows in all), which are all the side beads from the base layer. Figure 3 shows how the piece will look from the end.

THIRD LAYER

3. The third layer has a larger circumference than the base layer, so two beads will be added on each side instead of one. The top bead of the second layer will become the side bead of the third layer. Figure 4 shows an end view of the three layers and Figure 5 shows two rows looking down at the bead's new surface. This layer is stitched in the same direction as the base layer, working with the tubular right-angle weave from row 1 to row 5.

Larger beads may be used in this layer; a 3- or 4-mm fire-polished bead would work well.

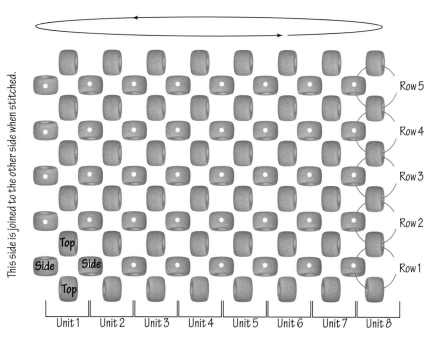

This side is joined to the other side when stitched.

Row 5
Row 4
Row 3
Row 2
Row 1

Top
Side Side
Top

Unit 1 | Unit 2 | Unit 3 | Unit 4 | Unit 5 | Unit 6 | Unit 7 | Unit 8

The beads with the white dots will be used as the base beads for the second layer.

Figure 1

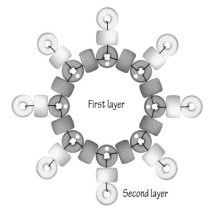

View of bead from the end showing first and second layers

First layer

Second layer

Figure 3

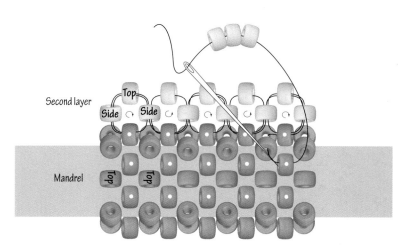

Second layer

Top
Side Side

Mandrel

Top Top

Figure 2

View of bead from the end showing first, second, and third layers

Third layer -
dark beads on outside

First layer -
dark beads on
inside

Second layer - light beads
perpendicular to first and third layers

Figure 4

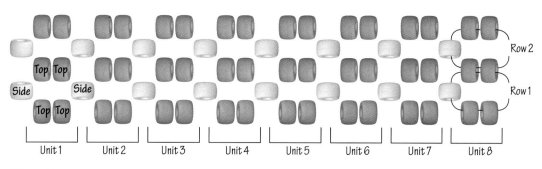

Row 2

Row 1

Top Top
Side Side
Top Top

Unit 1 | Unit 2 | Unit 3 | Unit 4 | Unit 5 | Unit 6 | Unit 7 | Unit 8

Figure 5

Spiral Ropes

MATERIALS

11/0 seed beads:
  15–18 grams each of two colors, depending on length desired
Accent beads of choice
Beading thread in a color to blend with beads
Beading needle, size 12
Scissors

Beads are joined in such a fashion that they spiral around each other in a soft rope. Spiral rope is an instant gratification stitch that everyone can do. You can use any size bead—the combinations are endless—and the results, even for a beginner, are beautiful.

Figure 1. Thread a needle with 60 inches (1.5 m) of thread. String on a stop bead, and put it 7 inches (17.8 cm) away from the end of the thread. Loop back through the stop bead, being careful not to slit the thread inside the bead.

Using 11/0 seed beads, pick up four core beads and three outside beads for the spiraling part of the pattern. Contrasting colors for the core and spiral make the process easier for the beginner. Pass the needle back up through beads 1, 2, 3, and 4.

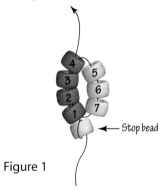

Figure 1

Figure 2. Pick up one core bead (8) and three spiral beads (9, 10, and 11). Slide the beads to the previous work, and pass the needle back up through beads 2, 3, 4, and 8. Turn the work counterclockwise to get ready for the next stitch.

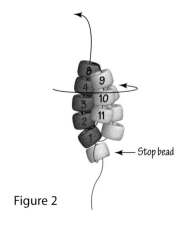

Figure 2

Figure 3. After the initial set of beads, all stitches consist of one core bead and three spiral beads. When passing back up core beads, use the previous three core beads and the new one being added. (See Figure 3.) String on bead 12 (the core bead) and beads 13, 14, and 15 (the spiral beads), and push them to the work. Pass the needle back through core beads 3, 4, 8, and 12. Continue stitching in this manner, rotating the spiraling beads counterclockwise until you have the desired length.

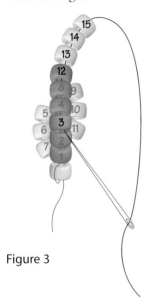

Figure 3

Figure 4. The addition of larger beads or other fancy beads to the spiral rope can add interest and texture to your piece. Work the spiral rope to the length desired, string on the large bead, and push to the work. Pick up four core beads and three spiral beads, and push those so that they sit tightly against the large bead. Keeping everything snug, pass the needle back up the four core beads, creating the first spiral of the new segment.

To reinforce and strengthen the stitching, pass the needle back down through the spiral beads 5, 6, and 7, the large bead, and into the last spiral beads (A, B, and C) of the previous segment. Now go back up the four core beads, the

Figure 4

large bead, and the four core beads of the new segment. If the large bead is very heavy and you've enough room in all of the beads, repeat the process of weaving back into the previous segment, then back up to the new segment.

SPIRAL ROPE VARIATIONS

Here are a few variations to get your creative juices flowing. The bead sizes you choose, as well as how you use color, can change the look of spiral rope. The stitch can also be done to look flat or to have branches.

Variation 1. Combining size 11/0 beads for the core and size 15/0 beads for the spiral produces a look that's a little more delicate than the basic spiral. Pick up three 11/0 core beads and four 15/0 spiral beads, and stitch as usual. (See figure 5, page 148.)

Variation 2. This design uses 15/0 seed beads for the core and one 15/0, one 8/0, and one 15/0 for the spiral, creating a very textured spiral. (See Figure 6, page 148.)

Variation 3. Figures 7 and 8 on page 148 show how to take Variation 2 a little bit farther. Space out the texture by putting two regular spiral stitches between the ones with the 8/0 beads.

Variation 4. Besides adding larger beads to the basic spiral, you can add texture to the surface of the spirals.

Add a picot; complete a stitch, pass the needle back into bead 5, pick up three beads (A, B, and C), and weave back through beads 5, 6, 7, 1, 2, 3, and 4. (See Figure 9.). Continue in this manner for the desired length. In this sample the surface work is on bead 5, but it could sit over beads 6 or 7 instead.

Variation 5. This surface texture is very similar in technique to Variation 4; however, the look is quite different.

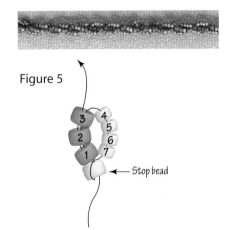

Figure 5

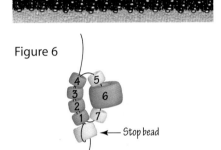

Figure 6

Figure 7

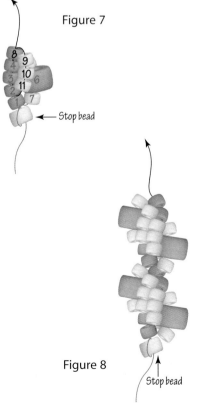

Figure 8

Stop bead

After completing a stitch, pass back through bead 5, and pick up one 6/0 bead and one 11/0 bead. Slide the beads to the work, pass back down through the 6/0 bead (A), and weave through beads 5, 6, 7, 1, 2, 3, and 4. (See Figure 10.) Continue in this manner for the desired length.

Variation 6 / Flat Spiral. The basic pattern is one 8/0 core bead and six 15/0 spiral beads, passing through three core beads. To start, pick up and loop through a stop bead; position it 6 inches (15.2 cm) away from the end of the thread. Add three core beads and six spiral beads to the thread, and weave back up through the core beads. Now pick up one core bead and six spiral beads, and pass back through the last three core beads; continue in this manner for desired length. (See Figure 11.)

Because the 15/0 beads are so much smaller than the 8/0 beads, the spiral is very loose and doesn't cover the core very well at all, but you can use this to your advantage. Using your fingers, push the first two spirals around to the left, and push the next two spirals to the right. Divide all the spirals in this manner.

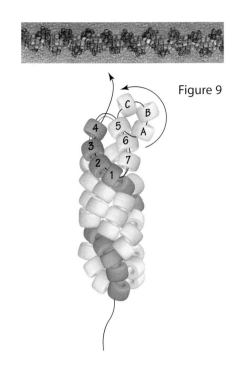

Figure 9

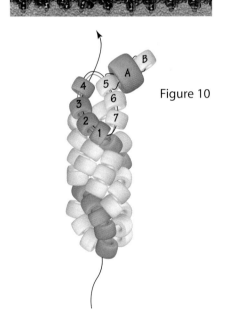

Figure 10

148

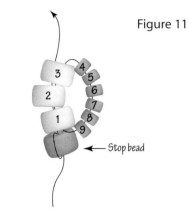

← Stop bead

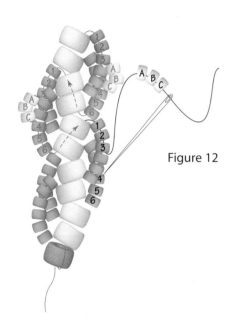

Figure 12

Using the needle and thread at the end of the chain, pass through the first three beads of the last spiral. Pick up three 15/0 beads, and pass through the last three beads of the next spiral, joining the two spirals together (see Figure 12 for the thread path). Weave over and up two core beads, then repeat the process of joining the two spiral sections together. Work down the length of the chain, joining the spirals on the left and right.

Variation 7. This variation produces a spiral that completely covers the core, except for the last four core beads. Instead of adding a drop bead to the surface of a spiral bead, add it to the place where the spiral beads meet the core beads. Use a lightweight thread, as you'll be passing through each stitch twice.

Make the basic spiral with 11/0 seed beads, then weave through the spiral beads (5, 6, and 7) again, pick up a 3.4-mm drop bead, weave back up the core beads, and pull tightly. (See Figure 13.) Continue with the basic spiral, adding a drop bead at every stitch. The drop beads will protrude from the spiral. (See Figure 14.)

Variation 8. To achieve another look, use tiny 3.4-mm drop fringe beads for the core and 15/0 seed beads for the spiral. Pick up four drop beads and six 15/0 beads, and weave back up through the drop beads. Pick up one drop bead and six 15/0 beads, slide them to the work, and pass back through the last four drop beads. With this pattern of beads you'll have to be careful and make sure that the drop beads stay at the surface as you stitch.

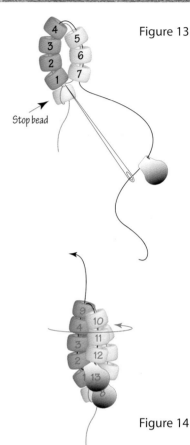

Stop bead

Figure 13

Figure 14

Branched Spiral Rope Lariat

FINISHED SIZE
30 inches (76.2 cm) long

MATERIALS
11/0 seed beads:
 7 grams lined topaz/brown
 7 grams transparent gold luster
  dark amber
 5.5 grams lined topaz/khaki
 5.5 grams lined green/
  dark olive
15/0 seed beads"
 25 grams (total weight)
 7 grams matte transparent
  brown

7 grams matte transparent
 dark brown
5.5 grams matte metallic
 yellow green
5.5 grams matte olive
70 Czech fire-polished beads,
 3 and 4 mm, a mixture of:
  Olivine
  dark olive
  crystal gold capri
50 leaf-shaped beads, a mixture of:
  greens
  pinks
Brown beading thread, size B
Beading needles, sizes 12 and 13

FIRST HALF OF THE LARIAT
1. Thread the needle with 60 inches (1.5 m) of thread. String on a stop bead, and loop back through it, 12 inches (30.5 cm) away from the end of the thread (this tail will be used later to start the other half of the necklace). Combine the two brown colors of 11/0 beads, and put them in a dish. Combine the two brown colors of 15/0 beads, and put them in another dish. Picking randomly from the different colors of brown for the core and the spiral, stitch 4 inches (10.2 cm) of spiral rope, using three 11/0 beads for the core and four 15/0 beads for the spiral. (See Figure 1.)
Note: All branches are made with the green 11/0 beads and the green 15/0 beads randomly combined, as the browns are for the spiral rope. Start adding the leaf beads when you get to the sixth branch, adding them to the longest point.

ADDING A BRANCH
2. String on seven green core beads and four green spiral beads, and pass back up through the core beads 5, 6, and 7. (See Figure 2.) Pass back through core beads 5, 6, and 7 six more times, adding four green spiral beads to each stitch, and totally covering the core beads. (See Figure 3.) Pick up a 3- or 4-mm fire-polished bead and a 15/0 bead, and pass back through the fire-polished bead, the seven core beads that make up the branch, and the next three core beads in the main work (labeled A, B, and C in Figure 4). Pull everything snug, but not tight—just enough so that there isn't any thread showing. Pick up bead D (a 15/0), and pass the needle back through beads C, B, and A. (See Figure 4.) Now you're ready to begin the spiral rope again; move the branch out of the way, and

continue stitching. Bead D, used to make the turn, blends right into the work. (See Figure 5.)

Do eight spiral rope stitches between the branches. Make a total of seven branches, ending with eight stitches after the last branch.

ADDING A DOUBLE BRANCH

3. To make a double branch, string on nine core beads, and encase the last three with 15/0 beads, as you did for the single branch. Add the fire-polished bead and the 15/0 bead, and pass back down seven of the core beads. The needle should exit bead 3; snug up the thread.

4. String on five core beads and three spiral beads, and pass back up through the last two core beads. Cover the two core beads with 15/0 beads, add a fire-polished bead and a 15/0 bead, and pass down through all of the core beads in the second branch. Weave through beads 2 and 1 of the main branch and beads A, B, and C of the spiral rope. Pick up the 15/0 (D), and pass through beads C, B, and A. (See Figure 6.)

Do four spiral rope stitches between the double branches. Make a total of 14 double branches, ending with four stitches after the last double branch.

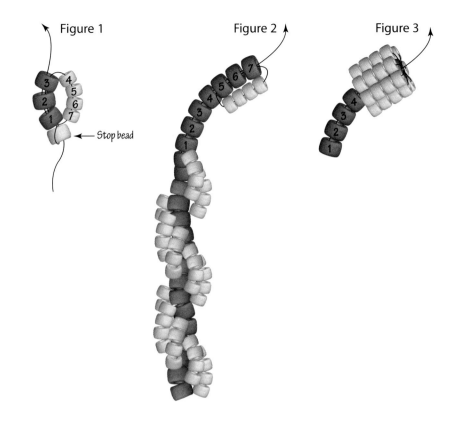

Figure 1

Stop bead

Figure 2

Figure 3

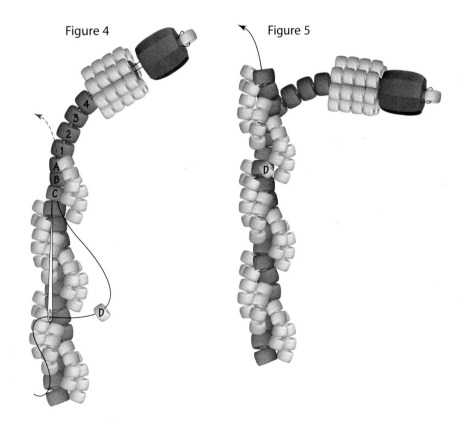

Figure 4

Figure 5

ADDING A TRIPLE BRANCH

5. To make a triple branch, string on 11 core beads, and encase the last three core beads with 15/0 beads, as you did for the single branch. Add a trim bead and a 15/0, and pass back through core beads 11, 10, 9, 8, 7, 6, and 5. Add the second branch between beads 5 and 4 of the main branch, and add the third branch between beads 3 and 2 of the main branch. Make the second and third branches the same size as the second branch shown in figure 6.

Do four stitches between triple branches. Make a total of seven triple branches, ending with a triple branch.

THE SECOND HALF OF THE LARIAT

6. Remove stop bead, and thread a needle onto the thread. Stitch 4 inches (10.2 cm) of spiral rope. *Note: If you need to make adjustments to the length of the necklace, do it here. Increase or decrease the length of the plain spiral rope as needed.*

7. Continue stitching the other half of the necklace, repeating steps 2 through 5. To wear the necklace, place it around the neck and tie the ends together in the front.

Figure 6

152

Daisy Chain Anklet

FINISHED SIZE

9¼ inches long

MATERIALS

11/0 seed beads:
- 32 light blue
- 24 gold
- 32 light green
- 24 medium green
- 32 lavender
- 24 orange
- 32 light pink
- 31 red
- 24 turquoise
- 24 yellow

Claw clasp
10 mm ring
Sewing needle
Off-white thread
Scissors

Note: Each unit of the chain is composed of nine beads, eight "petals" of the same color in a circle around one "center" of a different color.

1. Thread needle with a 24"–30" length of thread (additional lengths of thread can be added if necessary), allowing a long thread end at beginning of weave. Note: You may tape the end of the beginning thread to a flat surface for stability.

2. Slip eight beads of first color on needle. Run needle back through first bead on thread as shown in diagram. Slip red bead on for "center." Then run needle through lower left bead of circle of eight. (See Figure 1.)

3. Slip one bead of second color on needle. Run needle through lower right bead of first "flower." Slip one more bead on needle and run needle through first bead of second color. Slip six more beads on needle. Slip red bead on for "center." Then run needle through lower left bead of circle of eight.

4. Repeat step 3 for thirty-one flowers—each a different color than the previous one. Run thread through lower left bead of last flower.

5. Sew clasp on one end of length and ring on remaining end, running thread through adjacent beads three times. Bury thread ends in weave by running each thread end back into last bead. Trim excess thread, taking care to avoid cutting weave threads.

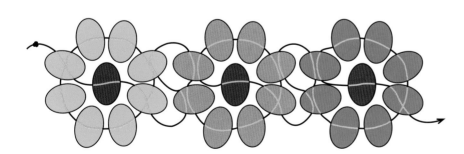

Figure 1

Buried–Bugle Cords

MATERIALS

Bugle beads (make sure they do not have sharp edges or they will cut the thread)

Cylinder beads (if using size 11/0 cylinder beads, they often disappear into the hole of a larger bead, so add a size 11/0 seed bead between the two to act as a stopper)

Triangle beads, or any fancy beads of your choice

11/0 seed beads

Beading needle

Thread to blend with beads

Scissors

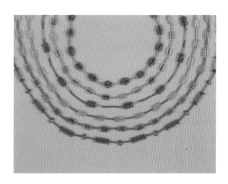

Wrapping beads around other large bugles or beads is given a new slant here, making cords that can be worn as jewelry, used as handles for tiny bags, or serve as fringes for anything.

1. Put a needle on the end of a very long thread, go through the hole in a bugle or a large bead and tie the two ends together at one end, leaving a 6-inch tail to finish off later.

2. Pick up a grouping of 3 to 5 beads that match the length of the large bead or bugle, and take the needle through the hole again. Pick up the same combination of beads again and go through the hole. Five or six groupings of beads will be about all that you can get through the hole before it is blocked up with thread.

3. String on some beads for spacers, then another large bead or bugle, and cover it again in the same way.

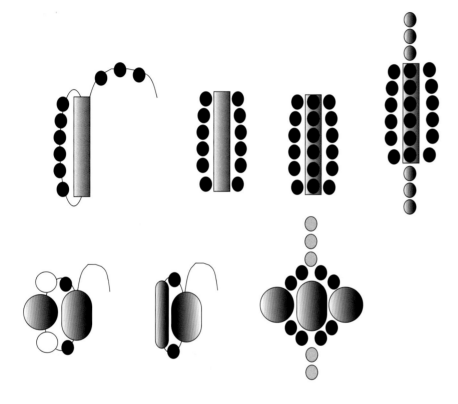

Crazy Chain

MATERIALS

Beads and bugles of your choice
Beading needle
Beading thread to blend with your beads
Scissors

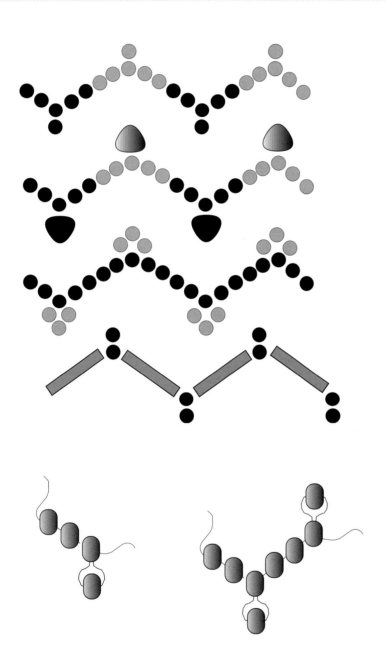

This chain is based on one seen in Malacca, Malaysia, but the original had loops instead of the beaded picots. The picots are worked as you go along, forcing the string into a zigzag. Don't put a heavy bead on the bottom, as it will weigh down the chain too much; this chain should be bouncy.

1. Pick up four seed beads. Skip the fourth bead and take the thread back through the third bead again, making a picot. Pick up six more beads, skip the sixth bead and take the thread back through the fifth bead again, making a picot. Repeat this row for the length of the chain you want.
2. Experiment with using a bugle bead instead of seed beads between the picots; the picot beads could be larger or a different shape, or you could work a 3-bead picot.

Beaded Link Chains

MATERIALS

11/0 or 15/0 seed or cylinder beads
Beading needle to suit size of beads
Thread to blend with bead colors
Scissors

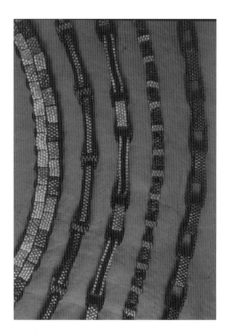

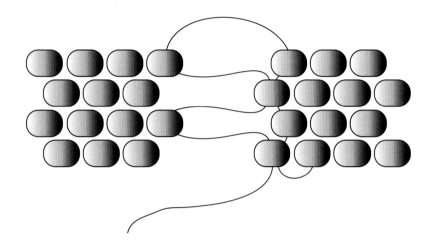

Strips of beading can be joined into rings and the rings linked together to make chains of enormous variety. The rings can be wide or narrow, short or long, folded in half and doubled, or even have strips of beading threaded through them. The small size of the rings rules out any complex pattern, but stripes of different-colored beads are easily incorporated or random color mixes can be used.

1. Make a four-bead strip of peyote stitch about 1½ inches long. Join the two ends together and finish the thread off.
2. Make a second strip the same size, but before joining the ends pass one end of the strip through the first link you made. Join the ends of the second strip. Continue in this fashion until your chain is the length you want.
3. If you have gone merrily on making links and forgotten about linking them, just make more strips and pass them through two links before joining the ends.

Beaded Braids
& Cords

MATERIALS

11/0 or 15/0 seed, tubular, or cut beads
Piping or braided cord in the diameter of your choice
Needles
Thread to blend with cord and beads
PVA glue
Scissors

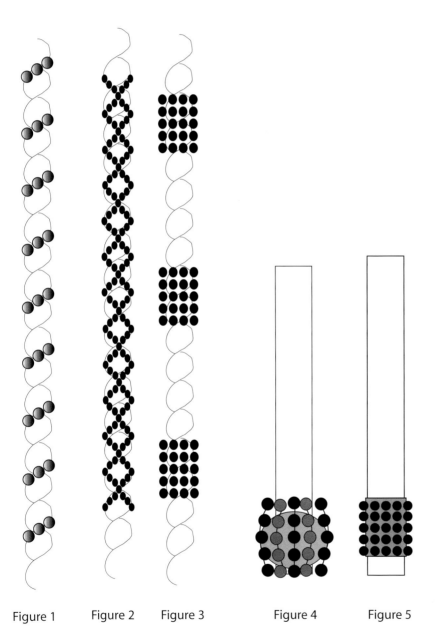

Figure 1   Figure 2   Figure 3   Figure 4   Figure 5

Twisted cord, whether store-bought or homemade, can be enriched by the addition of beads. Here are some possibilities:

1. Thread a needle and sew the end firmly into the end of the cord. Pick up about 6 beads on your needle and wind the beads around the cord, letting them fit into the groove. (See Figure 1.) Sew through the cord and back through the last bead. Pick up more beads and continue this process.
2. Make a bead strip and coil it around the cord, attaching it at either end. (See Figure 2.) If the cord is long, you will need to sew the bead strip to the cord at intervals for it to be secure.
3. Wrap a grouping of beads over the cord at intervals. (See Figure 3.)

FINISHING CORD ENDS

4. Knot the end of a cord and stitch groups of beaded thread vertically over the knot to hide it. If you are still doubtful about the cut ends of yarn, dab a little PVA glue on them. It will dry clear, so it won't really show. (See Figure 4, page 157.)

5. Wrap the end of the cord with yarn or strong thread to secure the ends; then wind a string of beads over the wrapping and sew both ends of the thread into the cord. (See Figure 5, page 157.)

BEADING OVER CORDS

6. Peyote-covered cord: Odd-count peyote continues around the cord in a spiral. Tubular odd-count peyote can be used to make a cord without anything inside it or to cover a ready-made cord. The slight bump at the top and bottom from using odd-count peyote hardly shows on a cord.

   String enough beads to go around a length of piping cord, and take the needle through the beads again to make a ring. There should be an odd number of beads. Work tubular peyote stitch until the cord is covered.

7. Brick stitch cord: Brick stitch can be used by itself or over a cord and, because it is stiffer than peyote, it is useful as the handle of a bag or tote. Make a ladder strip and join it into a ring. Work brick stitch into the loops until the cord is long enough.

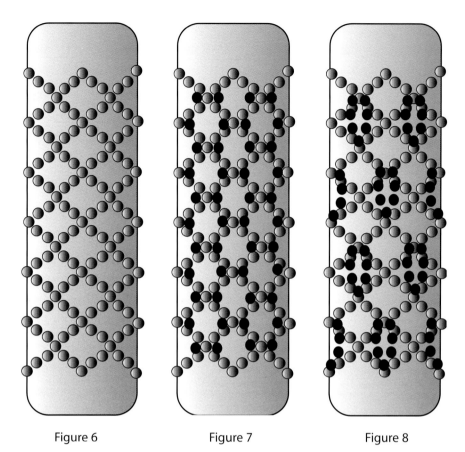

Figure 6   Figure 7   Figure 8

ADDING TEXTURE

8. Netting: A beaded or fabric cord can have a netting overlay. Pick up enough beads to go around your cord, making sure you have a number that is divisible by 3 or 4. Work a 7- or 9-bead netting into every third or fourth bead. If you are netting over a beaded cord it is probably not worth working a smaller netting, because you will hide the original beading. (See Figure 6.)

9. Picots or loops: After you have made the cord, you can sew extra beads or loops on and they will add "crunch" texture or movement to the cord and strengthen the netting. (See Figures 7 and 8.)

Humbugs

MATERIALS

11/0 or 15/0 seed or cylinder beads in 2 or 3 colors
Smooth, round, unsharpened pencil in a plain color
Dowel or mandrel about 1½ inches (4 cm) in circumference
Chunky knitting wool for stuffing humbugs
Beading needle
Thread to blend with bead color
Scissors

These little tassels are fun—soft because the beaded shapes are stuffed with wool. If you use cylinder beads, the tassels come out quite tiny. Seed beads make a larger size. You will be using an even-number tubular peyote stitch.

LARGE HUMBUG

1. Pick up 30 beads on the needle and make a ring by going through the beads again. Tie both ends of the thread tightly. Secure the non-working end of the thread with an elastic band to an end of the larger-diameter stick. Continue working tubular peyote stitch for 20 rounds (10 beads deep). If using seed beads, you might need 2 to 4 beads less, and 2 to 4 rounds fewer, depending on their shape. Make one large humbug.

2. Sew across one opening, fitting the beads together like the teeth of a zipper. Take 5 or 6 wraps of chunky yarn around your finger, cut yarn and stuff into large humbug. Sew up the second opening at right angles to the first to make the humbug shape.

3. With needle and thread at last corner, pick up 10 beads for a hanging loop, taking the thread through twice for strength. Weave thread end into work and trim.

SPIRAL PATTERN ON LARGE HUMBUG

4. For a varied effect, use 30 beads, threading them on in two colors (two of color A, four of color B) repeated 5 times. If using a different stick, or different beads, thread them on in multiples of 6. Work 20 rounds, or fewer if using seed beads, working spiral pattern. Stuff and sew up so that the stripes continue without a break across the seam. Make loop as above.

SMALL HUMBUGS

5. Pick up 18 to 20 beads on the needle and make a ring by going through the beads again. Tie both ends of the thread tightly and secure non-working end of the thread with an elastic band to the unsharpened end of the pencil. Work 12 to 14 rounds (6 beads deep); perhaps 11 rounds, if using seed beads. Make 9 small humbugs.

6. Stuff humbugs with short lengths (2 wraps of yarn around your forefinger) of chunky wool yarn. Sew up as for large humbugs.

7. Thread beads onto one corner of each of the small humbugs, and sew three of them to each corner of the large humbug (but not onto the fourth corner with the loop on it). Try threading 10 beads onto one humbug, 20 onto the second, and 30 onto the third so they hang at different lengths from each corner.

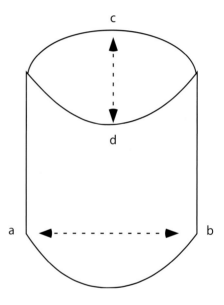

USING DIFFERENT-SIZED STICKS

Tie on an even number of beads so that they fit exactly around the rod or dowel. Calculate two-thirds of the number of beads and work that many rounds: e.g., 36 beads and 24 rounds, or 42 beads and 28 rounds. You will need fewer rows if you are using seed beads.

Tiny Flowers

MATERIALS

11/0 or 15/0 seed beads in colors of your choice
Beading needle to suit size of beads
Thread to blend with colors of beads
Scissors

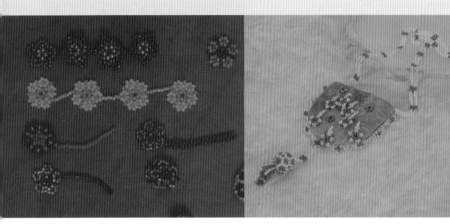

3rd round. Add 1 bead (color A) through each bead.

4th round. Add 1 bead (color B) through each bead.

5th round. Go through 2 beads, add 2 beads (color B) through the next bead. Repeat to the end, having added 15 beads. (See Figure 1.)

THREE-COLOR METHOD

2. Thread 5 beads (color A), make a ring, and go through the ring again, slipping through a couple of beads. Then, slip forward 1 bead at the end of every round following:

1st round. Add 1 bead (color A) through each bead.

2nd round. Add 2 beads (color B) through each bead. (10 beads)

3rd round. Add 1 bead (color C) through the next bead, then 1 bead (color A) through the next bead. Repeat to end of round.

4th round. Add 1 bead (color B) through each bead.

5th round. Add 1 bead (color A) through the first bead, 2 beads (color B) through the next, then repeat to end. (15 beads)

6th round. Thread 1 bead (color A) through each bead.

7th round. Thread 1 bead (color A) through each bead.

8th round. Thread 1 bead (color A), 1 bead (color A), 1 bead (color B). Repeat to end of the round. (See Figure 2.)

The flowers can be sewn back to back, perhaps with a bead between them to add bulk, or they can be piled up on top of each other, each one a different color. They may also be linked in chains, hung on strips or braids. (See Figure 3.)

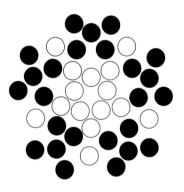

Figure 1

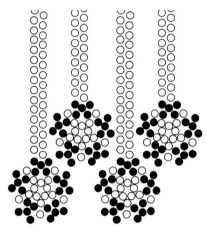

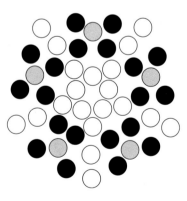

Figure 2

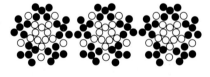

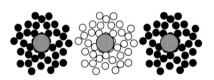

Figure 3

TWO-COLOR METHOD

1. Thread 5 beads (color A), make a ring and go through the ring again, slipping through a couple of beads. Then, slip forward 1 bead at the end of every round following:

1st round. Add 1 bead (color A) through each bead.

2nd round. Add 2 beads (color B) through each bead. (10 beads)

Blackberries

MATERIALS

11/0 seed or cylinder beads:
  25 (minimum)
Needle to suit size of bead
Thread to blend with bead colors
Scissors

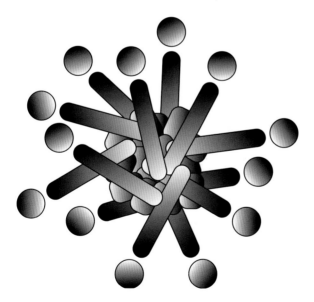

Figure 1

Figure 2

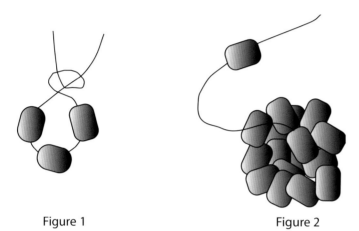

Figure 3

Note: You can hide your not-so-nice beads in the center of any sort of blackberry. If you are going to make more than one, you will need to count the number of beads each time to make sure they are the same size.

1. Put a 15-inch length of thread through your needle and pick up three beads. Leaving a 5-inch tail, tie both ends together in a knot. (See Figure 1.)

2. Pick up one bead and take the needle through the cluster of beads, not through a hole in a bead. Pick up another bead and take the needle through the cluster, back to the other side. (See Figure 2.) Continue like this, picking up one bead at a time.

3. Roll the blackberry around in your fingers as it gets bigger, to keep it in a nice shape. If there is a hollow, bring the needle up into the hollow and put a bead in it.

VARIATION

Try using different beads for the outside layer—perhaps triangles, or even cubes. If you use bugles, you will need to pick up one bugle and one seed bead, skip the bead, and go back through the bugle into the cluster. (See Figure 3.)

SECTION V

Embroidery With Beads

Bead-Embroidered Collar

MATERIALS

11/0 seed beads:
   1 gram medium green
   18 pink
   4 turquoise
6/0 seed beads:
   16 light pink
#2 bugle beads:
   38 light blue
   24 light green

20 freshwater pearls, 4–5 mm
2 flat amethyst beads, 12 mm
4 light jade chips
4 turquoise chips
between needle, #10
embroidery needle, #9
Embroidery transfer pencil
Purchased shirt with collar
Thread to blend with colors

1. With a dark pencil, trace Collar Adornment Pattern design. Turn tracing paper over and retrace your pencil lines using a transfer pencil. Iron transfer pencil lines onto collar points.
   Note: Choose any color of fabric that coordinates with the beads you have chosen. Select a garment that has a pointed collar and is made of a tightly woven fabric; knit fabrics are not suitable.

2. Thread needle with a 30-inch length of thread. Beginning with large lower flower, position turquoise chip on collar. Bring needle from back of collar to front. Slip chip on needle, letting it slide down thread until it rests flat against collar. Slip one turquoise seed bead on needle and take needle back through hole in chip. Pull thread taut until seed bead acts as an anchor on surface of chip, forming flower center. (See Figure 1.)

3. Sew nine pearls around turquoise chip to form flower. Sew three light blue and three light green bugle beads on opposite sides of flower to form leaf clusters.

4. Using method in Step 2, attach jade chip with medium green seed bead. Work stems in medium green seed beads toward remaining flowers. Run backtracking thread through beads to stabilize curves.

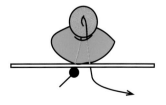

Figure 1

5. Attach amethyst flat bead with pink seed bead. Sew thirteen light blue bugle beads around amethyst bead to form flower. Sew three light green bugle beads on side of flower to form leaf clusters. Attach jade chip with medium green seed bead.

6. Work short stem in medium green seed beads to next flower. Sew one pearl at stem indicated to form flower center. Attach six light pink 6/0 beads with pink seed beads around pearl to form flower. Sew three light green bugle beads on side of flower to form leaf clusters.

7. Continue in this manner for both collar points.

A garment that has been beaded may be hand-washed and line-dried if the manufacturer's label says that the fabric is washable.

If a very lightweight fabric such as silk, satin, or taffeta is used for beadwork, a backing such as cotton broadcloth or lightweight felt should be fused onto the fabric to stabilize it. Following manufacturer's instructions, use lightweight fusible webbing to adhere a backing onto project fabric before beading.

If a hoop is used to stabilize fabric on which you are beading, make certain that the entire area to be beaded fits within the hoop. Once beads are sewn onto the fabric, it cannot be shifted, as the beads will get in the way.

Collar Adornment Pattern & Key

#2 bugles light blue
#2 bugles light green
11/0 medium green lines
4–5 mm freshwater pearl
6/0 light pink
12 mm amethyst
turquoise chip
light jade chip

Bird of Paradise Leather Book Cover

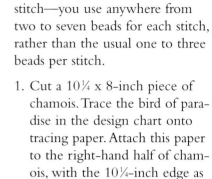

FINISHED SIZE

10½ x 8½ inches

MATERIALS

11/0 Japanese seed beads:
  5 grams emerald
  5 grams matte emerald
11/0 Delica Japanese tubular beads:
  4 grams matte emerald, #859
  4 grams lined lime green, #274
  2 grams silver-lined violet,
    #610
  2 grams opaque royal blue
    luster, #216
  2 grams matte tangerine, #855
  2 grams dyed matte transparent
    watermelon, #779
  2 grams dyed matte transparent
    red, #774
  2 grams Ceylon light yellow
    (off-white), #203
  2 grams lined pale yellow, #053

2 grams dyed opaque squash,
  #651
2 grams opaque yellow, #721
2 grams silver-lined teal, #607
Small bugle beads:
  4 grams matte emerald
  4 grams silver-lined green
8/0 seed beads:
  3 grams, matte green
  3 grams matte dark green
10 x 12-inch piece of golden
  deer chamois
½ yd red cotton fabric
6 yds ⅛-inch (3mm) red ribbon
White nylon beading thread,
  size D
Several beading needles, size 10
Thimble
Tracing paper
Mini leather punch set
Hammer
Leather matte knife
Leather glue
Pliers

The great look of beads on leather has its price—lots of broken needles! Have plenty of extra needles handy, and use pliers to help pull the needle through the leather. This project is done in a variation backstitch—you use anywhere from two to seven beads for each stitch, rather than the usual one to three beads per stitch.

1. Cut a 10¼ x 8-inch piece of chamois. Trace the bird of paradise in the design chart onto tracing paper. Attach this paper to the right-hand half of chamois, with the 10¼-inch edge as the top, by basting around the edges of the tracing paper.

2. Knot beading thread and pull up through the back of the piece onto the section of the outline you want to start on. String from two to seven beads, depending on the straightness of the line; the straighter the line, the more beads you use. For a curve, you would string fewer beads. PNDT leather. PNUT leather at a point between the last two beads strung. PNBT the last bead strung. (See Figures 1–4.)

3. Using the backstitch, outline the design in the Japanese tubular beads according to the design chart. After all the outlines are beaded, carefully tear off tracing paper.

4. For the veins on the leaves, use the small bugle beads. The main vein runs down the center of the leaf and the secondary veins are perpendicular to the main one. The silver-lined green bugle beads are used for the front leaf, and the matte emerald bugle beads are used for the back leaf. The bugle beads are strung two at a time for all veins.

Design Chart

☐	Lined lime green
☐	Silver-lined teal
☐	Matte emerald
☐	Ceylon light yellow
☐	Lined pale yellow
☐	Matte tangerine
☐	Opaque yellow
☐	Opaque squash
☐	Matte transparent watermelon
☐	Matte transparent red
☐	Silver-lined violet
☐	Opaque royal blue luster

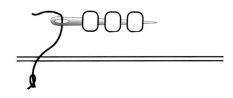

Figure 1

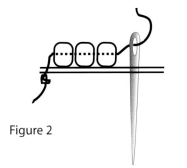

Figure 2

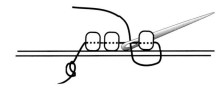

Figure 3

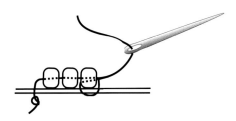

Figure 4

5. After you have the veins out-lined, fill in the leaves with the size 11/0 and size 8/0 beads. The rows are parallel to the secondary veins. The size 8/0 beads will go in the middle of the veined-in areas and the size 11/0 beads will be used to fill in around them.

6. The rest of the piece (flower and stem) are done in the Japanese tubular beads. Use the backstitch to fill in all the areas with the colors according to the design chart. Place the bead rows parallel to the outline rows.

7. When all the embroidery is fin-ished, punch holes about ⅛ inch apart all along the outer edge of the leather with a mini leather punch. Whipstitch the ribbon through the holes. (See Figure 5.) Leave about 2-inch ends, which will be glued under later.

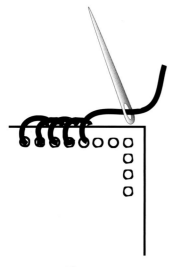

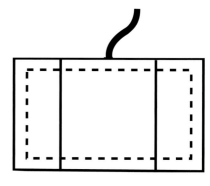

| Figure 5 | Figure 6 | Figure 7 |

FABRIC CASE (LINING)

8. Cut a 9¾ x 34-inch piece of the fabric. Fold in half with the right sides together so that the piece measures 9¾ x 17 inches. Pin a 14-inch length of ribbon in between the fabric right in the middle of the folded-in-half piece. (See Figure 6.)

9. Sew around three edges with a ½-inch seam allowance. Don't sew on the fold edge. Make sure the ribbon inside doesn't get sewn into the seam, and leave a small space open along the middle bottom edge for turning. Clip corners.

10. Turn the fabric right-side out and press with an iron. Fold in short ends 2¾ inches and iron flat. This will form the pockets for the book's cover. Now top-stitch all around, ⅛ inch from outside edges. This will sew the pockets down and close up the space you left open for turning the fabric. (See Figure 7.)

11. Lay fabric flat with the pockets down. Glue the wrong side of the leather cover onto the back of the fabric. For best results, place a large, heavy book on the cover until glue has dried.

Backstitched Shoe Pin

MATERIALS

11/0 seed beads:
  3 grams red
  2.5 grams metallic gold
  0.5 gram rose
  15 light aqua
  15 light blue
  15 medium blue
#2 bugle beads:
  7 lavender
  10 red
1 lavender crystal bead, 8 mm

2 freshwater pearls, 6 mm
Thick, white bath towel
Between needle, #10
Embroidery needle, #9
White card stock
Scissors
Double-sided fusible webbing
Fabric for backing
Iron and ironing board
Jewelry glue
White paper
Pin back, 1¼ inches
Coordinating color thread

1. Color photocopy Shoe Pin Pattern directly onto card stock. You may also trace pattern and transfer to card stock by putting a layer of carbon paper between the card stock and the tracing paper and retracing the design. Another method is to use a transfer pencil to trace the design first, then iron it onto the surface, remembering that the design will come out in mirror image. Trim the card stock around pattern edge, leaving ½-inch border all around, and keeping corners somewhat rounded to avoid catching thread.

2. Thread needle with a 30-inch length of thread. Place a bugle bead on card stock directly over its photocopied symbol. Bring needle from back of card stock to front at one end of bugle bead. Slip bugle bead on needle and let it slide down thread until it rests on surface. Take needle from front of card stock to back, pulling until bead rests firmly against surface.
   Note: Bugle beads are almost always sewn on individually.

3. Place crystal on surface directly over its photocopied symbol so one cut facet lies flat against sur-face. Bring needle from back of card stock to front. Slip crystal on needle and let it slide down thread until it rests on surface. Take needle from front of card stock to back at other end of crystal.

4. Since freshwater pearls have extremely fine holes, use #10 between needle and check to see that pearl slips over needle before marking card stock surface for it. Place pearl on surface directly over its photocopied symbol so flatter side lies against surface. Bring needle from back of card stock to front. Slip pearl on nee-dle and let it slide down thread until it rests on surface. Take nee-dle from front of card stock to back at other end of pearl.

5. Sew lines of rose, light aqua, medium blue, and light blue seed beads onto card stock. For each color, bring needle from back of card stock to front at desired starting point. Slip sev-eral beads on needle. Lay line against surface and check to see that they comfortably fill desired space. Take needle from front of card stock to back. Secure line using couching technique (see page 26 for review).

6. For curves and outlines, seed beads may be sewn on two at a time. Bring needle from back of card stock to front about two bead lengths ahead of desired starting point (A). (See Figure 1.) Slip two metallic gold seed beads on needle and let them slide down thread until they rest on their sides on surface. Take nee-dle from front of card stock to back to secure beads (B). Bring needle from back of card stock to front two bead lengths ahead of second bead in line (C). Slip two more beads on needle and let them slide to surface. Take needle from front of card stock to back in first hole made (A). Repeat for length of line.

Red Shoe Pin Pattern & Key

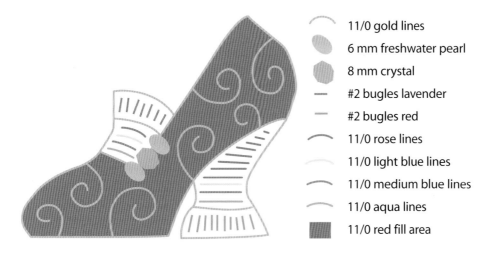

- 11/0 gold lines
- 6 mm freshwater pearl
- 8 mm crystal
- #2 bugles lavender
- #2 bugles red
- 11/0 rose lines
- 11/0 light blue lines
- 11/0 medium blue lines
- 11/0 aqua lines
- 11/0 red fill area

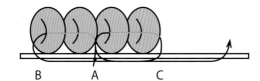

Figure 1

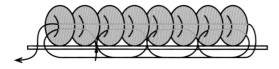

Figure 2

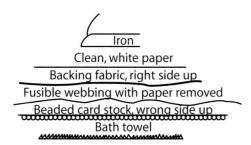

Figure 3

7. Strengthen metallic gold seed bead line with backtracking by bringing needle from back to front just beyond last bead in line and running thread back through all beads in line—run through only three beads at a time, particularly if line is curved. (See Figure 2.) Tighten line until smooth and neat, but not puckering. Take needle from front to back and secure thread.

Note: If beads being backtracked have very fine holes, use a #10 between needle.

8. Using the same method as in Step 7, fill in red areas with red seed beads. For small areas and tight curves, sew seed beads onto card stock individually.

9. To finish back of surface-beaded project, layer and center in order, from bottom: bath towel, beaded card stock wrong side up, fusible webbing with paper removed, backing fabric right side up, and clean white paper. (See Figure 3.) Press iron flat on white paper for five seconds. Shift iron and press for two more seconds to eliminate any steam holes. Allow to cool.

10. Trim excess fabric from edges of beaded project; take care not to accidentally cut a long string of beads near the edge. Apply a thin line of diluted glue around trimmed edges to secure.

11. Glue pin back onto back of shoe. Sew through holes on pin back to front of beaded project and secure.

Celtic Knot Necklace & Earrings

MATERIALS

11/0 seed beads:
   3 grams pewter
   1.5 grams dark bronze
   1.5 grams metallic gold
   12 black
10 mm fire-polished crystals:
   7 bronze
4 mm round matte beads
   14 gold
Barrel clasp

Card stock
Craft scissors
Double-sided fusible webbing
2 Celtic-type Pattern Ear findings
Embroidery needle #9
2 Head pins: .22-diameter,
   1¼ inches long
3 inches square of lightweight
   leather for backing
Round-nosed pliers
Wire cutters

PIN

1. Color photocopy Celtic Knot Pattern directly onto card stock (or see alternate methods in Step 1 on page 169). Trim the card stock to ½ inch all around pattern edge, keeping corners somewhat rounded to avoid catching thread.

2. Thread needle with a 30-inch length of thread. Sew metallic gold and pewter 11/0 seed beads onto card stock, following method for curves and outlines, in Step 6 on page 169. Run backtracking thread through beads. Review Backstitch technique on page 26, if necessary.

3. Fill in background areas with black and dark bronze 11/0 seed beads.

4. For one drop on pendant, bring needle to front surface at one dot. Slip beads of each drop on needle. Skipping last seed bead, run thread back through all beads. Repeat for each drop. (See Figure 1.)

5. For one necklace strand on pendant, bring needle out at either dot on top left edge. Slip four pewter seed beads, one matte gold round bead, one firepolish crystal, one matte gold round bead, and one dark bronze seed bead on needle. Slip pewter seed beads on needle to a 7½-inch length.

6. Sew one part of clasp onto bead strand, looping thread back through last few beads until clasp is secure. Run thread back through all—except last four seed beads—on strand. Add four more pewter 11/0 seed beads and take needle through remaining dot. Bury thread in back of stitching and trim excess close to project. Repeat Steps 5 and 6 for necklace strand on top right edge of pendant.

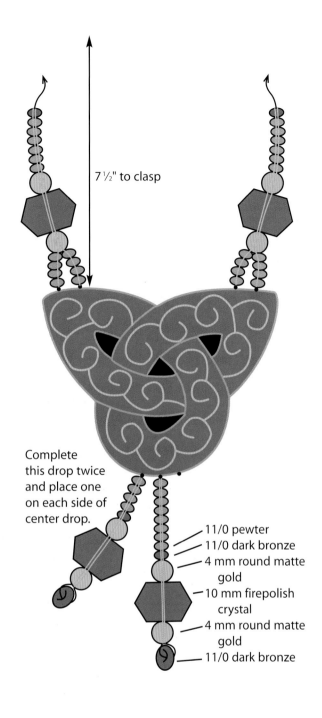

7 1/2" to clasp

Complete
this drop twice
and place one
on each side of
center drop.

— 11/0 pewter
— 11/0 dark bronze
— 4 mm round matte
     gold
— 10 mm firepolish
     crystal
— 4 mm round matte
     gold
— 11/0 dark bronze

Figure 1

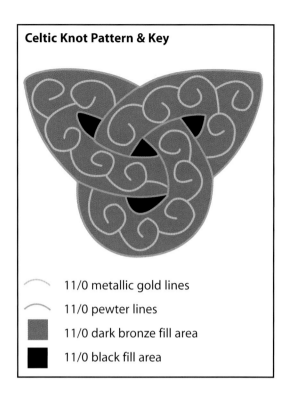

Celtic Knot Pattern & Key

⌒ 11/0 metallic gold lines

⌒ 11/0 pewter lines

▨ 11/0 dark bronze fill area

■ 11/0 black fill area

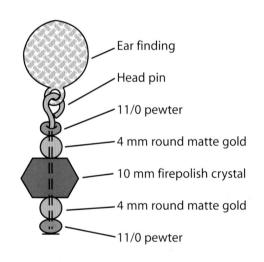

— Ear finding

— Head pin

— 11/0 pewter

— 4 mm round matte gold

— 10 mm firepolish crystal

— 4 mm round matte gold

— 11/0 pewter

Figure 2

FINISHING

12. To finish back of surface-beaded project, layer and center in order, from the bottom: bath towel, beaded card stock wrong side up, fusible webbing with paper removed, leather right side up, and clean white paper. Press iron flat on white paper for five seconds. Shift iron and press for two more seconds to eliminate any steam holes. Allow to cool.

13. Trim excess fabric and leather from edges of beaded project, being careful not to nick a beading thread. Apply a thin line of glue around the trimmed edges to secure.

EARRINGS

14. To make earrings, slip beads for each drop on head pin. Using wire cutters, trim head pin to 3/8 inch. Using round-nosed pliers, form an open loop. Slip loop of head pin on ear finding and carefully close loop. (See Figure 2.)

Backstitched Elephant Necklace

FINISHED SIZE

8 inches wide x 11 inches long

MATERIALS

11/0 Delica Japanese tubular
beads:
  10 grams matte metallic
    silver-gray, #307
  10 grams matte dark gray,
    #306
  10 grams transparent
    silver-gray luster, #114
  7 grams transparent gray iris,
    #107
  4 grams Ceylon gray, #252
  4 grams Ceylon light yellow,
    #203
10 metallic dark gray seed beads,
  size 6/0
2 concave bicone silver beads
8 crystal chips
1 silver rose bead, ½ inch
  (for clasp)
Black nylon beading thread,
  size D
Medium gray felt, 12 x 12 inches
Thin gray leather, 12 x 12 inches
Two beading needles, size #10
Sturdy sewing needle
Tracing paper
Glue gun
Scissors

Done in the backstitch, the elephants are first embroidered on felt and then glued onto leather. See page 26 to review backstitch technique. When you come to a tight curve or small space, use one or two beads at a time instead of three.

1. Using the Line Chart, trace the outline design of the elephants onto tracing paper and pin the tracing paper onto the felt. Use a thick needle to make pinholes along the outlines. Don't make the holes too close together or the tracing paper will fall apart. Go over these holes with chalk or watercolors. This should go through the holes and onto the felt. Remove the tracing paper and draw along the dotted lines with a fabric pencil to make them more permanent.

2. Backstitch along the outlines with the dark gray beads, but do not outline the tusks. The tusks are embroidered with the Ceylon light yellow beads. Starting with the top of a tusk, keep your rows of beads perpendicular to the edges of the tusks. Curve the lines a bit to give the tusks a cylindrical look. Wait to do the eyes until you are embroidering the heads of the elephants.

3. Using the color chart as a guide, fill in all areas with the backstitch. Keep your rows fairly perpendicular to the edges of the areas. Start with the bottom of the legs of the front elephant and work your way up. Then do the trunk and head. Follow the curves of the tusks for three rows above the tusks to give an appearance that the tusks are under the skin. Do the ears by lining up the rows with the ear ruffle outlines.

4. Next, start with the trunk of a side elephant and work your way up. Then do the other side elephant.

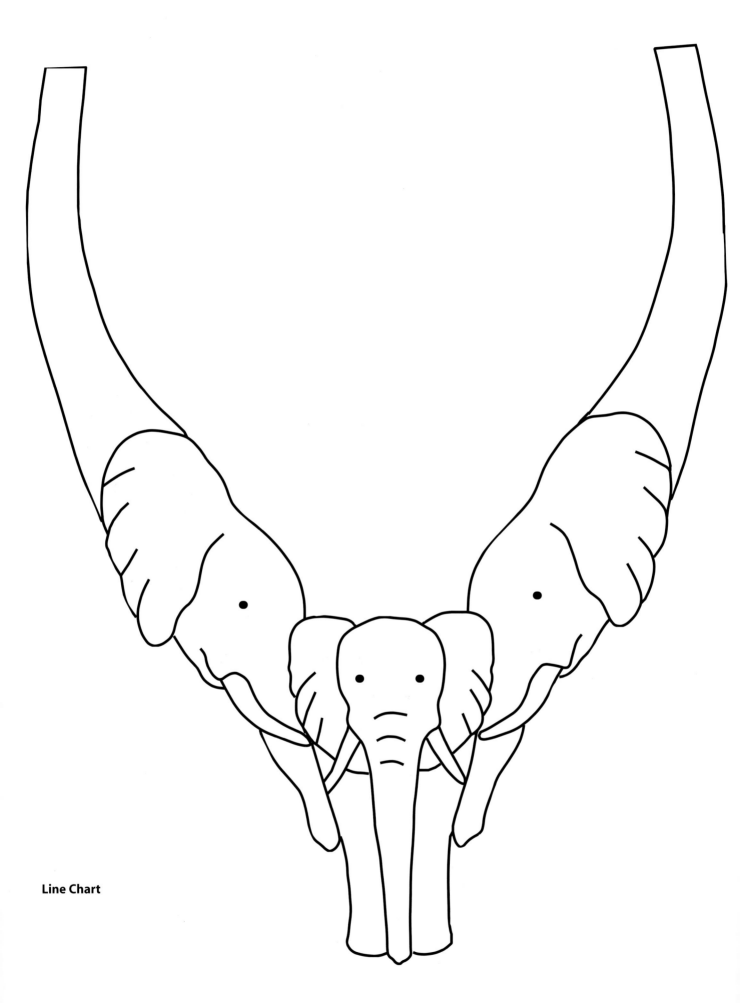

Line Chart

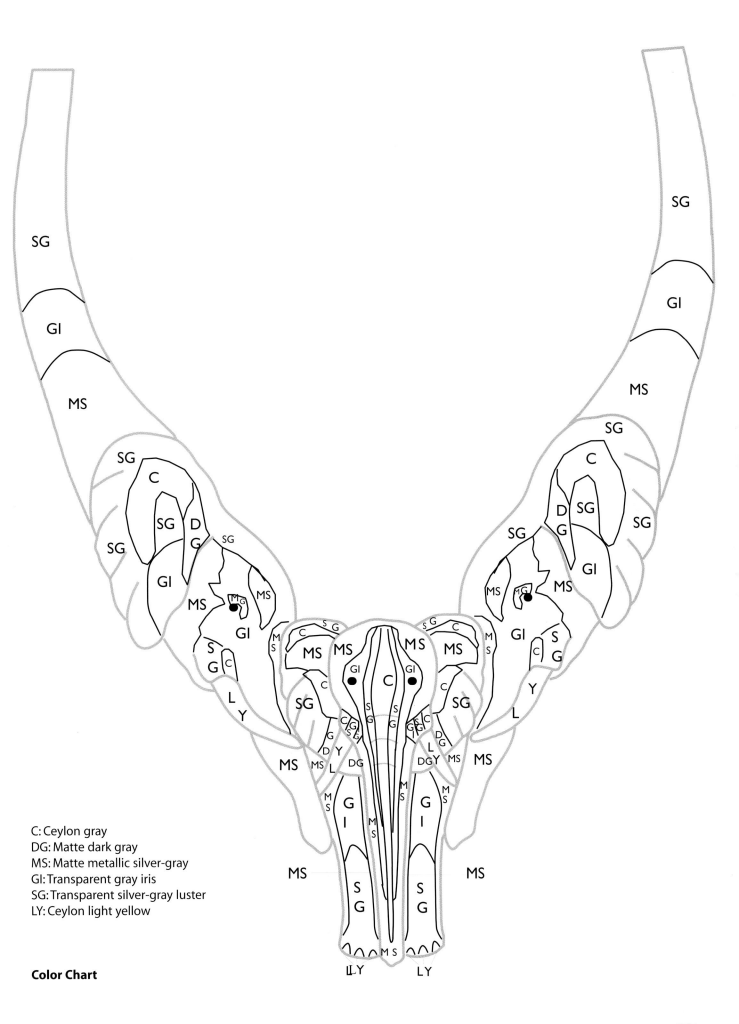

C: Ceylon gray
DG: Matte dark gray
MS: Matte metallic silver-gray
GI: Transparent gray iris
SG: Transparent silver-gray luster
LY: Ceylon light yellow

Color Chart

175

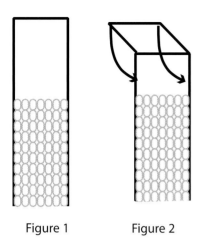

Figure 1   Figure 2

5. Cut the felt around the elephants, leaving a ¼-inch edge. Fold the edge to the back of the design so you can't see it from the front and glue in place. Gluing felt onto felt can be tricky if you don't have good, strong glue. You might want to use a glue gun for this.

6. Next, glue the elephants onto the leather. When the glue is dry, cut the leather as close as you can get around the elephant design with a pair of scissors, leaving a ½-inch leather tab at each end. (See Figure 2.) Fold the tabs in half to the back of the work and glue in place. (See Figure 3.)

7. When the glue is dry, punch a small hole into the center of the tabs with a sturdy needle, ¼ inch from the top. Take a length of thread about 3 feet long and thread each end with a beading needle. Pull one needle through the hole in the leather tab. Position the leather tab to the middle of the thread. Tie a square knot above the tab. Using both needles, string three metallic beads size 6/0, one silver bicone bead, and two metallic beads size 6/0.

8. Separate the needles and on each needle string eight matte metallic silver-gray beads. Next, using both needles, string one crystal chip. *On one needle, string eight transparent gray iris. Do the same with the other needle. Then, using both needles at the same time, string on one crystal chip.* Repeat between asterisks, using eight transparent silver-gray luster beads. Repeat again using eight Ceylon gray beads.

9. Next, on one needle, string one Ceylon gray bead, five transparent silver-gray luster beads, five transparent gray iris beads, five matte metallic silver-gray beads, five transparent gray iris beads, five transparent silver-gray luster beads, and one Ceylon gray bead. Take the other needle and PNBT the beads in the opposite direction, forming a loop. Pull tight and tie the threads with a surgeon's knot. Hide excess threads down through the beads and cut.

10. Repeat this design on the other side, but don't form the loop. Instead, secure a ½-inch silver rose bead right after the last crystal chip. Hide excess thread back down through beads and cut.

Water Lily Mirror

FINISHED SIZE

3 inches in diameter

MATERIALS

11/0 Delica Japanese tubular beads:
  4 grams Ceylon light yellow,
    #203
11/0 seed beads:
  14 grams metallic light green
  6 grams silver-lined transparent
    dark blue
  6 grams turquoise white heart
  9 opaque red-orange
  15 iridescent opaque yellow
  23 opaque orange
8/0 seed beads:
  1 gram iridescent light green
White nylon beading thread,
    size D
Light green felt, 6 x 6 inches
    (if you use an embroidery hoop,
    you may need a larger piece)
Two beading needles, size 12
Round wooden or plastic mirror
    3 inches in diameter
Small embroidery hoop (optional)
Scissors
Glue

This stylized water lily was inspired by the rosettes done by Native Americans. It is worked in the couching stitch.

Thread two needles with separate lengths of thread and knot ends. One needle will be used to string the beads, and the other will be used to sew the beads to the felt. (See Figure 1.)

Note: It is essential to keep your project flat as you work, or it won't lie flat when you're done. If this is hard for you, you may wish to use a small embroidery hoop to keep your work flat.

Pull both needles up through the center of the felt. String nine red-orange beads on one needle. Sew down first bead to create the center. Arrange the other beads in a circular pattern around the center bead, sewing down the beads with the other thread between every two or three beads. (See Figure 2.)

To end a round, use the bead thread and PNT the first two beads in the round. Pull tight. Take the needle down through the felt and back up where next round will begin. (See Figure 3.)

Round 2: Use about fifteen yellow beads or enough to fit around the first round. String seven or eight beads at a time. (It is difficult to predict exactly how many beads will be needed to fit around any given round, because seed beads tend to be irregular in size.) Tack down the yellow bead strand between every two or three beads. Don't forget to end this round and every round hereafter as shown in Figure 3.

Opaque orange

Opaque red-orange

Iridescent opaque yellow

Turquoise white heart

Silver-lined transparent dark blue

Metallic light green

Ceylon light yellow

Design Chart

Round 3: Use about twenty-three orange beads. Fit around yellow round, tacking down between every two or three beads.

Round 4: String about thirty-one Ceylon light yellow beads and tack down.

Round 5: String two turquoise beads, four Ceylon light yellow beads, two turquoise beads, four Ceylon light yellow beads, two turquoise beads, five Ceylon yellow beads, two turquoise beads, four Ceylon light yellow beads, two turquoise beads, four Ceylon light yellow beads, two turquoise beads, and five Ceylon yellow beads.

Note: When you are running low on thread on either needle, take the needle to the back of the work and tie a knot. Cut the thread from the needle. Thread the needle with a new strand of thread, tie a knot at the end, and pull the needle up from the back of the work at the same place where you left off. Continue as usual.

Round 6: Follow the design chart and make sure the groups of two turquoise beads line up with the groups of two turquoise beads in the previous round. Adjust the number of Ceylon light yellow beads according to the space available between the groups of turquoise beads.

Rounds 7–19: Follow the design chart, adjusting the number of beads for each color according to the space available.

When you have finished Row 19, cut the felt around the beads, leaving an edge of about ¹⁄₁₆ inch. Be careful not to cut any threads. For the last round, use the iridescent light green beads, size 8/0. String the beads and position them so they hide the felt edge. Attach the beads to the felt using the couching stitch. Bring sewing needle up through the felt at a slight outward angle and, after catching the beading thread, take the needle back down at the same angle. Finish the round and bring the needles to the back of the work. Tie a knot and trim thread ends. Glue beadwork to the back of the mirror. Place a flat, heavy object on top of the mirror to hold the beadwork in place while the glue dries.

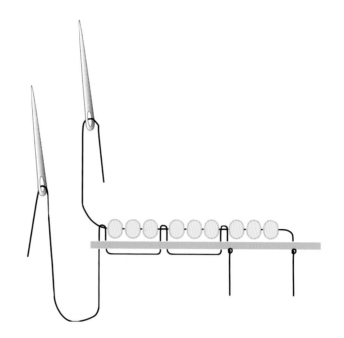

Figure 1

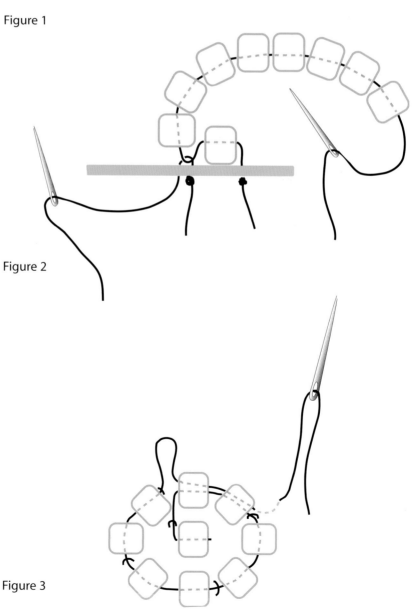

Figure 2

Figure 3

Oriental Carpet Eyeglass Case

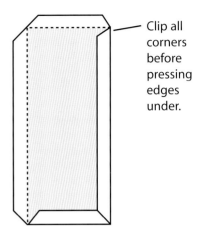

Clip all corners before pressing edges under.

Figure 1

MATERIALS

11/0 seed beads:
  11 grams pink
  10 grams aqua
  10 grams dark blue
  10 grams yellow
  3 grams pale blue
  3 grams light purple
  3 grams medium purple

3 grams red
1 gram light green
Embroidery needle, #9
Fabric for lining and backing
  (⅛ yard each)
Fabric scissors
Interlock needlepoint canvas
  #14, 5 x 9 inches
Steam iron and ironing board
Off-white thread

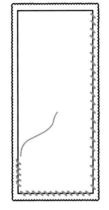

Stitch lining fabric onto back of beadwork.

Figure 2

1. Refer to page 27 for technique review, if needed. Following Oriental Carpet Pattern, work from top row to bottom row. *Note: The last row charted is the center row in the design.*

2. Turn chart 180° and continue working design from center row—but not repeating center row.

3. Using steam iron, steam back of work and reshape it so it is squared. *Note: Take care when handling glass beads that have been under the iron as they can be quite hot to the touch.*

4. Trim canvas to ½ inch around design and clip corners. Using pressed and trimmed beadwork as a template, cut two pieces from lining fabric and one from backing fabric. (See Figure 1.)

5. Press canvas edges under finished beadwork. Press edges of remaining three pieces under to same size. Stitch one lining piece onto back of beadwork, hiding raw edges. Stitch remaining lining and backing pieces so raw edges are together. (See Figure 2.)

6. When both backing and beadwork have been lined, stitch them together, leaving one edge open to form eyeglass case.

Stitch backing and beadwork together.

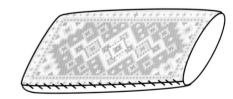

Figure 3

Oriental Carpet Pattern & Key

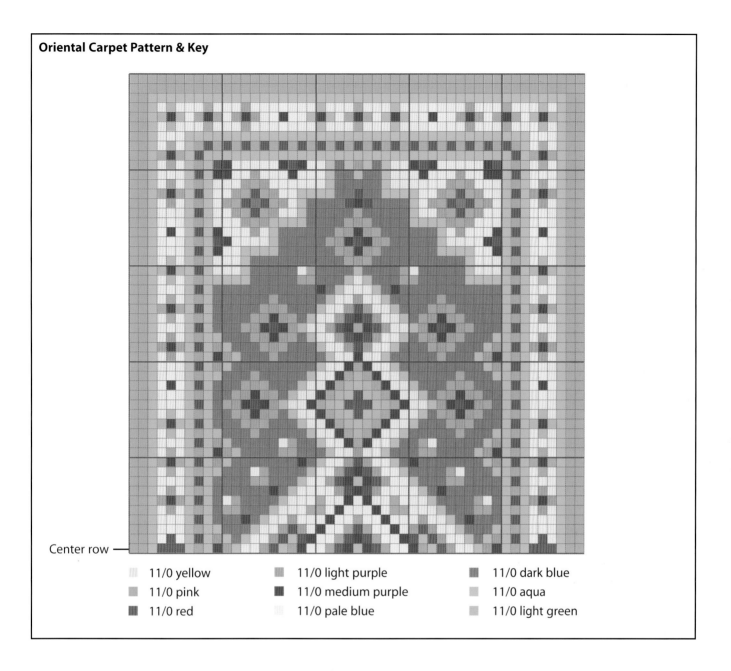

Center row

▦ 11/0 yellow	▦ 11/0 light purple	▦ 11/0 dark blue	
▦ 11/0 pink	■ 11/0 medium purple	▦ 11/0 aqua	
■ 11/0 red	▦ 11/0 pale blue	▦ 11/0 light green	

Beaded Cross-Stitch Anniversary Oval

STITCH COUNT
88 x 68

MATERIALS
25-count linen
DMC embroidery floss, #822, #815, #561
Fine gold metallic embroidery braid
Tapestry needles, #26, #28

All beads listed may be obtained from Mill Hill, P.O. Box 1060; Janesville, WI 53547-1060; phone: (608) 754-9466; fax: (608) 754-0665; or visit the website at *www.millhill.com*.

Follow graphs by symbol. For a review of Cross-Stitch techniques and stitches, see pages 28–29.

Special Instructions: At the dots around the yellow beads (for the white flowers, bottom center), using one strand of floss (822), pick up nine beads (3021). Return the needle in the first bead, go down in the same hole to form a loop.

After the entire project has been stitched and beaded, attach the glass treasures with the designated floss or beads.

Mill Hill Treasures

	SYMBOL	ATT W/BEAD/FLOSS	#PKGS
12143	◣	40161/822	4
12158	⬮	40161/822	1
12155	⬮	40161/822	3
12011	✳	168/822	2
12115	*see note	40161/822	1
12137	*see note	40161/822	1

Note: Refer to graph for treasure placement.

Mill Hill Beads

	SYMBOL	ATT W/FLOSS	#PKGS
2005	⠶	822	1
252	○	822	1
3035	U	822	1
332	I	561	1
3028	◆	561	1
367	▣	822	1
3034	■	822	1
168	✛	822	1
3004	◤	822	1
2002	▫	822	1
2012	♦	822	1
553	ヽ	822	1
145	–	822	1
3021	▫	822/bead loops (9)	1
40161	UWT	822	1

DMC Floss

	XS	BS
561	G	
815		⌐

Kreinik

	XS	#SPOOLS
002 #4 Braid	◢	1

Top left

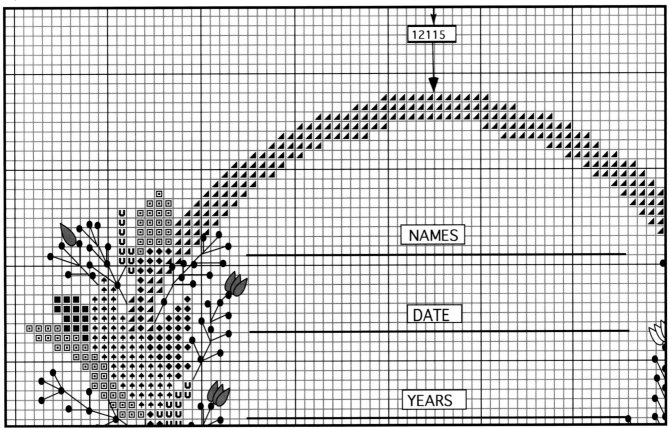

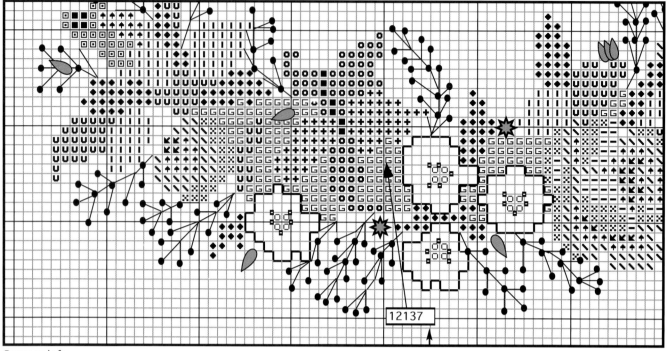

Bottom left

Top right

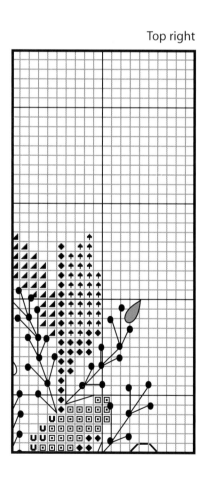

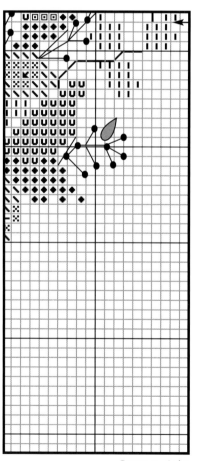

Bottom right

Acorn Sampler

STITCH COUNT

115 x 175

MATERIALS

25-count linen

DMC embroidery floss, #315, #646, #3024, #3740, #3750, #3787

Tapestry needles, #26, #28

All beads listed may be obtained from Mill Hill, P.O. Box 1060; Janesville, WI 53547-1060; phone: (608) 754-9466; fax: (608) 754-0665; or visit the website at *www.millhill.com*.

Follow graphs by symbol. For a review of Cross-Stitch techniques and stitches, see pages 28–29.

Note 1: For Herringbone border, work back and forth in rows. Begin four threads down from the upper left corner of the section (top row is already charted). Work from top to bottom in the following sequence of floss: 315, 3740, 3787, 3750, 3740, and 315. Some compensation may be necessary at the end of the row.

Mill Hill Beads			
	SYMBOL	ATT W/FLOSS	#PKGS
556	○	3024	2
3013	⁙	3024	5
3011	⧗	3024	1
3025	●	3024	4
3036	∪	3024	1
40161	UWT	3024	1

DMC Floss			
	XS	SS	HB
3787	╱		*
3750	◢		*
646	▌	▁▂▃	
315	▪		*
3740			*see note 1
3024	UWB-UWT		

Mill Hill Treasures			
	SYMBOL	ATT W/BEAD/FLOSS	#PKGS
12199	▧	/3024	10
13002	✸	40161/3024	1
13024	◈	/3024	7
12196	*see note 2	40161/3024	1

Note 2: Refer to graph for treasure placement.

Top left

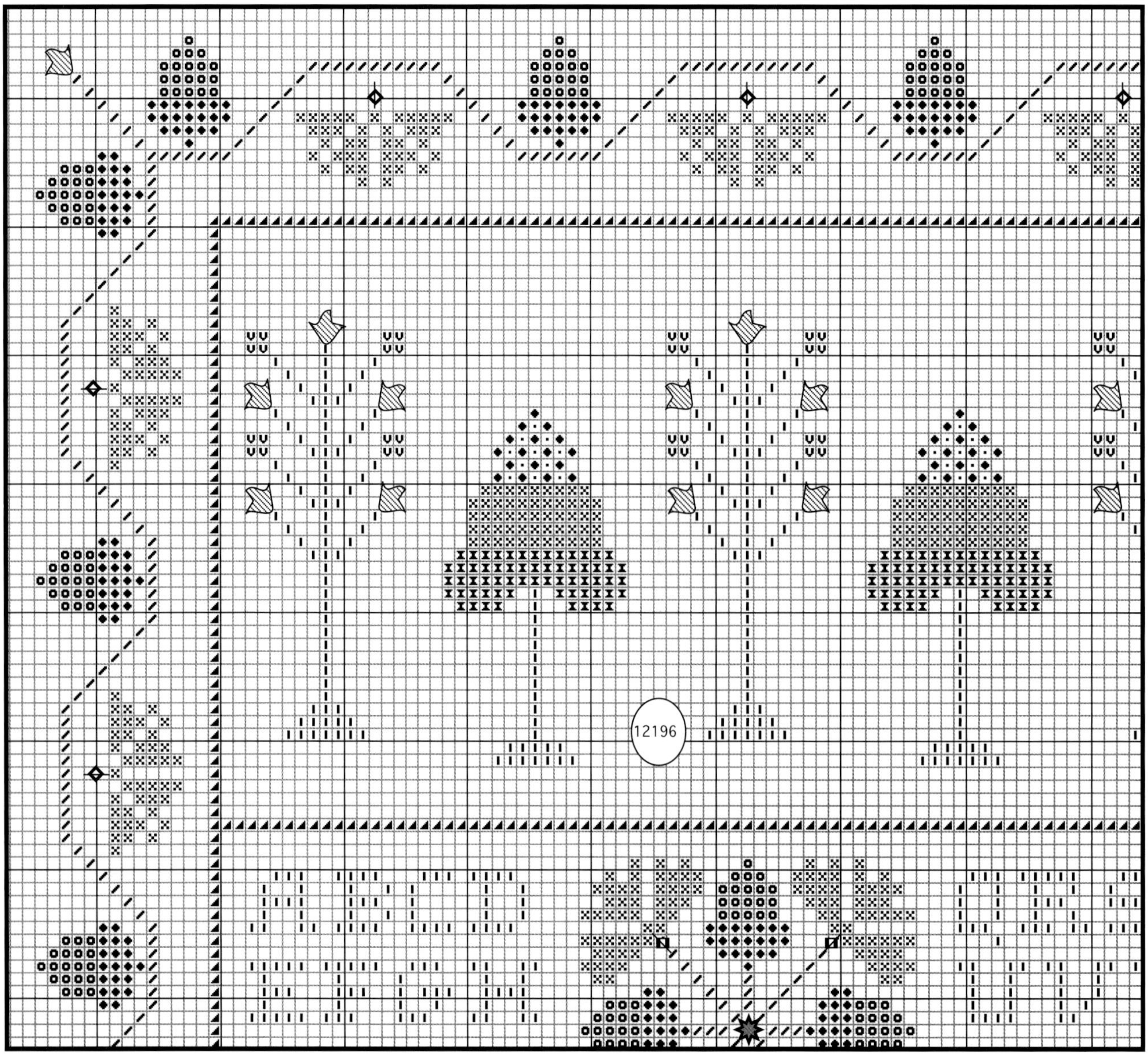

Top right

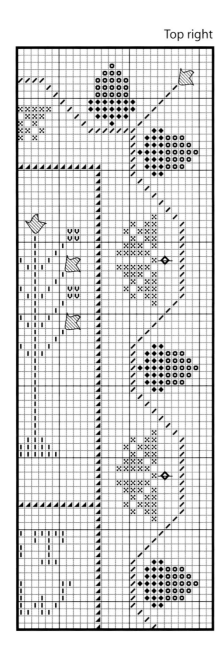

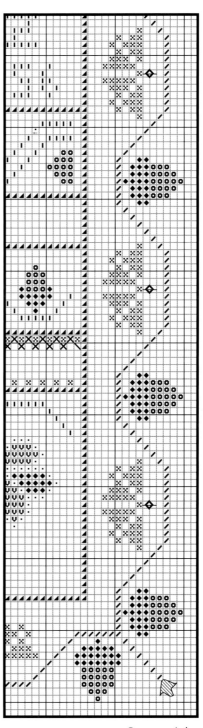

Bottom right

187

SATIN STITCH BORDER

HERRINGBONE BORDER

START HERE

Bottom left

Glossary

Amulet Also called a charm or fetish. An object believed to have magical powers to protect its owner from evils, such as disease or sorcery, or to attract good luck. Made of plant material, stones, or metal, sometimes marked with symbols or words.

Antique beads A brand of Japanese glass beads with large center holes and a tubular shape. The size 11/0 antique bead is similar to a size 13/0 seed bead. It also comes in a 3.3-mm size, which compares to a size 8/0 seed bead. Antique bead also refers to any bead not currently manufactured.

Backstitch An embroidery stitch used to sew a string of beads onto fabric or leather. Two or three beads are strung on at a time and a stitch is made to secure them to the fabric or leather. Then the thread is brought back through the last bead strung.

Bead A bead is a small pierced object used for stringing onto a thread, string, or wire. The word bead is derived from the Old English words bed and gebed, which mean prayer, and the Middle English word bede, which means prayer.

Beading needle A thin, straight needle 1¼–3 inches long with a long, narrow eye. It is made as thin as possible so that it can pass through the small holes of beads.

Bi-cone bead A bead that is cone-shaped at either end.

Big eye needle A beading needle with an eye that is as large as the whole center section of the needle. The long center eye makes threading the needle very easy.

Blocking A wetting and drying process that is done to knitted, crocheted, or needlepoint projects in order to shape them, smooth out stitch irregularities, and flatten curling edges.

Brick stitch A beading technique that gets its name from the appearance of the beads in the finished work, which resembles a brick wall. This stitch was frequently used by the Commanche Native Americans and, thus, it is sometimes called the Commanche stitch.

Bugle bead An elongated tubular glass bead ranging in size from ⅛ inch–2 inches long. It can be straight or twisted and comes in the colors and finishes of a seed bead.

Cathedral bead A bead made of clear glass. Also called a transparent bead.

Ceylon A shiny, pearlized finish on an opaque bead.

Charlotte bead A seed bead, usually size 13/0, that has one hand-cut facet.

Couching A type of appliqué work where a string of beads is appliquéd or sewn onto fabric or leather. Two needles are used in this technique. The beads are strung onto the thread with one needle and sewn down to the fabric with the other.

Delica beads A brand of cylindrical glass beads with large center holes that make them excellent for needle-weaving techniques because of their consistency in size and shape and because their large holes will accommodate several passes of thread. They are made in Japan and come in two sizes. The size 11/0 are similar to a size 13/0 seed bead. The 3.3-mm size is close to the size 8/0 in seed beads.

Drawn-glass bead A bead made with the drawn-glass technique. A tube of molten glass is pulled so that it is long and thin and is then cut into small pieces or "beads." The edges are then polished smooth.

Drop bead An accent bead in the shape of a tear drop or a pressed, or molded, shape, such as flowers or leaves. The hole is drilled either through the side at the small end of the bead or vertically through the center.

Faceted crystal beads Made of fine quality glass (usually with a high lead content), these beads are shaped by a mechanized cutting process and have a wonderful diamond-like fire. Available in many shapes and sizes, from 4 mm cone-shaped beads to 18 mm ovals, they are available in a good range of colors (mostly transparent). They are expensive but readily available.

Faience bead The first bead made with man-made materials. It was made in ancient Mesopotamia by heating quartz sand and some form of alkali or clay. Historians believe that the faience bead was the forerunner to glass, which is made of the same ingredients as faience except with more alkali.

Fancy glass beads Sometimes called Treasures. All varieties of shapes and colors. Most bead stores and mail-order catalogs will have hundreds of different styles.

Findings Metallic objects used in jewelry making, such as earring wires, clips, posts, clasps, headpins and eyepins, hooks and eyes, chains, hair clips, brooches, and pins.

Greasy finish A glass bead finish that leaves a semi-opaque bead with a dirty kind of shine.

Hank Several strands of beads tied together and sold as one unit. The number of beads per strand and strands per hank depends on the size and weight of the beads.

Herringbone stitch In bead-weaving—an off-loom beading technique that creates a woven-looking glass fabric; an old African stitch from the Ndebele tribe. In cross-stitch—a series of wide, overlapping cross-stitches that create a herringbone pattern.

Hex bead A faceted seed bead in which the glass is not cut but is extruded through a mold, leaving the beads with five or six sides. They have large holes and very thin walls. They are similar in size to Delicas, also excellent for weaving, but the range of colors and finishes is quite a bit more limited.

Iris finish A glass bead finish that creates a rainbow iridescence on the surface of the bead. It is also called the Aurora Borealis (AB) finish when it is used on transparent beads.

Lined bead A transparent or translucent bead with a hole that is lined with silver, gold, or paint. Sometimes the hole is etched.

Loom A frame or structure that supports the thread used for weaving beads.

Loom work Beadwork that is done on a loom.

Luster finish A glass bead finish that leaves the bead glossy with a whitish tinge.

Matte finish A glass bead finish that creates a dull surface. This is done by an acid wash or a tumbling of the beads.

Micro bead Another word for seed beads. Any glass or metal bead with a diameter of .04 to .24 inch.

Micro bugle A bugle bead smaller than ⅛ inch long.

Metallic finish A glass bead finish that gives the bead an extremely shiny surface.

Natural Beads Carved beads made of bone, wood, semiprecious stones—in chips of varying grades such as turquoise, amethyst, cinnabar, citrine, and some hard quartzes—and finished beads of assorted shapes and sizes.

Netting An off-loom beading technique that creates an open mesh of beads.

Off-loom work Beadwork that is done without a loom or structure to support the thread.

Opalescent bead A bead made of glass that has a slightly clouded appearance. Also called translucent bead.

Opaque bead A bead made of glass that is a solid color and lets no light through.

Peyote stitch Also called gourd or twill stitch. An ancient off-loom beading technique used by Native Americans for hundreds of years. Some tribes reserve the term "peyote" stitch for projects sacred to their culture and refer to all else as gourd stitch. It can be made into flat, circular, or tubular objects. It creates a solid, flexible fabric of beads.

Pony bead A bead larger than a seed or micro bead but with the same shape and usage as one. It is any seed bead size 6° or larger. It was a popular bead among the Europeans used for trading with the Native Americans of the Southwest.

Pound bead This was the name given to small drawn-glass beads by the bead trade long ago when they were sold by weight rather than number.

Rocaille A tiny glass bead or seed bead. *Rocaille* means "little stones" in French.

Rosette A circular beadwork design that is common among the Native Americans. It is done with the couching stitch.

Satin bead A bead made with satin glass, which is created by putting air bubbles in the molten glass or by fusing layers of the same color glass to the hot gather before pulling the gather into a tube. This gives the bead a deep satiny look.

Seed bead Also called a micro bead. Any glass or metal bead, round or oval in shape with a centered hole, between 15/0 (very tiny) and 6/0 (the largest seed bead).

Three-cut bead These extruded beads have irregular cuts made all over their surface to form flat shiny planes that give them a faceted look. Three-cuts come in two sizes, 12/0 and 9/0—they are favored on elegant evening clothes because of their extreme sparkle and shine. *Note: The holes may be inconsistent, so buy extra, as a good percentage might be unusable.*

Two-cut bead A bead with two or three facets on the sides.

Twisted needle A beading needle made of a thin wire twisted together, leaving a large, collapsible eye. It does not have a sharp point and is very flexible.

Warp The vertical group of threads stretched across a loom.

Weft The threads of a loom that carry the beads and run horizontally across the warp threads.

Index

3/17/05

Credits and Rights Information
(continued from p. 4)

The publishers of *The Pattern Companion: Beading* gratefully acknowledge permission for the use of material from the following previously published works. Information, illustrations, and/or projects from:

Beading for the First Time, by Ann Benson © 2001, by Ann Benson, with photographs by Kevin Dilley for Hazen Photography appear on pages 14–15, 27 (illustration), 32–33, 82–83, 90–95, 98–99, 109–111, 153, 163–165, 169–172, 180–181, 189–190.

Beaded Cross-Stitch Treasures, by Gay Bowles © 1999 by Chapelle Limited, with designs from Mill Hill Designs, appear on pages 28–29, 182–188.

Beaded Tassels, Braids & Fringes, by Valerie Campbell-Harding © 1999 by Valerie Campbell-Harding, with photographs by Peter Read, appear on pages: 154–161.

The Art of Seed Beading, by Elizabeth Gourley, Jane Davis & Ellen Talbott © 1999 by Elizabeth Gourley, Jane Davis & Ellen Talbott, with photographs by Myra Nunley, appear on pages 8, 13, 17–27, 29–30, 38–39, 62–75, 84–89, 100–108, 112–120, 166–168, 173–179, 189–190. Designs by Elizabeth Gourley, 62–75, 84–89, 166–168; by Jane Davis on 112–119; by Ellen Talbott, 100–108, 173–179.

The Art & Elegance of Beadweaving, by Carol Wilcox Wells © 2002 by Carol Wilcox Wells, with photographs by Evan Bracken, appear on pages 7, 9–12, 15–16, 29–31, 37, 40–61, 76–81, 97, 121–152. Designs by Martha Forsyth, Pat Iverson & Kathryn Black on 121–123; Leslie Frazier on 79–81; Suzanne Golden on 56; Ella Johnson-Bentley 15; NanC Meinhardt, 57–58; Gail Naylor, 144–145; Rebecca Peapples, 59–61.